New Releases from IRM Press

Business to Business Electronic Commerce: Challenges and Solutions

Table of Contents

Section III. Value Chain Networks and Research Issues

Preface

The growth in the importance of electronic commerce (eCommerce) has been nothing short of phenomenal. Thousands of new companies have created new marketplaces and new opportunities worldwide. The most visible impact to the average consumer is in the explosion of digital content availability and the plethora of new etail sites to purchase everything from books to airline tickets to groceries. However, the growth of business-to-business electronic commerce (B2B eCommerce) has been (and will continue to be) a much more significant business activity of far higher value and will impact nearly all organizations in the long run.

B2B eCommerce activities primarily consist of two categories–those that facilitate the procurement of goods and services and those that provide business infrastructure. Within the broad first category are all the activities and processes that are related to the supply chain. Manufacturing companies purchase raw materials, components, and subassemblies from their suppliers upstream in the supply chain. They also sell their products to other companies who add value through other processes–further assembly, distribution, or sale to consumers. The downstream supply chain partners may include other manufacturers, distributors, wholesalers, dealers, franchisees, retailers (and etailers), and consumers who may "buy direct" from a B2C website such as Dell.com. Manufacturers are not alone–all companies must purchase materials, supplies, and services from various sources. Comprehensively, this network of companies may be termed the *value chain* or *value network*. All final sales to consumers of all goods and services are the culmination of a series or network of value-added processes, which include tangible improvements to physical items and less tangible improvements to the value proposition for the consumer.

This first category of B2B eCommerce includes single acts of procurement by one company from another ("one-off sales") as well as organized online trading exchanges. The exchanges may be operated by an individual company as an avenue to facilitate interaction with all its suppliers. Exchanges may also be organized by an industry consortium using an industry standard set of data representation schemes and protocols. (These have their roots in the electronic data interchange (EDI) efforts in previous decades.) Or they may be created and operated by third-party intermediaries who typically seek profits based on a transaction fee or a subscription fee for participation in the exchange. (Several chapters described below will elaborate on this taxonomy.)

The second category of B2B eCommerce (business infrastructure) includes a variety of business interactions not directly related to the traditional purchase and sale of goods and services in the supply chain or value chain. The value-added services provided through these digital networks create the digital business infrastructure for New Economy companies. In this highly interconnected environment, firms focus on more narrowly defined core competencies and outsource many processes to firms specializing in providing these real-time digital services. These include adserver networks, digital content syndication and configuration, content delivery maximization, website hosting and maintenance, customer acquisition (through affiliate relationships), real-time data mining, order fulfillment, payment processing, encryption, and many other digital processes. In addition, many companies outsource physical processes related to electronic commerce, such as outbound logistics (delivery) and even order fulfillment. Thousands of new companies have been formed in the last four years to provide these digital services (also known as web services or eServices). Some are generic services available to all, while others are industry-specific. These value chain networks will be addressed in the final section of this book.

This book addresses managerial and research issues related to all aspects of B2B eCommerce. The 13 chapters of this volume cover the environment of B2B eCommerce, supply chain management issues, value chain networks, and related research issues in three sections. Topics include EDI, exchanges, trust, manufacturing connectedness, automated tendering, virtual alliances, and B2X networks. The chapters are lively, with examples from industry. They also provide new scholarly perspectives on these important new markets and the processes that create and support them.

The contributions within this book are written by a collection of respected academic scholars from leading universities around the world and also by consultants with extensive experience creating, advising, and evaluating the new companies in this emerging field. Their work will be helpful to *managers* who seek guidance and insight into the strategic and operational questions arising from participation in this dynamic new environment. The findings contained within these chapters also constitute a valuable resource to *researchers* who seek to extend their understanding of the principles describing these networks and processes. Further, *educators* can use this book as a source of teaching material and classroom discussion to prepare tomorrow's leaders for this emerging New Economy. Finally, *public policy analysts* and *public leaders* need to understand this important new driver of economic growth. All students of business from all perspectives will benefit from the rich analysis contained within the chapters of this book.

The first section of this volume addresses the Business-to-Business Electronic Commerce environment. The first chapter provides a valuable framework for understanding the exchanges that have evolved within these emerging marketspaces. An exchange is a new organizational form residing in digital space that acts as an intermediary to enable firms to conduct and engage in online relationships. This chapter proposes a classification scheme for B2B exchanges that attempts to capture the chaos and complexity of today's B2B relations. It uses multiple implications of this taxonomy for managers to consider, and proposes guidelines for selecting the appropriate exchange mechanism for various business conditions.

The next chapter in the first section presents some valuable managerial considerations related to the establishment of B2B applications. By looking at recent examples, this chapter reveals a number of difficulties and challenges related to technology infrastructure and selection of viable business models. It outlines three specific business models and presents a framework to describe some of the managerial challenges that must be considered. The third chapter furthers this section's look at the B2B environment by providing an overview of critical issues associated with crafting a valuable and sustainable electronic marketplace. After a review of B2B markets, the issues of price presentation and price setting are introduced. The chapter then explores factors associated with participant motivation regarding the key issues of liquidity formation and maintenance, exchange ownership and governance, and the delivery of value-added services.

The final chapter in the first section addresses the issue of "impersonal trust" in establishing successful B2B relationships–the type of trust that is created by structural arrangements, rather than from repeated interaction and familiarity. It cites the institutional structures that B2B exchanges enable through signals and incentives. The antecedents of impersonal trust are presented–accreditation, feedback, monitoring, and legal bonds–and the role of trust in increasing satisfaction, reducing risk, encouraging continuity, and promoting favorable pricing is also discussed. Finally, the impact of these issues on the management of B2B sites and activities is discussed.

The second section of this book covers issues related to Supply Chain Management within B2B eCommerce. The initial chapter in this section provides an account of the history of EDI and Internet-based Supply Chain Management activities in the nation of Singapore. It also presents challenges in implementing B2B eCommerce in procurement and transportation. The goal is to prevent future failures resulting from the pitfalls identified in this chapter. The following chapter also addresses manufacturing connectedness issues in the context of B2B eCommerce. It argues for the involvement of managers at all levels, especially senior managers, in inter-organizational linkage efforts. Some of the issues include the role of standards, the use of cross-functional sourcing teams, and organizational buy-in. The evolution of highly connected virtual organizations is also addressed in this chapter. The next chapter in Section II introduces lessons in Supply Chain Management from the Chemical Industry. It argues that basic underlying problems in the supply chain must be solved before firms can successfully adopt formalized online procurement processes. Digital exchanges will not have a great impact until managers address internal problems, such as ERP implementation. If a company wishes to move from an "available-to-promise" functionality to one of "capable-to-promise" via the Internet, it must be able to plan production nearly in real time. The final chapter in this section addresses the electronic tendering process for B2B online auctions. The authors describe how the activities of buyers, sellers, and brokers, such as tender invitation, tender return, and negotiating, can be automated with various auction mechanisms to improve the efficiency and effectiveness of B2B exchanges. The chapter proposed a three-layer solution which uses a natural language ontology with dedicated agents to implement an automated tendering support system.

The third and final section of this book contains chapters which develop themes related to value chain networks and eServices, along with some emerging research issues in B2B eCommerce. The first chapter in this section presents an important new research perspective that is designed to improve upon the traditional perspectives from economics and network analysis. It seeks to explain more effectively the unfolding nature of B2B intermediaries and emerging marketspaces. This chapter proposes Structuration Theory as an alternative perspective, which examines the impact of B2B intermediaries not just on economic indicators, but on process outcomes such as mutual trust, coordination, innovation, and utilization of shared knowledge. It also evaluates the alignment of technology and interorganizational structure, and presents examples of the application of this theory. It concludes with some research questions and suggestions for future research approaches.

The second chapter in Section III provides a taxonomy of eCommerce business models and an evaluation of the role of agent technologies in various eCommerce processes. It distinguishes between the characteristics of value networks and dynamic markets. Finally, it presents the evolving standards established by the European Community (EC) designed to foster interoperable business systems. The third chapter discusses powerful new business alliances that offer services and products by utilizing the autonomous infrastructure provided by independent partners. These "extended corporations" integrate their business processes and systems with integrated value chains that support extended enterprises. It also provides a framework for managers encompassing the use of adaptive business objects and eServices to provide flexible eCommerce solutions. The next chapter in the final section provides perspective on the creation of virtual alliances through Value Chain Management. Using a three-stage investigation, this analysis defines the strategy and structure for an eBusiness enterprise as a value alliance network capable of flexibility and adaptability. Virtual markets are evaluated, and opportunities for electronic intermediation are examined. Supply chains, demand chains, and value chains are related to the evolution of a virtual value chain, which is then used as a basis for the development of effective organizational structures. This approach is then reviewed in the context of the retail market and interactive home shopping systems, and illustrated with an example from the eGrocery business.

The final chapter presents a new way of thinking about outsourcing in the age of digital end-to-end process integration. The evolution of eServices which can be "snapped together" by agile virtual corporations make entirely new business forms possible and have created entirely new marketspaces. Many of these "business-to-exchange" (or B2X) networks are discussed, and some suggestions for the future of B2B eCommerce are presented. The Internet will soon become a standards-based pool of "plug-and-play" processes that allow companies to simply connect to a "data tone" or "applications tone" to build their virtual enterprise that rapidly bring new value to markets.

Acknowledgments

In closing, I want to thank the many individuals who contributed to the success of this volume. First, I want to acknowledge all of the authors for their creative ideas and outstanding scholarship. Their participation made the editorial process enjoyable and rewarding. The diversity of author perspectives has made this volume a truly valuable resource for many types of readers.

All of the authors also served, along with other individuals, as blind reviewers for the articles submitted for consideration for this book. Thanks to all the reviewers for their constructive and thoughtful assessments and suggestions. Among the authors, Paul A. Pavlou was especially helpful in his contribution to the review process. In addition to the authors, I wish to thank a few reviewers who performed extra duties reviewing multiple papers for me – Akhilesh Bajaj of Carnegie Mellon University, Ravi Bapna of Northeastern University, Vijayan Sugumaran of Oakland University, and Peter Tarasewich of University of Massachusetts-Boston.

I also wish to thank Mehdi Khosrowpour at Idea Group Publishing for his leadership and sponsorship of this project. The entire staff at IGP has been helpful with all phases of this book's publication life cycle. Special thanks go to Michele Rossi at IGP for her guidance and assistance with the administrative processes during this project. Her attention to detail and her humor ensured that this book was a pleasure to develop.

I want to thank my parents for instilling in me a perpetually inquisitive nature and for teaching me the value of asking "Why?" My father was my greatest teacher and I will always be in debt to him. Finally, I want to thank one individual most of all for her endless support and important role in all of my work. My wife, Kim, is a true partner in so many ways, and I could not have completed this project without the joy in my life that she alone creates. Thank you, Kim.

Merrill Warkentin
Mississippi State University

Section I

The B2B eCommerce Environment

Chapter I

A Classification Scheme for B2B Exchanges and Implications for Interorganizational eCommerce

Paul A. Pavlou and Omar A. El Sawy
University of Southern California, USA

The Internet is transforming and reshaping the nature of interorganizational commerce by enabling many new types of interfirm electronic exchanges. A B2B exchange is defined as a new organizational form residing in digital space that acts as an interfirm intermediary that enables firms to conduct and engage in any-to-any online relations. This chapter proposes a classification scheme for B2B exchanges that attempts to capture the chaos and complexity of today's online B2B relations. This typology integrates several theories of interfirm relations from the information systems, marketing, and organizational economics literatures to propose a parsimonious but comprehensive taxonomy that encompasses neutral markets (many-to-many) and dyadic relations (few-to-few), and also the concept of biased relations, monopolies (few-to-many) and monopsonies (many-to-few). This chapter discusses the implications of the proposed taxonomy for interorganizational eCommerce that ensue from the alternative types of B2B exchanges. Furthermore, the influence of product, organizational, and market characteristics on B2B eCommerce is discussed, and guidelines for appropriate selection of exchange type and particular B2B exchanges are proposed.

INTRODUCTION

Intense competition in electronic markets and the growing number of web-based B2B marketplaces have made interorganizational eCommerce important and challenging. The notion of B2B eCommerce is not new, but its scale and scope has proliferated with the advent of B2B exchanges, which provide a facilitating structure for virtual relationships by enabling an easier identification and selection of suppliers and products, lower transaction costs, and more integrated supply-chain management compared to traditional channels (Dai and Kauffman, 2000). With over 1,000 currently established Internet B2B exchanges and an expected online transaction volume of over $6 trillion by 2004 (Bermudex et al., 2000), a primary issue associated with research on B2B exchanges is their proper classification (Kaplan and Sawney, 2000). Most B2B exchanges have substantially different characteristics in terms of their industry and product focus, the type of relationships and power asymmetries between buyers and suppliers, and type of product sourcing. The complexity of B2B exchanges calls for a complete but parsimonious typology that can bring order to the chaotic space of B2B eCommerce. Before being able to make some systematic efforts to capture today's chaotic B2B environment and build new theories, an academic-oriented classification scheme should be introduced to link the existing literature into the new landscape. Hence, the primary purpose of this chapter is to establish a comprehensive and versatile typology to capture and explain the scope of today's B2B exchanges, illustrated by existing real-life examples.

An important application of B2B eCommerce has been the interorganizational information system (IOIS) through which multiple firms interact online to identify and select trading partners, negotiate, and execute business transactions (Bakos, 1991). Internet-based IOIS can be considered as an extension of traditional EDI-based systems that enable firms to transact without investments in dedicated assets. Nonetheless, perhaps the most important development of an IOIS is the web-based B2B exchange, which is *not* merely a more advanced information system that acts as an interfirm intermediary, but it also offers an *organizational arrangement* with certain institutional structures to coordinate interfirm relations. A B2B exchange is defined as a new organizational form residing in digital space that acts as an interfirm intermediary that enables firms to conduct any-to-any online relations. Transacting through web-based exchanges may reduce transaction costs, increase the availability of products and suppliers and reduce dependencies on a few trading partners and products. Moreover, B2B exchanges may offer several secondary services towards integrating purchasing, distribution, and inventory processes, streamlining the entire transaction process, thus allowing better inventory management, quality control, and supply chain processes. Finally, many exchanges may offer collaborative services for joint planning, design, and forecasting (McKinsey, 2000). Therefore, B2B exchanges become more flexible coordinating mechanisms with fewer inefficiencies and faster operations compared to physical undertakings. By participating in B2B exchanges firms can significantly increase their transaction efficiencies; hence, without loss of generality, firms can achieve cost-savings by employing B2B exchanges in their eCommerce efforts.

Given the power of B2B exchanges to support business exchanges and offer several services, any firm could leverage their capabilities to receive value through eCommerce. The low cost of Internet-based eCommerce increases the scope of B2B exchanges to touch all firms irrespective of size, nature of business and relationship orientation. Therefore, since B2B exchanges redefine how firms interact with each other, it is important to understand how firms can benefit from B2B eCommerce through their participation in these exchanges. The academic and business literature has primarily focused on the efficiency-based cost savings associated with eCommerce (Bakos, 1998), mainly resulting from lower transaction costs, higher speed and less 'friction'. While participation in multilateral markets meant loss of electronic integration, the power of B2B exchanges enables markets to achieve comparable levels of technical and business integration as traditional dyadic relationships (Choudhury, 1997). Therefore, both buyers and suppliers benefit from these efficiencies. Nevertheless, perhaps the greatest value derived from B2B eCommerce can be absorbed by buyers through effective eProcurement resulting from better and more informed decisions in selecting suppliers and products, superior planning and forecasting, and obtaining more competitive pricing, better delivery terms, and higher product quality (Kalakota et al., 1999). While efficiency considerations may not greatly depend on exchange type, effective eProcurement mainly results from the selection of an appropriate B2B exchange that dictates the supplier consideration set, the amount and quality of industry and product information, and accompanying services. Therefore, exchange type selection should have a significant impact on eProcurement effectiveness, which is usually determined and measured in terms of supplier performance-competitive price, timeliness of delivery, supplier flexibility, and product quality (Heide and Stump, 1995).

The information systems, marketing and organizational economics literatures on interfirm relations provide many moderating factors that may affect the selection of appropriate B2B exchanges (e.g., Choudhury, 1997; McQuiston, 1989; Williamson, 1975). These factors can be broadly classified into three main categories–product, organizational, and market characteristics. Product characteristics include asset specificity and product complexity, among others. Company characteristics include procurement importance and novelty, switching costs, and purchase formalization and centralization. Market situational characteristics include a firm's bargaining power, market liquidity, product availability, relationship reciprocity (trust), uncertainty, and bargaining power. Finally, the importance and novelty of the purchase to the firm also affects the procurement process. These moderating factors should be taken into account in the selection of appropriate types of B2B exchanges following the proposed classification.

The existing literature covers a broad spectrum of relationships from basic buying and selling (price-driven transactions) to joint ventures and network firms (relationship-driven transactions), in addition to exchanges governed by power asymmetry (Frazier and Stewart 2000). Drawing from the literature on interorganizational relations, we attempt to develop an all-inclusive typology for alternative types of B2B exchanges. This classification scheme is proposed to link existing theories into the new Web-based B2B cyberspace and pave the road towards successful eCommerce strategies. Some illustrative real-world examples are also given to better explain each proposed type. Moreover, we discuss several moderating factors such as product, company, and market characteristics that influence the choice of B2B exchange type. In sum, this chapter attempts to answer the following questions: (1) How can B2B exchanges be classified? (2) How do product, company and market characteristics affect the selection of the type of B2B exchanges?

CONCEPTUAL DEVELOPMENT

Selecting B2B exchanges is a challenging decision for most firms given the number of alternatives available in today's eCommerce environment. Other than an IOIS, a B2B exchange can be considered as a structural arrangement for the governance of economic activity. Following Williamson and Ouchi (1981), governance refers to the "mode of organizing transactions," which includes elements of structuring relationships, as well as their enforcement. Malone, Yates, and Benjamin (1987) proposed two forms of governance structure for B2B exchanges based on Transaction Cost Economics (TCE): electronic markets with price-driven transactions, and electronic hierarchies where firms form dyadic relationships through managerial authority. Similarly, according to Macneil (1980), interfirm relations could be classified into discrete versus relational exchanges. Discrete exchanges are characterized by independent transactions that only involve a transfer of ownership, whereas relational exchanges are described by a mutuality of interests between firms where the historical and social context matters. From a marketing perspective, a relational exchange or dyadic relationship is embedded into the social context, which modifies the nature of the relationship based on cooperative norms rather than pure self-interest (Dwyer, Schurr and Oh, 1987).

The marketing and economics literature has focused on markets and relational exchanges (hierarchies) (Heide, 1994; Malone et al., 1987). Drawing on this distinction, B2B exchanges can thus either take the form of participation in an electronic market or participation in an electronic hierarchy. Nonetheless, this simplistic classification cannot adequately capture the whole spectrum of B2B exchanges, which have substantially different characteristics in terms of (a) their industry and product focus (vertical vs. horizontal), (b) relationship concentration (impersonal vs. relational), (c) asymmetries between firms (biased vs. neutral) and (d) type of sourcing (systematic vs. spot). Consequently, the immense complexity of today's B2B exchanges requires a more multifaceted classification. Choudhury (1997) proposed a typology of IOIS that consisted of electronic monopolies, electronic dyads and a multilateral IOIS such as the electronic market. Kaplan and Sawhney (2000) classified governance structures for B2B exchanges in terms of manufacturing and operating goods (vertical vs. horizontal), and spot against systematic sourcing. Bakos (1991) proposed various types of functional structures that interconnect suppliers, customers and intermediaries. These taxonomies may be able to capture a sufficient portion of the spectrum of B2B exchanges, but none of them is able to independently cover all types of B2B exchanges. Therefore, an all-inclusive classification scheme needs to be designed to cover the entire spectrum of B2B exchanges. Rather than attempting to inductively determine a classification scheme, a deductive approach should be employed drawing on the fundamental dimensions of interfirm relations.

Three primary structural dimensions–reach, range and reciprocity–can be assumed to span the dimensions of interorganizational relations (El Sawy and Nissen 1999). The dimension of *reach* is proposed to measure the number of potential partners to which a firm has likely access. The *range* dimension is proposed to measure the variety of products within the firm's reach. The *reciprocity* dimension measures in aggregate the strength and directionality of the interfirm relationships. Based on these fundamental structural dimensions, we attempt to link interfirm relations with B2B exchanges. Hence, reach would specify the number of a firm's potential trading partners in a B2B exchange (exchange participants), range would dictate the availability of products in the exchange, and reciprocity would state the nature of the buyer-supplier relationships in the exchange. Therefore, these three dimensions should be able to adequately determine the type of B2B exchange and propose a versatile classification scheme.

The dimension of reach is proposed to classify B2B exchanges in an all-inclusive typology, and implicitly account for the range and reciprocity dimensions. Reach measures the number of potential partners to which a firm has likely access in a given exchange, relating positively to the number of opportunities that a firm can potentially pursue. Combining the reach dimension from the perspective of both buyers and suppliers, a two-dimensional classification scheme arises which measures the *proportion* of buyers to suppliers, or vice versa. The proportion of buyers to suppliers can create a 2X2 typology that distinguishes the type of exchange based on the number of participating firms. Despite the relative simplicity of this typology, it has the immediate benefit of an all-inclusive, yet parsimonious classification scheme. This typology includes all previously suggested types such as markets, dyads, monopolies, monopsonies and relational exchanges, and implicitly encompasses previous dimensions such as product focus, relationship concentration, asymmetries between buyers and suppliers and type of sourcing.

When any participating buyer or seller in a B2B exchange views an equal number of potential partners, there is a balanced proportion of firms, dictating a neutral exchange that may be one-to-one, few-to-few, or many-to-many (suppliers-to-buyers). Similarly, when there is an imbalance proportion, exchanges become progressively biased that may be many-to-few, few-to-many or more extreme (many-to-one or one-to-many). This approach gives a two-dimensional classification scheme with four extreme points and four distinct quadrants, as shown in Figure 1. First, when the reach dimension is many for both buyers and suppliers (many-to-many), markets arise, covering the upper left quadrant. The opposite extreme point arises when the reach of each buyer and supplier is only one (one-to-one), signifying a traditional dyadic relationship. The lower right quadrant spans a region where few qualified firms form a reserved exchange (few-to-few). The two other outermost points in the 2X2 matrix are extreme situations where a single firm having a great reach of potential partners dominates the exchange. The upper

Figure 1: Graphical Representation of the Proposed Typology for the Forms of B2B Exchanges

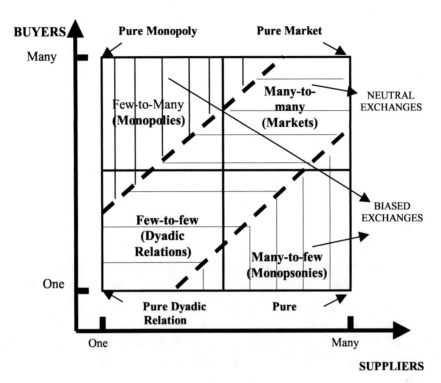

left corner (one-to-many) shows a monopoly where a single supplier may sell to many buyers. Equally, the lower right corner shows the case of a monopsony exchange where one buyer purchases from a great number of suppliers. Similarly, the two adjacent quadrants cover the area of biased exchanges (few-to-many and many-to-few), respectively.

The proposed classification scheme is an all-inclusive, two-dimensional typology that covers all types of alternative forms of B2B exchanges. It is robust to encompass the notions of neutrality and bias, and it readily relates to concepts from organizational economics (markets, monopolies, and monopsonies) and marketing (dyadic relationships). Furthermore, its conceptual simplicity and parsimony make it superior to previous descriptive taxonomies since many factors of interfirm exchange behavior (product, organizational, and market characteristics) can be linked into a coherent theoretical framework. Finally, despite its reliance on a single dimension, the other two fundamental structural dimensions of range and reciprocity can be integrated. The dimension of range covers vertical markets that deal with industry-specific products, and horizontal markets carry products that all industries can use. Despite earlier attempts to classify exchanges as vertical and horizontal (Kaplan and Sawney 2000), recent findings showed that both types of products are often traded within the same B2B exchange (Dai and Kauffman 2000). Based on network externalities, the greater range of products available in the same exchange, the greater benefits a firm receives from streamlining its operations through B2B exchanges dealing with both vertical and horizontal markets. Moreover, the proposed types of exchanges usually reflect the range of products traded. Therefore, there is no need to draw an additional dimension for range when the theory of network externalities dictates that the extant dimensions may cover product type. Similarly, the dimension of reciprocity is related to the number of participating firms (Heide, 1994) and power bias (Kumar, Scheer and Steenkamp 1995). Therefore, the proposed taxonomy also encompasses interfirm reciprocity.

Neutral Exchanges

Neutral exchanges are either large-scale marketplaces that enable many buyers to reach many suppliers, or small-scale marketplaces that enable one or a few buyers to reach a small number of selected suppliers. Many-to-many B2B exchanges are usually public markets where firms interact with either a dynamic or static pricing, whereas one-to-one or few-to-few B2B exchanges are usually private, firm-driven markets with negotiated or hierarchical pricing.

Many-to-Many (Markets)

B2B exchanges have radically transformed interfirm relations by allowing electronic integration among multiple buyers and sellers where the cost of searching, participating and transacting is sufficiently affordable. A many-to-many exchange allows a virtually infinite number of firms to transact electronically with minimal costs. Such B2B exchanges allow buyers to choose among a large number of suppliers for a set of products, whereas sellers have many buyers to promote their products. However, the presence of a great number of firms in this type of exchange precludes strong interfirm relationships. Despite the lack of high reciprocity, information sharing, feedback mechanisms, and accreditation efforts can be insured through the exchange, which enables a basic level of impersonal trust. Therefore, many-to-many B2B exchanges benefit from high reach, whereas they are usually low in the range and reciprocity dimension. Many-to-many exchanges create value by matching many firms through negotiated prices (dynamic pricing), and also by aggregating a large number of firms (static pricing). The matching mechanism is particularly effective in true price discovery, delivery terms, and product quality as firms dynamically interact through the process of supply and demand or the auction mechanism. Aggregation is effective when multiple suppliers post their products through a catalog, and buyers are able to conveniently search for the best prices, quality and delivery terms.

Dynamic Pricing (Matching)

When many firms interact in a B2B exchange, a dynamic mode of pricing can be used to discover the market price of a product. Similar to stocks in the New York Stock Exchange, commodity goods enable supply and demand forces to find the Pareto optimal allocation of price, quality, and delivery terms. Many-to-many exchanges fit classical economic theory where perfect competition with infinite suppliers and buyers exists, entry and exit barriers are low, and the focal good is low in asset specificity (commodity). If enough liquidity is built into the system, an electronic market closely resembles the ideal market, which is theoretically the most efficient trading structure, or perfect competition (Varian, 1984). Nonetheless, high liquidity can be achieved only when a great number of firms transact particular commodities. Hence, the range of obtainable products is usually very low. However, dynamic pricing is only feasible in markets characterized by commodities, where trading is based on a limited number of product characteristics. Fluid pricing, quality and delivery terms that are based on interactive negotiation between buyers and suppliers who quickly adapt to changing market conditions characterize such B2B exchanges. Dynamic pricing can also take the form of an auction, but this mechanism may favor the supply side (forward auctions) or purchasing side (reverse auctions).

Neutral B2B exchanges with dynamic pricing may be economically efficient, but they are restricted by four factors: reach, range, power asymmetry and reciprocity. First, the availability of trading partners is a crucial issue. If firms do not have the required reach, markets will lack liquidity and will cause uneven pricing and other inefficiencies. Second, only a small number of commodities with simple descriptions can be traded. Product differentiation, which is usually driven by suppliers to gain a 'niche,' reduces liquidity. Third, large buyers or suppliers would use their negotiating power to receive better deals rather than getting the market price. Finally, to allow a true liquid and unbiased market, many-to-many exchanges require anonymity. However, many buyers seek high-reciprocity partnerships with suppliers to safeguard the integrity of the transaction, increase coordination and reduce uncertainty. Therefore, despite attempts to increase interfirm trust in such marketplaces, reciprocity is a critical factor that limits the extent of many-to-many dynamic B2B exchanges.

Altra.com (www.altra.com) is one of the most prolific many-to-many

B2B exchanges that connect multiple firms into a neutral dynamic-pricing marketplace, offering a real-time, online system for trading natural gas, power, natural gas liquids and crude oil. Similar to a stock exchange, buyers and sellers can view and exchange bids and offers quickly, remaining anonymous until they reach an agreement. Altra.com provides a great reach for its market participants by having more than 6,000 firms worldwide. In addition, high liquidity is another characteristic since a tremendous amount of energy is transacted through Altra's exchange. Moreover, the gas and power industry is fragmented with not many powerful traders being able to affect the market; hence, bias is a minimal issue. However, the range of products in this exchange is very small since only gas and power-related commodities are exchanged. In addition, the participants' reciprocity is rather low given that all transactions are anonymous until an agreement is reached. Nonetheless, this concern is addressed by allowing scheduling for purchases, viewing transactions, tracking energy positions, and generating invoices and remittance statements. Therefore, this B2B exchange offers a variety of secondary services to allow electronic integration, monitoring, physical scheduling and reconciliation of all completed transactions to establish a basic level of reciprocity among firms. In sum, similar to the characteristics of the proposed many-to-many dynamic market, the reciprocity among firms is rather low, the range of products is limited, but the reach and liquidity offered by Altra's B2B exchange is very high.

Static Pricing (Aggregation)

The most common type of many-to-many B2B exchanges is based on catalog aggregation using posted prices. Static markets are characterized by fixed prices and offers from many industry suppliers, where terms and conditions are usually posted to allow a convenient, one-stop procurement. While static pricing allows room for inefficiencies and uneven pricing, it also allows a greater number of similar products to be traded, increasing the availability of suppliers (reach) and products (range). These marketplaces can accommodate products with more complex description and greater specificity, allowing more product differentiation and less competition among suppliers. Therefore, the reach of the purchasing side and the range of products available in the aggregation mechanism are greater than in the matching mechanism. Static pricing can be particularly effective when search costs are high but the timeliness of the purchase is crucial. Therefore, buyers can receive a competitive price and quality through conveniently searching over a great number of competing suppliers and products, and also assure favorable delivery and warranty terms by selecting qualified suppliers. In terms of reciprocity, aggregating exchanges are rarely anonymous, allowing a certain level of reciprocity between firms.

Assetsmart.com (www.assetsmart.com) is a catalog-based B2B exchange with a comprehensive list of high-technology equipment. The static pricing model allows a great number of products from many suppliers to be traded in a single B2B exchange. In the Assetsmart.com marketplace, by allowing sellers to reveal their identity, reputable suppliers can still leverage their brand name while communication may occur before purchasing. Moreover, the exchange provides detailed information about products, thus reducing the products' complexity and specificity and making purchasing more accessible. In addition, an organized search engine makes finding products easy through a robust online catalog, automating the purchasing process from requisition to payment, and making purchasing possible. Finally, Assetsmart.com directly addresses reciprocity concerns by monitoring every step of the fulfillment process, streamlining the business processes and supply chain, notifying firms if any problems occur, and providing order fulfillment and status information.

Few-to-Few (Dyadic Relations)

Many industries depend on long-term relationships built over many years based on cooperative adjustments and mutual management of the supply chain. Even if many-to-many B2B exchanges receive a great deal of attention, few-to-few exchanges for coordinating transactions will also play a role in eCommerce. Close relationships between a small number of firms promote collaboration, coordination and expertise sharing. Few-to-few or one-to-one exchanges benefit from web-based technologies; while EDI has been the most common method for automating procurement, its extent was limited by its substantial cost that made it only accessible to large firms with recurring volume of purchases. However, the use of the Internet makes electronic integration economically accessible to small-scale B2B exchanges. Markets are assumed to be low in trust and fail when relationships must be deep to account for specific, specialty goods with complex and unique descriptions that require relationship-specific initial investments, such as interfirm learning (Williamson, 1975). Therefore, unlike markets that are driven mainly by the price mechanism, specialty goods require reciprocity among firms (Dwyer et al., 1987).

Dyadic relations are created when there is a cooperative relation between firms that extends beyond a single transaction. A strategic alliance is a form of exchange that requires close collaboration, coordination and exchange of private information between few firms (Bakos and Brynjolfsson, 1993). The initiation of dyadic relations is based on selective entry through quality screening. The relationship is maintained by communication that provides role specification, proactive planning, mutual adjustment through reciprocal negotiation, internal monitoring, a long-term incentive system and enforcement based on joint cooperation. Few-to-few exchanges usually have high levels of reciprocity that create value by capturing the long-term benefits of high-trust relations by enabling custom-made solutions that assure customized product quality, timeliness of delivery, and favorable pricing and warranty terms (Zaheer et al., 1998). These exchanges are effective when purchasing is of strategic importance and buyers wish to assure supplier reliability, competence and qualification, and also when switching to other suppliers is costly.

Buzzsaw.com (www.buzzsaw.com) offers customizable solutions for firms in the construction industry to meet, collaborate, design, plan and administer joint projects. A variety of collaborative services enabled by this exchange are most likely to maximize satisfaction while minimizing cost, especially for specialty products with complex specifications, features and options. Buzzsaw.com attempts to solve the problem of asset specificity by providing qualification, document sharing, extensive communication and one-to-one negotiation. Collaborative platforms facilitate communication, knowledge sharing and joint administration at every step of the construction process, promoting a high level of reciprocity among firms. Therefore, Buzzsaw.com provides the infrastructure and related services for relationship initiation, role specification, and joint design and planning. However, such services are primarily useful to close relationships and complex transactions; hence, the reach of participating firms and range of products are relatively limited.

Biased Exchanges

Whereas neutral exchanges may ideally be the most efficient governance mechanism, *bias* is an inevitable attribute of interfirm relations, since either side may possess buying or selling bargaining power because of industry structure, the nature of the focal product, or size. Auctions are well-understood examples of biased markets. Traditional forward auctions favor suppliers since many buyers compete for a single product and raise the product's price, whereas reverse auctions favor buyers by having multiple suppliers bidding downwards for a single purchase, thus dropping the product's price. For buyers, the greater reach to many suppliers and the greater number of products, the more value it can capture through more favorable transaction terms. A great reach of suppliers in a B2B exchange provides positive network externalities to the purchasing side that translates into more effective eProcurement. Conversely, a low reach of suppliers compared to the number of buyers can result in adverse network externalities and reduction in effectiveness to the procurement side.

Many-to-One (Monopsonies)

While it has been argued that eCommerce will eliminate power asymmetry and dependency among firms, traditional powerful buyers capture benefits by leveraging their existing physical power (e.g., reputation, size, purchasing volume) into online B2B exchanges. According to neoclassical theory, any form of power against a competing supply side could result in better outcomes for the demand side, and vice versa (Varian, 1984). Monopsony, which translates into *sole buying*, is the case of few buyers facing multiple sellers. Industries with pyramid shapes have a few big buyers and a fragmented mass of suppliers. Examples of such markets are the automotive and the apparel industry where a small number of large buyers (e.g., Ford, GM and Sears, Roebuck) have access to a great number of small suppliers. Many-to-one B2B exchanges occur when a single or few buyers support a marketplace with multiple competing suppliers. Monopsony allows the buyer to benefit from multiple competing suppliers, while facing no major antagonism from other buyers. Moreover, the range of products is limited to the assets at which the buyer has substantial power, and these purchases are important to its bottom line (Kaplan and Sawney, 2000). The dimension of reciprocity is still under debate; whereas monopsony has created long-term trusting relationships in some industries (Kumar et al., 1995), such dependency forces firms to leave the exchange or create coalitions to reduce the bargaining power of the other side. In general, the notion of bias is a challenging research issue; hence, it would be an interesting research area for B2B exchanges.

Covisint.com (www.covisint.com) is a B2B exchange that connects the major U.S. automakers (GM, Ford and Daimler Chrysler) with many fragmented suppliers in the automotive industry, through a supplier network, formerly known as the Advanced Network Exchange (ANX). The purpose of this B2B exchange is to facilitate and simplify trading between traditional big manufacturers and the more than 30,000 suppliers in the automotive industry. In Covisint.com, the supply side consists of few powerful players with tremendous bargaining power and a fragmented supplier side. This B2B exchange allows an enormous range of products to be traded, mainly based on contracts, reverse auctions and negotiations. The power asymmetry in this B2B exchange naturally results in substantial value for the big buyers in terms of pricing, quality and delivery terms. However, by implementing a powerful procurement system for transacting with many suppliers, the large automakers through investing in Covisint.com incurred a considerable ongoing expense to maintain such extensive technological platform. Therefore, whereas many-to-few exchanges favor the purchasing side, there are considerable expenses associated with running the B2B exchange, which need to be supplanted by the benefits than monopsony offers. Finally, given the long history of the automotive industry in the United States, the notion of reciprocity in this B2B exchange is still a debatable issue that draws from existing relationships. Therefore, the future of Covisint.com is interesting both from an academic and managerial perspective.

Few-to-Many (Monopolies)

Industries with inverse pyramid shapes have a few big suppliers and a fragmented mass of buyers. This mechanism is the primary model for business-to-consumer eCommerce, where a large supplier trades its products to many individual buyers (consumers). Monopoly exchanges have begun appearing in B2B markets initiated by large companies, such as Cisco, Staples and Grainger. From a theoretical perspective, monopolies are important coordinating mechanisms that received considerable attention (Varian, 1984). The range of products is undeniably restricted to the assets at which suppliers have some monopoly power. eProcurement in monopoly exchanges is usually ineffective and may result in poor transaction terms. Therefore, buyers may either seek to increase their reach through finding new suppliers, aggregate their power in many-to-many B2B exchanges or establish one-to-one relations with a specific supplier. Nevertheless, few-to-many exchanges are important coordinating mechanisms that suppliers should take advantage of. Similar to monopsony exchanges, bias creates an interesting issue associated with the dimension of reciprocity among participating firms.

Staples.com (www.staples.com) is a monopoly B2B exchange that promotes its office-related products. This one-to-many dynamic pricing configuration allows firms to buy specially configured systems with unique combinations of product features directly from this large supplier of horizontal products. This B2B exchange allows Staples.com to leverage its selling power in office products to target buyers of different sizes through a cost-effective marketplace. On the procurement side, buyers can take advantage of the increased buying flexibility offered by this exchange to transact with Staples.com, which expands its reach to many firms, allowing new avenues for incremental business. Therefore, monopoly B2B exchanges may provide flexibility towards streamlining the supply chain, even if it may not be the most effective eProcurement solution.

A table representation of the different types of B2B exchanges based on the proposed taxonomy along with some examples is shown in Table 1. It should be noted that this classification is not exclusive since a single B2B exchange may target various quadrants. For example, Fasturn.com (www.fasturn.com) operates simultaneously in both the one-to-many and many-to-many markets.

Factors Influencing the Selection of B2B Exchanges

Despite the significant efficiency improvements that B2B exchanges can offer, the most important aspect of eCommerce is perhaps effective sourcing solutions. Successful eCommerce is a combination of transactional efficiencies, information acquisition, partner selection and relationship management, and also optimum design, planning and decision-making, among others. Each exchange type determines the number of potential partners (reach), the availability of products (range) and the nature of the buyer-supplier relationships (reciprocity). For example, each exchange type shapes the nature of the services offered; few-to-few exchanges emphasize collaborative services, while many-to-many highlight search engines and transaction-facilitating services. In addition, through reach, range and reciprocity, exchange type influences transactional terms such as price, timeliness of delivery and product quality (Heide and Stump, 1995; Zaheer et al., 1998). For instance, few-to-few and many-to-few exchanges emphasize product quality, whereas many-to-many and few-to-many stress the importance of competitive price and delivery terms. Therefore, each type of B2B exchange has a dissimilar approach of creating value by differently affecting these terms.

Other than the dimensions of reach, range and reciprocity, there are also other factors that influence the choice of B2B exchanges, such as product,

Table 1: Typology of the Forms of B2B Exchanges

TYPE	Pricing	Orientation	Examples
Many-to-Many **(Market)**	**Dynamic** **(Matching)**	**Neutral**	**Altra.com** **Chemconnect.com**
	Static **(Aggregation)**		**Assetsmart.com** **Freemarkets.com**
Few-to-few **(Dyadic Relations)**	**Negotiated**		**Buzzsaw.com** **Citadon.com**
Few-to-Many **(Monopoly)**	**Posted**	**Biased** **(Supplier)**	**Staples.com** **Granger.com**
Many-to-Few **(Monopsony)**	**Static**	**Biased** **(Buyer)**	**Covisint.com** **AutoXchange.com**

organizational and market characteristics. In general, the factors related to product characteristics are asset specificity and procurement complexity; factors associated with organizational characteristics are purchase importance and novelty, formalization, centralization and switching costs; in terms of market characteristics, other factors are uncertainty and transaction activity. By taking into account these additional factors, a more informative selection of a B2B exchange could result in higher value creation.

Product Characteristics

TCE maintains that product *specificity* is the most critical dimension for determining the nature of cooperation in an economic transaction (Williamson, 1975). A product is highly specific if other firms cannot readily use this asset because of site, physical, human or time specificity. Where product specificity is great, firms usually make efforts to choose B2B exchanges with a long-term orientation and avoid spot transaction. Therefore, high product specificity is associated with smaller-scale B2B exchanges where quality is more important than price. The usual distinction of product specificity deals with commodities versus specialty items; many-to-many B2B exchanges may be more appropriate for commodities, whereas specialty items necessitate a small number of accredited suppliers. Purchase *complexity* is defined as the amount of information required in making an accurate evaluation of a product (McQuiston, 1989). Traditionally, product complexity discouraged electronic markets (Malone et al., 1987); however, electronic catalogs and search engines usually found in any type of exchange enable buyers to search for products irrespective of complexity. Nonetheless, products with complex descriptions are difficult to be transacted in a many-to-many exchange with dynamic pricing since liquidity requires simple descriptions.

Organizational Characteristics

Purchase *importance* is associated with the perceived impact of the purchase on firm profitability (McQuiston, 1989). While any type of B2B exchange could accommodate products that affect a firm's bottom line, important purchases may necessitate the establishment of private many-to-few or few-to-few exchanges with a trustworthy network of suppliers. In addition, important purchases might require a many-to-many exchange to avoid opportunity costs associated with relying on a few suppliers and ineffective pricing. Purchase *novelty* is defined as the lack of experience of a firm with similar procurement situations (McQuiston, 1989). When buyers are faced with novel purchasing situations, a normal approach is to acquire more information, decreasing the likelihood that buyers would rely on a small set of suppliers, and that they are likely to explore all potential opportunities, particularly electronic catalogs that provide a comparison-shopping. Purchase *formalization* refers to the formal procedures governing a firm's procurement process. The extent of formal organizational constraints imposes a disincentive to the buyer firm to search for all alternatives. Therefore, buyers will prefer to work with a small group of suppliers to avoid the pressure of formalization when new suppliers are selected. Purchase *centralization* refers to the concentration of decision-making authority for procurement to a small number of people at high organizational levels. The extant purchasing literature suggest that centralization leads to considering a large number of suppliers and selecting new ones.

Switching costs measure a firm's expected costs of crafting new relations. While the cost for participating in established exchanges is relatively low, the initial cost for establishing a private exchange may be considerable. Moreover, *technological compatibility* assesses the degree to which the compatibility of a B2B exchange with the buyer's existing internal system is an issue. In case of compatibility problems, firms incur costs to assure that an exchange is compatible with their legacy systems, costs that are commonly referred to as *transient disconnectivity*. Finally, firms face switching costs because of established relationships with particular partners that required specific investments. In sum, switching costs act as disincentives to explore new opportunities; therefore, an appropriate selection of a B2B exchange should take into account potential switching costs associated with it, and assure that the benefits outweigh these costs.

Market Characteristics

Uncertainty can arise from many factors, such as technological considerations and environmental conditions, and usually forces firms to rely on a small number of trustworthy partners. Uncertainty includes technological heterogeneity, which measures the diversity that characterizes the different dimensions of the product-related market. Another source is the pace of technological change, which measures the buyer's perceptions of the extent to which a product's dimensions are rapidly changing. In addition, market conditions and information asymmetry impose demands on the firm's processing capacity, which further increase the level of uncertainty. All these sources of uncertainty jointly contribute to fewer and more reliable suppliers. Finally, another important factor that firms need to consider in today's B2B eCommerce is transaction activity. The future of independent B2B exchanges depends on firm participation and activity. While there is probably not a theoretical interest, firms should ascertain that the chosen exchange is likely to maintain adequate transaction activities to remain in business.

Consortium Exchanges

Consortia are B2B exchanges that attempt to provide a technological and organizational platform to enable interaction among firms within an existing association or network. For example, Covisint.com (www.covisint.com) is considered a consortium exchange, built around an existing automotive association. Rather than joining a newly formed B2B exchange with new partners, firms usually prefer leveraging their existing relations into eCommerce. Following the proposed classification, consortium exchanges can lay anywhere along the proposed spectrum; for example, Covisint.com lies in the monopsony region. The future of consortium-based as opposed to public B2B exchanges is an interesting managerial and theoretical issue.

DISCUSSION

The major contribution of this research is the proposed two-dimensional typology that integrates alternative forms of B2B relations that were not adequately captured by previous taxonomies. Our typology covers the entire spectrum of B2B exchanges and attempts to implicitly account for all aspects that have not been adequately examined before, such as bargaining power and reciprocity. Moreover, by employing the single dimension of reach as the major sorting mechanism, the chaotic spectrum of B2B exchanges can be graphically represented on a straightforward 2X2 typology. Without loss of generality, the chaotic environment of today's B2B exchanges can be easily classified around two dimensions, representing a parsimonious and comprehensive typology.

A second contribution of this research is the incorporation of existing theories from Information Systems, Economics and Marketing into the proposed classification scheme. This scheme draws on previous research on B2B relationships from the economics and marketing literature to integrate IOIS into a coherent scheme that captures key features of eCommerce. First, the distinction between many-to-many versus one-to-one depicts the division between electronic markets and hierarchies from organizational economics (Williamson, 1981; Malone et al., 1987) and markets and dyadic relationships from marketing channel relationships (Macneil, 1980; Heide, 1994). Therefore, notions from the distinct disciplines of economics and marketing are integrated with Information Systems literature to produce a novel classification scheme that has strong roots in existing theory. Moreover, our typology also captures the practical dimensions of spot versus systematic sourcing (Kaplan and Sawhney, 2000). In sum, the proposed taxonomy takes into account various disciplinary approaches as well as practical dimensions.

A third contribution of this research is an attempt to link the proposed typology with additional factors present in interfirm relations. Several product, organizational and market characteristics need to be considered in the selection of the exchange type to achieve greater value from eCommerce. This chapter described these factors and discussed their importance with selecting a type of B2B exchange following the proposed classification scheme. These factors are drawn from existing theories from organizational economics and marketing, and hold substantial value in influencing interfirm relations. Therefore, there is considerable evidence to suggest that these factors should be applied to selection of both the general type of B2B exchanges and also for specific B2B exchanges. While our typology holds for eCommerce relations, it theoretically applies to B2B relations both in the physical and eCommerce. Our assumption is that web-based IOIS enable electronic integration of any-to-any relations and promote transactional efficiencies irrespective of the number of participating firms. Therefore, the dimension of reach can be readily applied to any type of B2B relations. Nevertheless, in the absence of low-cost, web-based IOIS, many-to-many exchanges are practically inapplicable.

CONCLUSION

Given the rapid development of electronic B2B exchanges, it is important to understand the complexity of interfirm relations based on a complete, parsimonious, and versatile typology. The proposed typology provides a simple and robust method to guide researchers and practitioners to identify alternative types of B2B exchanges in today's chaotic eCommerce. From a managerial perspective, not only can managers select the most appropriate type of B2B exchange, but they are also given a set of additional factors to consider in making their selection. Based on product, organizational and market characteristics, firms can appropriately weigh these factors in their decisions for both the type and particular selection of B2B exchanges.

ACKNOWLEDGMENT

This work was supported by the External Acquisition Research Program (EAR), sponsored by the Office of the Undersecretary of Defense (Acquisition, Technology and Logistics) and managed by the Naval Postgraduate School in Monterey, California.

REFERENCES

Bakos, J. Y. (1991). A strategic analysis of electronic marketplaces. *MIS Quarterly*, 15(3), 295-312.

Bakos, J. Y. and Brynjolfsson, E. (1993). Information technology, incentives and the optimal number of suppliers. *Journal of Information Systems*, 10(2), 37-51.

Bakos, J.Y. (1998). The emerging role of electronic marketplaces on the Internet. *Communications of the ACM*, 41(8), 35-42.

Bermudex, J., Kraus, B., O'Brien, D., Parker, B. and Lapide, L. (2000). B2B commerce forecast: $5.7T by 2004. Available on the World Wide Web at: http://www.amrresearch.com. Accessed September 28, 2000.

Choudhury, V. (1997). Strategic choices in the development of interorganizational information systems. *Information Systems Research*, 8(1), 1-24.

Dai, Q. and Kauffman, R. J. (2000). Business models for Internet-based eProcurement systems and B2B electronic markets: An exploratory assessment. *Proceedings of the 34th Hawaii International Conference on Systems Science*, Maui, Hawaii.

Dwyer, F. R., Schurr, P. J. and Oh, S. (1987). Developing buyer-seller relationships. *Journal of Marketing*, 52(1), 21-34.

El Sawy, O. A. and Nissen, M. E. (1999). The rolodex model: Understanding relationship complexity as a precursor to the design of organizational forms for chaotic environments. *Working Paper*, Marshall School of Business, University of Southern California.

Frazier, G. L. and Stewart, D. W. (2000). The boundaries of relationship marketing in channels of distribution. *Working Paper*, Department of Marketing, University of Southern California.

Heide, J. B. (1994). Interorganizational governance in marketing channels. *Journal of Marketing*, January, 58, 71-85.

Heide, J. B. and Miner, A. (1992). The shadow of the future: Effects of anticipated interaction and frequency of contact on buyer-seller cooperation. *Academy of Management Journal*, 35, 265-291.

Heide, J. B. and John, G. (1990). Alliances in industrial purchasing, the determinants of joint action in buyer-supplier relationships. *Journal of Marketing Research*, 37, 24-36.

Kalakota, R., Robinson, M. and Tapscott, D. (1999). E-business: Roadmap for success. *Addison-Wesley Information Technology Series*, Addison-

Wesley.

Kaplan, S. and Sawhney, M. (2000). E-hubs: The new B2B marketplaces. *Harvard Business Review*, May-June, 97-103.

Kumar, N., Scheer, L. K. and Steenkamp, J. B. E. M. (1995). The effects of perceived interdependence on dealer attitudes. *Journal of Marketing Research*, 32, 348-356.

Macneil, I.R. (1980). *The New Social Contract*. New Haven, CT: Yale University Press.

Malone, T., Yates, J. and Benjamin, R. (1987). Electronic markets and electronic hierarchies. *Communications of the ACM*, 30(6), 484-497.

McQuiston, D. H. (1989). Novelty, complexity and importance as causal determinants of industrial buyer behavior. *Journal of Marketing*, 53, 66-79.

McKinsey & Company. (2000). Coming into focus. *Internal Report*.

Varian, H. (1984). *Microeconomic Analysis*. New York: Norton.

Williamson, O. E. (1975). *Markets and Hierarchies*. New York: The Free Press.

Williamson, O. E. and Ouchi, W. G. (1981). The markets and hierarchies program of research: Origins, implications, prospects. In Van de Ven, A. H. and Joyce, W. F. (Eds.), *Perspectives on Organizational Design and Behavior*, New York: John Wiley & Sons, Inc., 347-370.

Zaheer, A., McEvily, B. and Perrone, V. (1998). Does trust matter? Exploring the effects of interorganizational and interpersonal trust on performance. *Organization Science*, 9(2), 141-159.

Chapter II

B2B Applications to Support Business Transactions: Overview and Management Considerations

Norm Archer
McMaster University, Canada

Judith Gebauer
University of California, Berkeley, USA

The use of Internet and Web technologies between organizations has gained much attention in recent years. Termed business-to-business (B2B) electronic commerce, the linking and integration of inter-organizational business processes and systems promises cost and time savings, as well as new business opportunities. The many examples of B2B applications cover a broad range of sales and purchasing processes, business models, industries, and products and services. Complexity ranges from simple message switchboards to sophisticated marketplaces handling a multitude of real-time transactions, integrated closely with the backend systems of the participants.

Using information technology (IT) to connect organizations is by no means a new phenomenon, but reaches back several decades to include electronic data interchange (EDI) systems and remote terminal applications. Still, systems based on Internet standards seem to be easier to set up technically and cheaper to interconnect. They might thus reach wider adoption and acceptance than many of the earlier initiatives, and as a result give smaller players a realistic opportunity to join in and reap benefits similar to their larger partners.

A closer look at recent examples, however, also reveals a number of difficulties and challenges. Besides shortcomings with respect to an adequate and affordable technology infrastructure, viable business models have not always emerged, and already project failures and market closures are being reported. A particular issue is that inter-organizational information systems always involve several independent decision makers whose interests have to be balanced very carefully.

After describing different forms of B2B electronic commerce systems and marketplaces, this chapter discusses a number of management challenges. The discussion includes earlier research on inter-organizational information systems.

INTRODUCTION

Despite recent signs for an economic slowdown, in particular concerning the so-called "New" economy, and despite the failures of many dot-com startups, many firms still plan to invest in new technologies, in particular to establish electronic links across organizational boundaries. In fact, the preponderance of Internet business is now business-to-business (B2B), estimated at more than five times the value of consumer-oriented electronic commerce (B2C), and predicted to grow to 10 times its value by 2003 (Forrester, 1999; Tedeschi, 1999). The Gartner Group estimates that by 2004, B2B eCommerce will represent seven percent of a forecast $105 trillion in total global sales transactions (McCall, 2000).

After an early emphasis on B2B applications to support selling processes (sell-side applications), electronic procurement systems have seen much attention (buy-side applications, Segev, Gebauer & Färber, 2000). Most recently, attention has shifted to Internet-based electronic marketplaces. In a recent study, market research company Jupiter Communications estimates that the investments to set up inter-organizational online markets will reach $80.9 billion by 2005, up from $2.1 billion in 2000.

An electronic marketplace is a virtual marketplace where buyers and suppliers meet to exchange information about prices and product and service offerings, to collaborate, and to negotiate and carry out business transactions. Numerous announcements of online exchanges, possibly involving many thousands of business partners, have been made in a number of industries, including automotive (Covisint), retail (Transora) and electronics (E2Open). Success is not always granted, however. In fact, B2B online markets often report difficulties in generating sufficient liquidity, and in some cases have already terminated their activities completely (Chemdex), providing evidence for the importance of carefully crafted management concepts (see www.netmarketmakers.com and www.b2business.net for overviews of current developments and up-to-date industry reports).

The discussion in this chapter will focus on the managerial issues of dealing with B2B applications, where participants may include buyers, suppliers, multi-firm consortia, independent third parties, as well as various providers of the technical infrastructure. To put the developments into perspective, we start our discussion with a brief overview of the history of Internet-based B2B applications.

The use of information technology (IT) to share information between organizations is not new. Since the early 1970s, IT has been deployed to link firms to their customers or suppliers, often through value-added networks (VANs). These make use of standard protocols such as ANSI X.12 or EDIFACT to share information and to automate the exchange of electronic documents relating to purchasing, selling, shipping, receiving, inventory, financial and other activities. As such, they are commonly referred to as electronic data interchange (EDI) systems (Emmelhainz, 1993; Sokol, 1995). The application of Michael Porter's findings on competitive structures of industries (Porter, 1980) led to a number of large-scale inter-organizational systems (IOS), set up to gain competitive advantage by locking in customers and business partners (Johnston & Vitale, 1988).

Many of the early examples, in particular basic EDI applications, typically had little to offer in terms of end-user interaction, support and flexibility. Because they were proprietary, complex and costly, only a relatively few large organizations undertook their installation, sometimes requiring their smaller trading partners to implement them as a prerequisite to doing business (Krcmar, Bjørn-Andersen & O'Callaghan, 1995; Mukhopadhyay, Kekre & Kalathur, 1995; Pfeiffer, 1992).

With the availability of low-cost Web interface designs and the ubiquity of the Internet as a common interconnection facility, EDI connections have become more affordable. Advantages include flat rate pricing for information communication, cheap access, common mail standards and public key encryption standards to ensure privacy of EDI transmissions over public networks. Non-proprietary solutions enable users to choose the level of service needed. For example, a VAN operating over the Internet can provide unbiased intermediary services that may be legally necessary, such as providing transaction time stamp verification to ensure non-repudiation of transaction events.

In addition to merely substituting proprietary lines of communication, emerging technologies and public networks have also facilitated new business models and new forms of interaction and collaboration, in areas such as collaborative engineering or the joint offering of complex, modularized products.

In cases where the Internet and World Wide Web are utilized to connect organizations, IOS are now commonly referred to as B2B systems, and the business that is being conducted based on the new infrastructure is termed B2B electronic commerce or B2B electronic business. Acknowledging the relevance of past experiences with establishing and managing IOS can be of great value in managing current B2B initiatives.

OVERVIEW OF B2B APPLICATIONS

We start our discussion of B2B application support of business transactions with a high-level overview of different business models and their functions. Many classification schemes are available (Choudhury, 1997; Kaplan & Sawhney, 2000). Instead of proposing yet another one, we start with a functional focus and distinguish between sell-side, buy-side and neutral/market-type applications. We then include more variables and propose a schema that can be used to characterize individual examples.

Buyers and sellers conduct business transactions to exchange goods and services. Figure 1 depicts a simple transaction process, where sellers interact with buyers through their marketing and sales distribution functions, with the support of internal processes such as manufacturing, logistics and accounting. Buyers interface with sellers through the procurement function, linked to supporting internal processes such as receiving, accounts payable and operations. In addition, intermediary functions can provide a multiplicity of services, including brokerage, payments, logistics, legal or consulting. Information technology is available to bridge each of the relevant interfaces.

In line with the general theme of this book, our chapter emphasizes the external connections between buyers, sellers and possibly third-party service providers. Each of these groups has slightly different needs and requirements regarding functionality, system layout and integration with backend systems. Depending on the primary focus of the application, we distinguish between sell-side applications and buy-side applications. A third group of applications marketplaces provides equal support for both supplier and customer.

Figure 1: B2B Transactions and Participants (Source: Ware et al., 1998, p. 156)

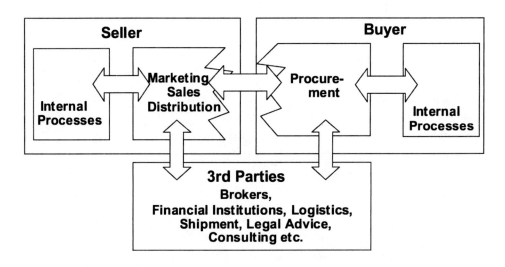

Sell Side

Early B2B applications feature online catalogs, made available to the Internet community by distributors and manufacturers, such as wholesale distributors W.W. Grainger (www.grainger.com, www.orderzone.com), Works.com (www.works.com) and computer manufacturer Dell (www.dell.com). Similar to corresponding applications in the B2C-world, online catalogs are complemented by additional features, such as shopping baskets and payment functionality. In addition to online catalogs these systems usually include online ordering, and provide for customized and secure views of the data, based on business rules from contract agreements with individual customers. In some cases, buying processes of the customers are supported, including features such as approval routing and reporting.

When setting up a sell-side system, the seller controls its content and administrative features, such as compliance with corporate identity, etc. (see Figure 2). For the initiators, the systems often represent an innovative part of an established multi-channel distribution strategy, resulting in cost savings, and possibly broader customer reach and closer relationships. Cisco currently handles over 80 percent of all orders through its Web site, resulting in a $500m bottom-line impact, relative to equivalent telephone sales and service operations, on $9.5b revenue in 1999 (Solvik, 1999).

While more sophisticated sell-side implementations typically link into the backend systems of the sellers, most implementations are not integrated with the information systems at the customer side. From the buyer perspective, the purchasing process is thus not supported in a seamless fashion.

Figure 2: Sell-Side System

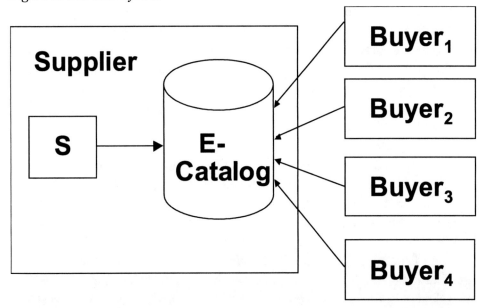

Another limit of current systems concerns the complexity of the goods they can handle. While some sophisticated applications exist to support collaborative forecasting or the configuration of complex products, most sell-side systems handle simpler transactions, such as maintenance, repair and operation (MRO) supplies.

While sell-side systems allow selling organizations to interface with a multitude of customers, buying organizations may have to integrate their systems with multiple different solutions, depending on the number of suppliers. Benefits for the buying organization stem from enhanced customer value through cost/time savings and continuous availability, compared to traditional solutions. Suppliers work to increase the reach of their solutions and provide sophisticated and easy-to-use systems. They also try to lock-in customers with additional functions to complement the transaction, providing the basis for comprehensive one-stop shopping sites. Intermediaries may participate in the solution by providing additional services to the controlling supplier organization. This includes electronic funds transfer (EFT) transactions by banks, and other functions that can be provided by eCommerce specialist firms, such as expertise in the design, development and/or operations of the application.

Buy Side

Buy-side applications provide the logical counterpart to sell-side systems, primarily supporting the procurement process, hence often termed electronic procurement systems. In this case, Internet technologies are utilized to move ordering processes closer to the end user, alleviating structured workloads in functional departments, such as purchasing and accounts payable, freeing them to handle more complex, strategic tasks. Examples of such systems are intranet-based procurement systems that have been initiated by numerous larger corporations, such as Cisco Systems, Chevron and the County of Los Angeles (Segev, Gebauer & Färber, 2000; Segev & Gebauer, 2000; see Figure 3 for an overview of the functionality). For smaller companies, an affordable alternative is to work through hosted solutions, using Internet browsers to access procurement functionality provided by a third party vendor or application service provider (ASP).

Some applications provide functionality beyond the automation of highly structured procurement processes, including production tendering (General Electric's Trading Process Network), large-scale online auctions (Freemarkets) and the multi-step generation of requests for proposals, as they are relevant for the procurement of freelance and management services (eLance, Webango and Menerva).

Interfacing end-user purchasing systems to internal information systems such as enterprise resource planning systems (ERPs) makes it possible to automate a substantial fraction of transactions, thus greatly increasing the speed of handling transactions, as well as reducing processing costs. On the software vendor side, a number of strategic partnerships of business eCommerce

Figure 3: Desktop Purchasing System (Buy-Side)-Key Functions and Connectivity Options

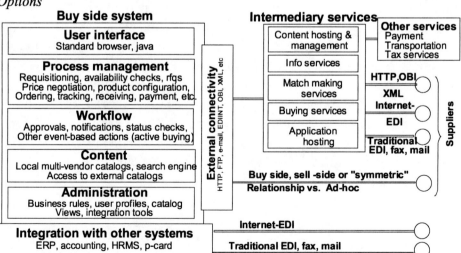

solution developers with ERP vendors have been formed (e.g., Ariba, i2 & IBM, and Commerce One & SAP) to take advantage of opportunities in this field.

Buy-side solutions are typically set up by the purchasing organization, which then also takes control of catalog content, data format and backend system functionality. The benefits include streamlined purchasing operations, including sizable fractions of transactions that can be fully automated. This results in time and cost savings, and freeing purchasing and accounts payable personnel from clerical work for more strategic tasks. As information quality and market transparency is improved, maverick buying (end-user purchasing from non-standard suppliers) can be reduced, enabling more favorable contracts with fewer suppliers. For example, an industry study (Aberdeen, 1999) showed a resulting five percent to 10 percent reduction in prices for goods and services through lower material and service costs, reduction of acquisition and order fulfillment cycle times of 50 percent to 70 percent, reduction of requisition processing costs of 70 percent per order and improved inventory management practices.

Suppliers typically benefit from long-term relationships, as in most cases the relationships between the buyer and its suppliers are put in place well before the system is established, including possible sole sourcing agreements. In some cases the solutions provide automated transaction and data uploading procedures. Still, suppliers wanting to participate in multiple buy-side solutions may have to deliver their data in multiple different formats, and adhere to multiple underlying business processes.

B2B Electronic Markets

A third group of applications does not focus on one transaction party specifically, but provides support for buyers and sellers, more or less equally. Often referred to as B2B electronic markets or hubs, this type of application can either resemble traditional exchanges bringing together multiple buyers and sellers on an ad hoc basis, or support more permanent relationships (equivalent of IOS). From formerly being a trading medium for financial and investment products only, electronic marketplaces have recently been proliferating across many industries from airlines to automobiles and a wide array of product categories from industrial components to lab supplies (Phillips & Meeker, 2000; Sculley & Woods, 1999).

A wide range of business models exists. Some electronic markets are supplier-led (e.g., Global Healthcare Exchange for medical products and Rooster.com for agricultural products). Other exchanges are buyer-directed (e.g., Covisint in the automotive industry and the Worldwide Retail Exchange for retailers). Some are independent of buyers and sellers and set up by intermediaries, such as distributors, retailers or brokers, financial institutions such as banks, as well as technology providers (VerticalNet and i2i's industry trading communities). They feature auctions, electronic catalogs and auxiliary value-added functions, such as industry news and online forums. The initiator typically controls the catalog content, aggregates supplier input and provides additional functionality and standardized data access to buyers (see Figure 4).

Some markets focus on specific groups of buyers, e.g., specializing in maintenance, repair and operational (MRO) supplies, and particular commodities (horizontal markets, e.g., Marketsite, Ariba.Net. and Works.com); others target users from specific industries (verticals), such as metals (Metalsite), automotive (Covisint), retail (GlobalNet Exchange), tire and rubber (RubberNetwork), and life sciences (SciQuest) (Phillips & Meeker, 2000).

In many cases, the exchanges are initiated by one group of market participants (suppliers, customers, technology providers), to be operated as separate companies with multiple ownerships (Covisint). While many of the early B2B marketplaces have been initiated by Internet pureplays (NetBuy, MetalSite, Chemdex), recent initiatives more often involve consortia of

Figure 4: Market Functions (Examples)

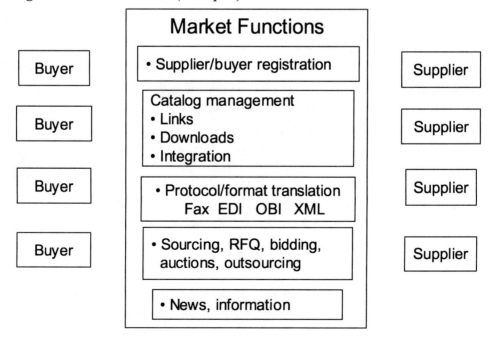

established brick and mortar companies, typically working very closely with technology providers. Covisint is an initiative of automotive manufacturers Ford, General Motors and DaimlerChrysler and software vendors Commerce One and Oracle, while Petrocosm, a marketplace for the petroleum industry, has been formed by oil giant Chevron, together with technology providers Ariba and IBM. Many other examples exist (see www.b2business.net for a directory of B2B marketplaces).

"Neutral" solutions provide benefits to both suppliers and buyers. First, they eliminate the need for market participants to link directly to their business partners, helping to circumvent the costly value-added network services of traditional EDI solutions. The savings from implementing only one interface to the intermediary instead of multiple interfaces to many suppliers or customers may in fact be quite substantial. Second, suppliers may deliver content in one standard format, while buyers access one integrated solution. Third, hubs can help increase flexibility if they support ad hoc transactions and provide access to suppliers and customers outside pre-established relationships. This may actually create competitive pressure on established relationships, leading to improved customer value.

The participation in third-party initiated e-procurement and marketplace solutions is often considered a low-cost alternative for small to medium enterprises that cannot afford to set up complex buy-side or sell-side implementations by themselves. One of the parties, or both, typically pay service charges to the intermediary that may depend on transaction volume and setup costs. How the costs are split between suppliers and customers basically depends on how market power is distributed among them, and is often a difficult problem to solve.

Characterizing B2B Applications

The preceding discussion of sell-side, buy-side and electronic market applications provided a brief overview of the many different applications and solutions that are typically subsumed into the category of B2B electronic commerce systems. Instead of reproducing the work of the many industry analysts (Phillips & Meeker, 2000), we close this section by proposing a scheme that we found useful to describe and categorize individual B2B applications and initiatives, as well as to identify related management issues and success factors (Table 1). Additional issues to be considered include the technical infrastructure as well as relevant business models.

Regularly, electronic marketplace initiatives prove to be more complex and difficult to set up and maintain than initially anticipated. Changes in business processes and relationships between participants within (purchasing

Table 1: Characterizing B2B Applications

Charact-eristics	Examples	Comments
Main initiator	Buyer Seller (manufacturer, distributor) Market maker Single organization Consortium	The initiator typically bears the majority of the investment, but is also its main beneficiary. In order for the investment to pay off, a number of participants have to agree to join in. The number of collaborating initiators (single organization vs. consortium) relates to internal management issues
Requirements to participate	Internet access/web browser Deployment of proprietary technology Adaptation of business processes	Depending on the underlying system architecture and business models, the amount of effort required to join the market can vary greatly. This allows predictions about the willingness with which participants will join (adoption) rate.
Main focus	Buy-side Sell-side Neutral	The focus can give clues of where the majority of the system features are to be found, including integration with backend systems, workflow support, ownership and maintenance of data
Target user group	Professional buyers, sales group Requisitioners, end users (horizontal) Industry experts (vertical)	Helps determine the system functionality, types of information and depth of expert knowledge required to provide adequate support for the target user group
Scope	Transactions, information, Negotiation, settlement Collaboration, community building Value added services Supply chain management Project management	The scope ranges from an EDI-like automation of structured processes to providing a platform that can combine online with offline, often unstructured, activities. It also helps determine the required level of system flexibility
Relationships	Ad hoc: spot buying and selling Long term, pre-established	Open vs. closed group of participants? Quality assurance of the participants and products integrated into the marketplace? The nature of the relationships prevailing in the market relates to the applicability of (economic) theories (transaction cost etc.)
Pricing scheme	Fixed Dynamic (negotiations, auctions)	Information about the role of the market (brokering?) as well as the inherent functionality of the underlying IT infrastructure
Primary business objective (of the initiator)	Saving process cost and time Reduce product prices and increase market transparency Improve process efficiency Generate revenue (as market maker) Lock in customers and partners	As part of the business model, the clear definition of business objectives is a crucial success factor
Types of goods or services	Commodities MRO-type supplies Direct goods Non-tangible goods and services Complex (project) products and services Capital goods	Information about the types of goods helps determine the requirements regarding the (technical) complexity of the system

vs. requisitioning) as well as between organizations have to be administered, in addition to the complex technical infrastructure that has to be put in place and maintained. A number of recently reported failures of a number of marketplaces, with life sciences marketplace Chemdex maybe being the most prominent example, only represent the tip of the iceberg.

MANAGEMENT CONSIDERATIONS

Characteristics of electronic marketplaces which are relevant to economic analyses include (Bakos, 1991): 1) EM systems can reduce costs of acquiring and communicating information about prices and products, 2) benefits to EM participants increase as more organizations join the marketplace, 3) EMs can impose significant switching costs on participants, 4) EMs typically require large capital investments and offer substantial economies of scale and scope, and 5) participants in EMs face substantial uncertainties in the benefits to be achieved by joining.

Many of the management issues of B2B electronic commerce systems stem from the fact that they have to integrate or at least coordinate decisions in more than one distinct and autonomous organization. Unlike in intra-organizational settings, the adoption and use of an application cannot be mandated by management, but has to be achieved through a favorable business model or other targeted strategies. Similarly, the level of risk regarding opportunistic behavior is greater when different organizations are involved than within one firm, where all efforts ultimately contribute to the same bottom line. Differing business processes, information systems and organizational cultures pose additional hurdles.

In the following, we address a number of management issues of B2B applications. For each of the issues, we include earlier research that can be applied to the current developments, and that can help increase understanding. Using a top-down approach, we include a look at industry structures, the role of intermediaries, system evaluation and adoption strategies, technical infrastructure and change management in the context of B2B applications.

Industry Structures

A number of researchers have published works on the economics of IOS and electronic markets by applying concepts from transaction cost theory (Williamson & Masten, 1995). This theory examines the economic efficiency of markets by considering different coordination mechanisms and the properties of the market, such as specificity of assets and products, bounded rationality of participants and uncertainty. The two main methods for coordinating the flow of goods and services are markets and hierarchies. Markets coordinate the flow through supply and demand forces with price as the main coordination vehicle, while hierarchies with pre-determined customers and suppliers, such as manufacturing assembly plants and their component suppliers, rely on managerial decisions to coordinate flows. Using the market mechanism requires significant effort, e.g., to locate vendors and products (search costs), to negotiate contracts, to ship items, and to track fulfillment and partner performance. The "equivalent of friction in physical systems" (Williamson, 1985) is summarized as transaction costs, or coordination costs (Malone, Yates & Benjamin, 1987).

Information technology can help to reduce transaction costs and the associated risks in electronic marketplaces, and many researchers have discussed whether this will lead to more markets and fewer hierarchies (read: smaller organizations) (Malone, Yates & Benjamin, 1987; Brynjolfsson et al., 1994). No final resolution has yet been proposed (Gurbaxani & Whang, 1991; Brynjolfsson, Malone, Gurbaxani & Kambil, 1994). While there is indeed a considerable trend towards the outsourcing of business functions (The Outsourcing Institute, 2000) and a concentration of organizations on core competencies, basic microeconomic theory also predicts that in an environment of perfect markets with full transparency and a very large number of suppliers and buyers, profit margins tend to fall towards zero. Given that this is an unacceptable scenario for any for-profit organization, it is not surprising that many organizations are concerned about preserving their unique selling propositions and business relationships in an environment that is characterized by intensifying and increasingly global competition.

Consequently perhaps, "mixed mode" network structures have emerged as an intermediate form of marketplaces blending hierarchical and market structures in a coordinated manner. To describe this development, Clemons, Reddi and Row (1993) coined the term "move to the middle," with evidence seen in the growth of outsourcing arrangements and more cooperative, integrated, inter-organizational relationships with a rather small number of preferred suppliers. Based on existing business relationships, collaboration between a limited number of partners is initiated dependent on the individual situation (Holland & Lockett, 1997; Powell, 1990; Thorelli, 1986).

Very large online markets basically only exist for a limited number of products that can be considered true commodities (e.g., energy, natural gas: Altra Energy, Enron). Most examples of Internet-based electronic markets feature a limited number of participants, often composed of closed groups (Segev, Gebauer & Färber, 1999). Contrary to the notion of the "perfect" marketplace of microeconomic theory, where ad hoc transactions occur and the identity of sellers as well as buyers is basically irrelevant, current online market structures tend to provide a controlled setting, combining the benefit of market coordination with reductions in coordination and transaction costs, while at the same time lessening product and service specificity (Alaniz, 1999; Forbes, 2000).

The application of earlier research on market structures to current developments is relevant for the initiators of B2B projects who might be tempted to base their calculations on a large number of participants. Instead they should be very careful to consider costs, risks and benefits of a particular B2B solution, from the perspective of each individual participant or group of participants. In addition, they will have to consider the fact that any organization will be hesitant at best to participate in an initiative that could ultimately be detrimental to their business models.

In addition, established business relations and the distribution of market power within any particular industry have to be taken into account. For example, a small number of powerful manufacturers in the automotive industry provide a much different setting from an environment characterized by a large number of smaller players (e.g., furniture industry).

The Role of Intermediaries

By its very nature, a market assumes an intermediary role supporting the trade between buyers and suppliers. Specifically, this role encompasses several functions, including (Bailey & Bakos, 1997): a) matching buyers and sellers, b) ensuring trust among participants by maintaining a neutral position, c) facilitating market operations by supporting certain transaction phases, and d) aggregating buyer demand and seller information.

The question of whether intermediaries have become less important in the age of the Internet has come up frequently, ever since the Internet reached widespread commercial use. With a fast-growing online population and more and more information available online, it became evident that the new medium could help businesses not only to disseminate information more broadly and reach a wider audience, but also to interact with customers, partners and suppliers on an individual basis. It allowed buyers to find products and vendors more easily than ever before. In addition, new business models started to evolve, re-creating the traditional role of intermediaries in the virtual space (Afuah & Tucci, 2001). This notion triggered expectations of shorter supply chains with direct links between manufacturers and end-consumers. With at least some of the middlemen and their margins cut out from the supply chain, an increase of customer value and/or profit margins of the remaining members of the value chain was expected (Benjamin & Wigand, 1995).

While these expectations have come true in some areas, it has also become evident that the developments are really more complex. At this point, researchers and practitioners tend to agree that the intermediary is here to stay. But the business models of electronic commerce are challenging its role(s), requiring a major rethinking and in many cases a re-orientation (Bailey & Bakos, 1997; Sarkar, Butler & Steinfield, 1995). There are several reasons for this notion.

First, the role of a real-life intermediary is often quite complex and not every aspect can yet be replicated online. For example, in the American real estate market, online startups have emerged that allow buyers and sellers of homes to connect via the Internet without the services of a traditional broker (Buxmann & Gebauer, 1998). At the same time, however, traditional brokers have also started to embrace the new medium. They make use of online technologies (Web sites, online newsletters) to intensify existing relationships with business partners and customers. As these relationships are among the key success factors of any real estate-broker, the new medium can help to strengthen their role (Sawyer, Crowston, Wigand & Allbritton, 2000).

Second, being a relatively novel phenomenon, the Internet has also created the need for new intermediaries. Conducting business in an online environment, where the business partner might not be known and/or thousands of miles away and business rules have not yet been established in the same fashion as in the offline world, opens up opportunities for intermediaries to establish trust, and to help ensure quality control. This includes technical instruments (security, privacy tools), as well as screening procedures for vendors and customers. In addition, there are ample opportunities to support the online user and provide guidance through the large amounts of information that are available online.

While the issue of intermediaries has first received significant attention in the context of consumer-oriented electronic commerce, it is also relevant in business-to-business environments. The need for conflict resolution has already become obvious, as more and more business partnerships are formed online (Gibs, 2000). In addition, compared to business-to-consumer applications, business-to-business systems tend to be more complex, regarding functionality as well as regarding the integration with backend systems. This generates a need for system providers and integrators at varying levels.

Once again, there is evidence that information technology should best be viewed as a tool to open up new opportunities, and that can be used in many different ways. It can indeed allow market participants to circumvent traditional intermediaries, as Dell is demonstrating with its business model of direct selling. Note, however, that Dell is also a very active supporter of online electronic marketplaces. In January of 2001, it announced a partnership with independent chip marketplace PartMiner's sourcing services to help locate hard-to-find electronic components (press release available from www.partminer.com). Furthermore, emerging technologies can also be used to strengthen the role of established intermediaries, as described for the real estate market and demonstrated by established distributors such as Grainger and Office Depot. Finally, the online world has opened much space for new intermediaries to provide tools and services that can help create an online environment comparable to business in the physical world, with regards to functionality, trust and security.

There are two key points in this discussion. First, it is important to understand industry structures, including the value that intermediaries currently provide to their customers. Only if these value propositions can be matched or even improved online, is there a chance that traditional intermediaries will become obsolete. Second, in order to be successful, any business, including an online intermediary, has to identify current "pain points" and inefficiencies of the value chain, thus providing a unique value proposition to its partners and customers.

From this point of view, it is not surprising that projects that combine very carefully the industry knowledge and market power of established industry players with the technology savvy and nimbleness of high tech startups have been most successful in setting up B2B electronic markets.

Evaluation and Adoption

In a model of search costs in a differentiated market with multiple suppliers and multiple buyers, it has been shown (Bakos, 1997) that suppliers as a group will have little incentive to introduce their own electronic markets. This is particularly the case where electronic markets reduce buyer search costs, resulting in markets that are significantly more transparent (note that this result typically only holds true for so-called buyer-markets, where there is no significant shortage in supply, and significantly less competition on the buyer side than on the supplier side). In these cases, suppliers may also want to control the information that is provided in the online market. For example, a supplier may want to emphasize descriptive information of products and services over price, making it difficult for buyers to purchase on the basis of price alone. Information provided through the online market can help to differentiate among products and services, even those normally regarded as commodities.

In this context, it is important to note that among the most distinguishing factors in inter-organizational systems is the fact that there is typically no centralized layer of management decisions, but rather that each of the participants decides independently on its level of participation and commitment. This means that adoption and system use cannot be managed in the same way as in intra-organizational settings, where all stakeholders are typically included. Instead, much care has to be taken to set up a system such that is beneficial for the main investor-initiator as well as for the participants

(Gebauer & Buxmann, 2000). In addition, a certain dependency on the commitment and collaboration of the business partners occurs as a result of a system-specific investment, such as the installation of access software and necessary changes in business processes. This poses a risk in inter-organizational settings (referred to as transaction-specific assets by Williamson [1985]). As a result, we would expect the threshold of a system that is considered beneficial by its stakeholders to increase, as compared to an investment where the benefits are dependent entirely on one organization's internal factors.

The task of evaluating an IOS becomes even more difficult once network effects are taken into account. These effects are due to the fact that the benefits from participating in any market-type setting is at least partly dependent on the number of fellow participants. The larger the network (read: market) becomes, the higher the incentives for the buyers to join in (Clemons & Kleindorfer, 1992). If the number of participants reaches a certain critical mass, it can even create a strategic necessity for potential participants to join.

As a result of these complications (dependence on the commitment of business partners, additional risk, external effects, etc.), the evaluation of an inter-organizational system is much more complex than information systems that are deployed only within one organization (Gebauer & Buxmann, 2000).

From the perspective of setting up a successful B2B application, two major groups can be distinguished: initiators and (potential) participants. Initiators bear the majority of the cost but on the other hand also enjoy the majority of the benefits, and they typically decide on the set up of the system, including technology infrastructure, types of systems used, corporate identity, representation of partners and selection of participants. This holds true for sell side as well as buy side solutions, and marketplaces. However, the success of the system and the recouping of the, oftentimes significant, investments is at least partly dependent on the participation of a critical mass of business partners. As a result, the question of how to sign on enough participants plays an important role. Assuming rational behavior of the actors, participation should yield a positive net benefit from the perspective of the individual organization. For a buy side solution, for example, the sign up costs for a supplier might include all investments necessary to prepare and upload catalog data, integrate with backend systems, train staff and adjust business processes. In sum, these efforts should not outweigh the benefits of participation (Gebauer & Buxmann, 2000). Depending on the individual arrangements, the benefits include reduced time and costs for order processing, improved customer service, increased customer reach in a globalized marketplace and the increase of revenues from long-term and trusted customer relationships.

As a result of these considerations, neutral intermediaries in such markets face a difficult balancing task, as they have to be careful to satisfy suppliers as well as buyers simultaneously. Before any party agrees to participate in a particular marketplace, its total costs should not outweigh the overall benefits it will receive from the arrangement. The intermediary on the other hand needs to choose a particular business model and to determine which suppliers and buyers to recruit as participants.

Four adoption strategies have been identified (Gebauer & Raupp, 2000): coercion, long-term commitment, subsidies and general system improvements.

1. *Coercion*: In the past, initiating organizations, in particular large ones, have frequently used their market power to demand participation in a particular inter-organizational solution (e.g., EDI). Business partners found themselves in situations where future business was dependent on their compliance with the demands put forth by the stronger partner (Mukhopadhyay, Kekre & Kalathur, 1995; Wang & Seidmann, 1995). If successful, this strategy leaves the initiator with a broad range of system design options as it puts the majority of the adoption efforts on the shoulders of the partners. The longer-term effects, from possibly straining the underlying relationship are unclear.

2. *Long-Term Commitment*: Another "low-cost" adoption strategy entices the participants with the promise of long-term business relationships (e.g., sole-sourcing agreements). Again, the majority of the adoption effort rests with the participants. The long-term commitment, however, brings with it a reduction of uncertainty for the partners and as a result mitigates the underlying risk, and possibly increases the willingness to participate (Bakos & Brynjolfsson, 1993). With this strategy, which basically shuts off the market mechanism to some extent, the long-term effects are unclear.

3. *Subsidies*: Some organizations have chosen to increase the number of participants by providing support to partners if they choose to take part in the solution. Subsidies range from direct financial support, to providing expertise, to physically hosting applications and managing network connections (Wang & Seidmann, 1995). While it can be shown that, in some instances, subsidies are superior to coercion, it tends to be suited well for situations where a relatively small number of participants is sufficient for reaching "critical mass." The participants might not have an incentive to reveal their true adoption costs, a problem that is referred to as "moral hazard" in the economics literature.

4. *System Improvements*: At the other end of the spectrum from forcing a partner into a B2B solution, the initiator can also choose to improve the system in a way that participation becomes beneficial for a sufficient number of participants, even without long-term relationships, direct subsidies or coercion. While this strategy can require significant investments for the initiator, it has become relatively popular in the context of the Internet (King & Anthes, 2000). It is particularly well suited for situations that require a large number of participants, precluding the management of individual subsidies.

As emerging technologies have brought along open standards, global markets and modular applications, the feasibility of lock-in and coercion-based strategies seems to have been reduced. While the different adoption strategies can well be combined, it is not clear which strategy or combination of strategies matches what type of situation best (Gebauer & Raupp, 2000). The initiators of B2B systems need to be aware of the perspective of their partners and customers, since reaching a critical participation mass is essential for the success of any B2B initiative.

Technical Infrastructure

In many cases, B2B electronic market-projects turn out to be more complex than initially anticipated, from an organizational and management standpoint, but also regarding the technical implementation.

Although available software products are maturing at a rapid pace, many and more complex functions are not fully developed yet. This includes functions such as collaborative planning, forecasting, and replenishment; negotiation and decision support; and procurement and asset management of complex and highly customizable items and systems (e.g., direct materials and services). The assembly of data from a large variety of different sources into a single electronic catalog, as well as the subsequent management of this data, is an unresolved issue, given the lack of widely adopted data standards and business procedures (Granada Research, 1999). Although the advent and diffusion of the structured document-standard eXtensible Markup Language (XML) is expected to help ease the problem, it does not by itself resolve the need for business partners to agree on the semantics of data structure and exchange processes (Shim, Pendyala, Sundaram & Gao, 2000).

As most organizations already have a fair amount invested in existing applications, integration with these legacy systems is also crucial, with serious technical and business process implications. The fact that issues of security and confidentiality tend to play a more critical role in an inter-organizational setting than internally adds to the complexity (Gebauer &

Schad, 1999). To meet these needs, significant customization might be required. In many cases the required investment in training, reorganization and business process reengineering may be large enough to outweigh initial software fees by several orders of magnitude.

At the bottom line, the initiation and implementation of a sophisticated B2B application typically requires massive investments in terms of financial and human resources, often resembling the ERP projects that many companies started during the 90's. Once again, this favors the primarily larger organizations that can afford the necessary financial and knowledge resources.

Simultaneously, many software vendors tend to cater to the "big fish." Given that the release of small-scale solutions and hosted applications as an alternative for smaller firms regularly lags behind, they typically end up with a much smaller range of available options.

B2B-Solutions for Smaller Firms

Handling B2B transactions through B2B eCommerce solutions is one way for smaller firms (SMEs) to make the transition to an IOS, but without a fully automated transaction management system. Another more recently available solution is hosted procurement applications, where the SME does not have to install any software, but can just use a browser to access procurement functionality. Procurement software vendors Ariba, Commerce One and Oracle have all started to offer hosted applications to complement their product lines, and other independent companies have entered this (Application Service Provider, or ASP) marketplace. To date, however, available hosted solutions are not yet very sophisticated. In particular, mixing and matching of modules and the integration of hosted applications with existing IT systems, such as databases or workflow modules, is less feasible in cases where different vendors are involved (Segev, Gebauer & Färber, 1999).

Supply side solutions with Web access can also be used as parallel channels for larger businesses to deal with small suppliers or customers that do not have the resources to commit to full IOS capabilities. While this allows the buying firm to automate a larger portion of its transactions, it does involve setting up and managing the additional communication channels, often using different technologies, differing levels of automation and generally lower cost efficiencies. For this reason, some larger firms refuse to do business with trading partners unless they use particular specified technologies.

When planning and designing any IT system, the project team has to decide on the scope of the application. How much of an underlying process should be automated, but how flexible does the system have to be at the same time? To what extent will alternate processes and solutions be required to handle exceptions? How much effort will be necessary to achieve participation from business partners and to reach sufficient liquidity in the market? Answering these questions carefully can have a significant impact on the project's bottom line.

In some cases, an 80% solution that consciously includes the perspective of the business partners can actually be more successful in the long run, compared to a "perfect" solution from the perspective of the initiator (Gebauer & Buxmann, 2000).

One important aspect in this context is the complexity of the business transactions. Complexity is determined by factors such as the number of sub-processes and organizational units that are involved, as well as their possible interactions, interdependencies and relationships with the process environment (Kieser & Kubicek, 1992). Since the type of goods or services involved in a transaction affects the complexity of handling the transaction, it is useful to classify transactions according to the objects being exchanged (Gebauer, Beam & Segev, 1998) (see Table 2). From the table, acquiring MRO supplies and services (Type 2), often referred to as indirect or non-production supplies and services, is the least complex type of transaction. Acquiring capital goods and making other types of ad hoc purchases (Type 3) tends to be the most complex because of their unique characteristics and infrequent occurrence.

To support transactions, typically a number of different IT infrastructures are available, such as EDI systems or Web-based ordering applications. The circumstances of future situations determine whether the chosen infrastructure can be used to process a specific transaction (standard situation) or whether an exceptional situation prohibits the use of the application at justifiable costs. Exceptional instances then need to be handled manually either totally or in part. The cost of handling standard or exceptional situations is determined by the specifics of the infrastructure in place (standard processing costs can be very low if processes are fully automated, but at the same time it might be difficult/expensive to handle exceptions). Managers need to decide which type of system (infrastructure) is suited best to handle all the instances that might occur throughout the lifetime of the system (a trade-off between automation and flexibility). All other things such as process structure and uncertainty being equal, automation will be more feasible for low complexity processes than for complex processes (Gebauer, 1997). In many instances, the best solution is a well-thought-out combination of process automation with non-automated elements, such as decision support.

Table 2: Transaction Classification According to Type of Object Exchanged

Type	Description
1	Raw material and production goods and services (large quantities, high frequencies, unique specifications, often just-in-time delivery)
2	Maintenance, repair, and operating supplies and services – MRO (low unit cost, low volume, off-the-shelf, relatively high frequency)
3	Capital goods, and ad hoc procurement for functions such as new product development (often outside the normal procurement process because of convenience, speed, and unique specifications).

Change and Project Management (Disruptive vs. Sustaining Technologies)

Given their scope and newness, B2B applications can have major impacts on inter-organizational business processes. Following the planning and design of the system business model and infrastructure, a careful plan of how to implement it, how to train employees and how to adapt business processes is the next step towards a successful project.

Early examples already show strong similarities with the ambitious enterprise resource planning (ERP) system implementations that were started during the '90s, that often turned out much more complex and risky than previously anticipated. Motorcycle maker Harley-Davidson has recently stalled the implementation of a central E-procurement system that was to bring together differing and incompatible systems, currently in use at the company's eight U.S. manufacturing sites (Gilbert, 2000a). The project turned out more difficult than anticipated when it came to coordinating differing views and requirements of internal functions, such as manufacturing, supply-chain management and accounting, plus those of the external partners (suppliers). The need to change established processes, the difficulty in extracting reliable data from incompatible systems and the complexities of direct (manufacturing-related) purchasing all led to the decision to put the project on hold until a more careful plan could be sketched out. Other firms have faced similar difficulties, and in many cases the expected number of users and partners could not be linked up in the anticipated timeframe. Partner adoption, catalog management and integration with a heterogeneous system of backend applications are frequently listed as major stumbling blocks (see Gilbert, 2000b, for more examples).

Naturally, as ePurchasing systems and electronic markets become more comprehensive, they also become more complex. Given the experiences with radical business process reengineering efforts during the 1990s, one practical approach is to start by implementing small parts of the process, and then adding more functions and increased integration (Hammer, 1990; Davenport

& Short, 1990; Davenport & Beers, 1995).

For example, an organization could start out by reengineering and then automating an inefficient process that causes long lead times and possibly frequent complaints, e.g., management approval of end user requests. As a next step, putting together an online catalog that contains the offerings of preferred suppliers can be useful as a first step to reduce "maverick" buying outside pre-established contracts. Online ordering, automated interfaces into backend systems and connections to open, electronic markets comprise additional features that can complement the solution. In addition, partial or complete outsourcing of technology development, and implementation, or application hosting should be considered (see Figure 5).

While the exact steps will depend on the situation within the individual firm, the stepwise approach will allow frequent adjustments to the project planning and implementation process, including the addition of new requirements. It can also allow learning effects to take place (Brynjolfsson & Hitt, 1998). Still, much research has to be done, until best practices for implementing online strategies will be commonly available.

The adoption of a B2B eCommerce solution is a strategic company decision and it is important to evaluate the potential overall impact of this innovation on the firm. As we have pointed out, this may require a substantial reengineering of the firm's business processes to be effective (Maull, Childe, Smart & Bennett, 1995). But this may be very risky, especially if the new solution is to operate in parallel with existing business channels. Pant and Hsu (1996) suggest a framework for considering business on the Web, from the

FIgure 5: Alternatives to Large-Scale Transformation-Incremental Mix and Match (Source: Segev, Gebauer & Färber, 2000)

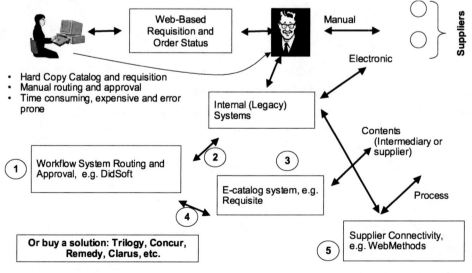

internal IT organization's point of view. This includes analyzing strategic and competitive advantages linked to company business strategy, and pursuing opportunities that support this strategy. Under the direction of senior management and users, the entrepreneurial approach (user innovations) is encouraged, resulting in simultaneous bottom-up development in the form of incremental change, combined with top-down analysis. However, the firm needs to address the strategic risks first if it is to avoid making large commitments of existing technical and operations staff and facilities to new technology and business processes with which the company is unfamiliar.

To evaluate the strategic risk involved in adopting an innovation, Christensen's model (Christensen, 1997) can be very helpful. This model evaluates the innovation in terms of a number of its attributes, helping to classify it as either "sustaining" or "disruptive" to the firm. By analyzing a particular proposal according to certain of its attributes, a company can make a reasoned judgment on how to proceed towards implementation. If a proposed solution is not categorized as disruptive, then it can be implemented within the firm's existing operations, linking them to online customers or suppliers. However, if several of the attributes of the proposed solution are classified as "disruptive," consideration should be given to mitigating potential disruptions to the company when it implements the innovation, by: a) spinning off a separate organization to implement it, b) outsourcing the proposed system, c) taking over an organization with the expertise to handle it, or d) forming an alliance with another company with technical competence and experience in the field.

Current dynamic developments in the context of electronic commerce are creating as much hope as confusion among organizations and individuals. Given the speed at which new technologies and applications are being announced, users feel the urge to react. Simple "me too" strategies, can be very risky, given the level of investment required by comprehensive and complex eCommerce applications.

SUMMARY AND OUTLOOK

Although new technologies bring about many changes, enable new business models and open new markets, many issues and laws from the old world remain valid and have to be taken into consideration to avoid failures. As Varian and Shapiro put it: "Technology changes, economic laws do not" (Shapiro & Varian, 1999).

In this chapter, we have provided an overview of recent, Internet-based B2B applications to support business transactions and discussed a number of management challenges that these applications bring about. After outlining three business models, we sketched out a framework that can be used as a starting point to describe some of the management challenges of B2B applications.

We showed that while emerging technologies allow organizations to facilitate electronic links with customers, suppliers and partners, reaping these opportunities is not easy. In addition to mastering the challenges with building the technical infrastructure, the management of inter-organizational applications today is just as difficult as it was before the advent of the Internet. Critical aspects include the development of a sound underlying business concept and careful planning of how to reach the critical mass of participants and traffic, which is required for the project to pay off. Industry structures, business relationships and the interaction between internal functions all have to be taken into account, as they will impact the success of potentially disruptive online initiatives.

Earlier research in the areas of inter-organizational systems, in particular on systems design, adoption strategies and network effects, project management and business process reengineering, as well as market structures, can all help to understand the current developments better. In addition, a clear understanding of the possibilities of emerging technologies is crucial to take advantage of the new opportunities. Still, many issues remain open to date. No widely adopted frameworks have been developed, to set up electronic catalogs and to facilitate electronic communication and boundary spanning business processes. Although technology is developing rapidly, it is still immature in many areas. In particular the integration with current IT infrastructures is often extremely complex when it comes down to the details.

From a researcher's perspective, this means that the area of B2B applications continues to be very interesting, and it provides a fruitful field for the application of prior work, while at the same time changing the rules of the game in very subtle ways.

REFERENCES

Aberdeen. (1999). *Business Resource Management: A Proactive Approach to Managing Operations*. Boston, MA: Aberdeen Group.

Afuah, A. and Tucci, C. L. (2001). *Internet Business Models and Strategies: Text and Cases*. Boston: Irwin/McGraw-Hill.

Alaniz, S. (1999). E-Procurement: A guide to buy-side applications. *Internet Research Industry Report*: Stephens, Inc.

Bailey, J. and Bakos, Y. (1997). An exploratory study of the emerging role of electronic intermediaries. *International Journal of Electronic Commerce*, 1(3), 7-20.

Bakos, J. Y. (1991). A strategic analysis of electronic marketplaces. *MIS Quarterly*, September 15, 295-310.

Bakos, J. Y. (1997). Reducing buyer search costs: Implications for electronic marketplaces. *Management Science*, 43(12), 1676-1692.

Bakos, J. Y. and Brynjolfsson, E. (1993). Information technology, incentives and the optimal number of suppliers. *Journal of Management Information Systems*, 10(2), 37-53.

Benjamin, R. and Wigand, R. (1995). Electronic markets and virtual value chains on the information superhighway. *Sloan Management Review*, 36(2), 62-72.

Brynjolfsson, E. and Hitt, L. M. (1998). Beyond the productivity paradox. *Communications of the ACM*, 41(8), 49-55.

Brynjolfsson, E., Malone, T. W., Gurbaxani, V. and Kambil, A. (1994). Does information technology lead to smaller firms? *Management Science*, 40(12), 1628-1644.

Buxmann, P. and Gebauer, J (1998). Internet-based intermediaries: The case of the real estate market. *Proceedings of the 6th European Conference on Information Systems (ECIS'98)*.

Christensen, C. M. (1997). *The Innovator's Dilemma: Why New Technologies Cause Great Firms to Fail*. Boston, MA: Harvard University Press.

Choudhury, V. (1997). Strategic choices in the development of interorganizational information systems. *Information Systems Research* 8(1), 1-24.

Clemons, E. K. and Kleindorfer, P. R. (1992). An economic analysis of interorganizational information technology. *Decision Support Systems*, 8, 431-446.

Clemons, E. K., Reddi, S. P. and Row, M. C. (1993). The impact of information technology on the organization of economic activity: The "move to the middle" hypothesis. *Journal of Management Information Systems*, 10(2), 9-35.

Davenport, T. J. and Short, J. E. (1990). The new industrial engineering: Information technology and business process redesign. *Sloan Management Review*, 31(4), 11-27.

Davenport, T. H. and Beers, M. C. (1995). Managing information about processes. *Journal of Management Information Systems*, 12(1), 57-80.

Emmelhainz, M. A. (1993). *EDI: A Total Management Guide (2nd ed.)*. New York: Van Nostrand Reinhold.

Forbes. (2000). B2B, the best of the Web. *Forbes*, July, 105-134.

Forrester, F. (1999). *Internet Commerce*. Forrester Research. Available on the World Wide Web at: http://www.forrester.com/ER/Press/ForrFind/ . Accessed in December 1999.

Gebauer, J. (1997). Modeling the IT infrastructure of interorganizational processes-automation vs. complexity. Paper presented at the *International Society for Decision Support Systems*, Lausanne, Switzerland.

Gebauer, J., Beam, C. and Segev, A. (1998). Impact of the Internet on procurement. *Acquisition Review Quarterly*, Spring, (14), 167-181.

Gebauer, J. and Buxmann, P. (2000). Assessing the value of interorganizational systems to support business transactions. *International Journal of Electronic Commerce*, 4(4), 61-82.

Gebauer, J. and Raupp, M. (2000). Zwischenbetriebliche Elektronische Katalogsysteme: Netzwerkstrategische Gestaltungsoptionen und Erfolgsfaktoren. *Interorganizational Electronic Catalogs-Strategic Options and Success Factors*, in German. Informatik Forschung und Entwicklung, 15, 215-225.

Gebauer, J. and Schad, H. (1999). Building an Internet-based workflow system-The case of Lawrence Livermore National Laboratories' Zephyr Project. *Annals of Cases on Information Technology Applications and Management in Organizations*, 1, 108-119.

Gibs, J. (2000). Conflict resolution, Jupiter Communications. *Executive Survey*, October 30.

Gilbert, A. (2000a). Rough road for eProcurement at Harley-Davidson. *Informationweek*, November 27.

Gilbert, A. (2000b). eProcurement: Problems behind the promise. *Informationweek*, Available on the World Wide Web at: http://www.informationweek.com/813/eprocure.htm. Accessed November 20, 2000.

Granada Research. (1999). *E-Catalog '99: Business-to-Business Electronic Catalogs*, Technology Report, Granada Research, Halfmoon Bay, and California.

Gurbaxani, V. and Whang, S. (1991). The impact of information systems on organizations and markets. *Communications of the ACM*, 34(1), 59-73.

Hammer, M. (1990). Reengineering work: Don't automate, obliterate. *Harvard Business Review*, 68(4), 104-112.

Holland, C. P. and Lockett, A. G. (1997). Mixed mode network structures: The strategic use of electronic communication by organizations. *Organization Science*, 8(5), 475-488.

Johnston, H. R. and Vitale, M. R. (1988). Creating competitive advantage with interorganizational information systems. *MIS Quarterly*, 12(2),

153-165.

Kaplan, S. and Sawhney, M. (2000). E-hubs: The new B2B marketplaces. *Harvard Business Review*, 78(3), 97-100.

Kieser, A. and Kubicek, H. (1992). *Organisation (Organization in German)*. Germany: de Gruyter.

King, J. and Anthes, G. H. (2000). How Enron built a $183 bullion e-business in less than a year. *Computerworld*, November, 45-46.

Krcmar, H., Bjørn-Andersen, N. and O'Callaghan, R. (1995). *EDI In Europe: How It Works In Practice*. Chichester, NY: Wiley.

Malone, T. W., Yates, J. and Benjamin, R. I. (1987). Electronic markets and electronic hierarchies. *Communications of the ACM*, 30(6), 484-497.

Maull, R. S., Childe, S. J., Smart, P. A. and Bennett, J. (1995). Current issues in business process reengineering. *International Journal of Operations and Production Management*, 15(11), 37-52.

McCall, T. (2000). GartnerGroup forecasts worldwide business-to-business e-commerce: GartnerGroup.

Mukhopadhyay, T., Kekre, S. and Kalathur, S. (1995). Business value of information technology: A study of electronic data interchange. *MIS Quarterly*, 19(2), 137-156.

Pant, S. and Hsu, C. (1996). Business on the Web: Strategies and economics. *Computer Networks and ISDN Systems*, 28, 1481-1492.

Pfeiffer, H. K. C. (1992). *The Diffusion Of Electronic Data Interchange*. Heidelberg: Physica-Verlag.

Phillips, C. and Meeker, M. (2000). *The B2B Internet Report*. Morgan Stanley Dean Witter.

Porter, M. E. (1980). *Competitive Strategy: Techniques For Analyzing Industries and Competitors*. New York: Free Press.

Powell, W. W. (1990). Neither market nor hierarchy: Network forms of organization. *Research in Organizational Behavior*, 12, 295-336.

Sawyer, S., Crowston, K., Wigand, R. T. and Allbritton, M. (2000). The social embeddedness of transactions: Evidence from the residential real estate industry. *Working Paper*, Syracuse University.

Sculley, A. B. and Woods, W. W. A. (1999). *B2B Exchanges*. ISI Publications.

Segev, A. and Gebauer, J. (2000). Emerging technologies to support indirect procurement: Two case studies from the petroleum industry. *Information Technology and Management*, 1, 107-128.

Segev, A., Gebauer, J. and Färber, F. (1999). Internet-based electronic markets. *EM-Electronic Markets*, 9(3).

Segev, A., Gebauer, J. and Färber F. (2000). The market for Internet-based procurement systems, *CITM Research Report WP-1040*, University of California, Berkeley (http://haas.berkeley.edu/citm/procurement).

Shapiro, C. and Varian, H. R. (1999). *Information Rules*. Boston, MA: Harvard University Press.

Shim, S. S. Y., Pendyala, V. S., Sundaram, M. and Gao, J. Z. (2000). Business-to-business eCommerce frameworks. *IEEE Computer*, October, 40-47.

Smith, M. D., Bailey, J. and Brynjolfsson, E. (1999). Understanding digital markets: Review and assessment. In E. Brynjolfsson & B. Kahin (Eds.), *Understanding the Digital Economy*. Cambridge, MA: MIT Press.

Sokol, P. K. (1995). *From EDI to Electronic Commerce*. New York: McGraw-Hill.

Solvik, P. (1999). *Time For Change. Context Integration*. Available on the World Wide Web at: http://www.context.com/epurchasing/eProcurement/sld001.htm. Accessed in December 1999.

Stepanek, M. (1999). Closed, gone to the Net. *Business Week*, June, 113.

Tedeschi, B. (1999). Real force in e-commerce is business-to-business sales. *New York Times*, January.

The Outsourcing Institute. (2000). *2000 Outsourcing Index*. Available on the World Wide Web at: http://www.outsourcing.com.

Thorelli, H. B. (1986). Networks: Between markets and hierarchies. *Strategic Management Journal*, 7, 37-51.

Wang, E. T. G. and Seidmann, A. (1995). Electronic data interchange: Competitive externalities and strategic implementation policies. *Management Science,* 41(3), 401-418.

Ware, J., Gebauer, J., Hartman, A. and Roldan, M. (1998). *The Search for Digital Excellence*. New York: McGraw-Hill.

Williamson, O. E. (1985). *The Economic Institutions of Capitalism: Firms, Markets, Relational Contracting*. New York: Free Press.

Williamson, O. E. and Masten, S. E. (Eds.). (1995). *Transaction Cost Economics (Vol. 1)*. Aldershot, England: Edward Elgar Publishing.

Chapter III

Online Exchanges and Beyond: Issues and Challenges in Crafting Successful B2B Marketplaces

John M. Gallaugher
Boston College, USA

Suresh C. Ramanathan
Koryak, USA

INTRODUCTION

Rapid advances are bringing new and efficient market mechanisms to industries as varied as aerospace and fish wholesaling. Digital marketplaces provide the opportunity to facilitate product and partner discovery, offer dynamic pricing and deliver a host of value-added services on a global scale. Early research in eCommerce pointed to the high cost of pioneering efforts such as EDI and private exchange formation as a limiting factor in realizing the benefits of electronic markets (Malone et al., 1987). However, a new generation of services is now being enabled by the ubiquity of the Internet, the open standards of XML, the wide use of third-party vendor-based solutions, and the rapid deployment and low maintenance costs of current systems (Gallaugher and Auger 1997). These advances have brought eCommerce to a much broader array of firms than previously thought possible, dramatically increasing the forecasts for global B2B eCommerce. With the development of increasingly sophisticated and more accessible technical solutions, the current challenge lies in developing and sustaining vibrant markets that attract active participation of both buyers and suppliers, and which generate value for all.

This chapter provides an overview of critical issues associated with crafting a valuable and sustainable electronic marketplace. In order to provide a foundation for examples and discussion, the first section reviews B2B markets and provides a simple classification mechanism. Next, the issues of price presentation and price setting are introduced as they relate to the classification framework. The second half of the chapter explores factors associated with participant motivation regarding the key issues of liquidity formation and maintenance, exchange ownership and governance, and the delivery of value-added services.

B2B MARKET MECHANISMS

Electronic Marketplaces provide the basic infrastructure to allow suppliers and buyers to interact in an online environment. By mid-2000 there were some 30,000 private exchanges in various stages of development and more than 600 public exchanges in operation (King, 2000). The rapid proliferation of B2B marketplaces has caused confusion in understanding the players and the effective use for various types of online marketplaces. A classification mechanism for understanding B2B marketplaces is offered by Kaplan and Sawhney (2000). This simple two-by-two scheme considers the dimensions of what firms purchase (manufacturing inputs or operating inputs) as well as how they purchase (spot buying or systematic buying), and classifies marketplaces accordingly (see Table 1). This mechanism allows us to examine when various types of exchanges are likely to emerge and how they might be used.

Table 1: Classifying B2B Marketplaces (Adapted in part from Kaplan and Sawney, 2000)

	Operating Inputs	Manufacturing Inputs	
Systematic Sourcing	MRO Hubs *low value goods with high transaction costs*	Catalog Hubs *non-commodity manufacturing inputs*	Aggregation
Spot Sourcing	Yield Managers *products have a high degree of price/demand volatility*	Exchanges *commodities or near-commodities used in production*	Matching
	Horizontal Markets	Vertical Markets	

Classifying B2B Marketplaces

Most contemporary electronic marketplaces can be classified as having elements of at least one of four types: MRO Hubs, Yield Managers, Exchanges or Catalog Hubs.

Operating Inputs that are purchased systematically are procured via *MRO Hubs* (maintenance, repair, operating). Since these sorts of products are likely to be used across industries, such markets are largely horizontal, supporting many industries on the buy side as well as numerous product categories on the sell side. MRO Hubs include those run by traditional distributors such as Grainger and new entrants like BizBuyer.com. The appeal of such exchanges is in lowering search and transaction costs in product categories where buyers require selection at the point of purchase (Bakos, 1991; Andersen, Day et al., 1997).

Yield Managers enable spot markets for non-manufacturing inputs. These sorts of markets are most appropriate when products or services exhibit either 1) a high degree of price and demand volatility, or 2) when such fixed-cost assets cannot be liquidated or acquired quickly. Advertising, utility markets, manufacturing capacity, manpower and warehousing space are all examples of products or services likely to be traded over Yield Managers.

Exchanges focus on spot sourcing for manufacturing inputs. Commodity-like products that are susceptible to supply or demand fluctuation are likely candidates for Exchanges. This is particularly the case where market-making mechanisms offer more efficient pricing than may be apparent via non-market schemes such as certain financial instruments, agriculture products, energy, and scrap or recycled materials (Malone, Benjamin and Yates, 1987).

Catalog Hubs enable systematic sourcing of manufacturing inputs. Since these inputs vary greatly from industry to industry, these markets are, by definition, vertical or industry-focused. The focus of such exchanges creates opportunities for the electronic marketplace to offer value-added services that exploit the uniqueness of the niche served. Such focus may be critical, as a lack of focus has been cited as one of the reasons for the failure of early players in the B2B space such as Industry.Net (Wildemuth, 1997). Chemdex, PlasticsNetwork and SciQuest are all examples of vertical markets served by Catalog Hubs.

Pricing Issues

Systematic sourcing and spot sourcing markets suggest two very different sets of pricing issues. Under systematic sourcing, pricing is largely determined up front, however the details of products, inventory, and pricing across a disparate and likely widely divergent product base present significant technical and coordination challenges. Under spot sourcing pricing is flexible, so one of the chief tasks of the exchange architect lies in crafting a mechanism that appropriately establishes a fair market price to the satisfaction of all participants. An introduction to these issues is offered below.

Systematic Sourcing and Price Presentation

MRO and Catalog hubs are targeted at systematic sourcing. Kaplan and Sawhney (2000) suggest a variety of conditions under which aggregation is appropriate. These include when products are specialized and not commodities; when prices are pre-negotiated, fixed or pre-determined, and market participants are unwilling to engage in dynamic pricing; when the supplier universe is highly fragmented; when product selection is large; and when the cost of purchase orders is high relative to product price.

The sheer variety of differentiated product offerings that many such exchanges attract requires an immense level of coordination among various parties and information systems. While fragmented markets make the economic case for aggregation, this fragmentation presents significant technical and organizational hurdles that must be overcome before systematic sourcing sites can move from concept to useful tool. To shed light on this difficulty, consider the seemingly basic task of offering an online catalog. In highly fragmented markets, a consolidated catalog that captures the information from numerous manufacturers can serve as a key competitive asset. Firms such as Aspect Development and TPN Register provide pre-aggregated and normalized multi-supplier catalogs to facilitate procurement of products across a wide variety of categories. However, the cost of creating a catalog can run well above $4.00 per item, depending upon complexity and sophistication required (Donahue, 2000). And this does not take into account the difficulty in maintaining catalog changes over time.

Online catalogs are created from numerous disparate data stores that are both electronic and paper based. The formats vary from catalog to catalog requiring a methodical approach to consolidation. XML (eXtensible Markup Language) can be used to facilitate catalog data exchange among suppliers, easing the development and maintenance burden. A consistency in XML tags is vital for this effort, but uniform standards are not available for the detail required by many marketplaces. As such, hubs may wish to work with trade associations or standards setting bodies to ensure that an appropriate standard is crafted and widely adopted.

The richness and the ease of use of the catalog can enhance the usage and purchase behavior of the user. Markets with a large number of highly divergent items must be particularly sensitive to interface design issues so that customers can appropriately manage the complexity of the site and quickly identify items of interest. The online building and contracting site Buzzsaw.com provides an example of targeting catalog design appropriate for different use as market participants migrate from the initial product location stage to subsequent reorder stages of use. Buzzsaw has used the services of Wiznet to create a content rich catalog that architects and engineers could easily use. Buzzsaw also created a separate bare bones transactional catalog for placing procurement orders (Donahue, 2000). The dual offerings are meant to appeal to different needs – rich for more detailed initial exploration, limited for fast, renewable transactions.

On top of the technical and design challenges, marketplace owners must ensure that mechanisms are in place for the regular and systematic updating of supply information. While supply-chain links can help in accurately presenting product availability and forecasting delivery time, updates, edits and removal of items require a commitment on behalf of participants to maintain information shared with the marketplace. Establishing this level of supplier commitment is difficult in situations when marketplaces are starting out and member firms are uncertain or unaware of the resources they must commit. Failing to address these seemingly mundane aspects of marketplace development and maintenance will make it impossible to cost-effectively represent available products and will doom an effort to failure. Issues related to additional value creation and marketplace appeal are detailed later in this chapter.

Spot Sourcing and Price Setting

The spot pricing used by Yield Managers and Exchanges requires a means for price-setting. In these environments, simple matching or auctions can be used to price-set. In traditional market exchanges, such as those employed via the electronic communications networks (ECNs) used in securities trading, buyers and suppliers arrive with each broadcasting their desired prices. Should a match be made, the exchange aligns partners and completes the transaction. If no match is made, market participants examine their prices relative to others in the market and may make adjustments accordingly, hold position or leave the market.

It is also possible that an intermediary (sometimes referred to as a dealer) may take possession of a product (Fan, Stallaert and Whinston 2000). Examples of dealer involvement in electronic markets include trading by Nasdaq market makers as well as Enron's active role in trading energy products and other commodities through EnronOnline. Enron has traded some $300 billion online in the first full year of the firm's online trading effort, including 60% of the world's natural gas. Dealers can foster market liquidity when a buyer/seller match is not immediately available. The absence of a dealer has been suggested as one reason for the lack of liquidity evident in early ECN-based after-hours securities trading in the United States.

Auctions allow a party to place a product or service out for bid. In *forward auctions*, the seller requests that buyers set the price. This is usually the case when the item being sold is scarce, allowing the sellers to leverage market control in their favor. In *reverse auctions*, buyers take bids for their business. Reverse auctions are effective in situations where the buyer has significant leverage, many supplier alternatives exist, there is slack or perishable inventory and the product being defined is largely a commodity.

While there are many variations of auctions, we can classify the most popular mechanisms into one of five primary categories (Hogan, 2000):

- *English Auction*: In this auction the bidding starts at the lowest acceptable price and bids are successively higher until the auction is closed. The highest bidder wins. This forward auction can also be conducted as a reverse auction.
- *Dutch Auction*: In the Dutch auction the bidding for one or a group of like items starts at a high price and is progressively lowered until all buyers have bid on all the items.
- *Vickrey Auction*: This is similar to the English Auction expect that the second highest bidder wins. This is intended to avoid "Bidder's Remorse."
- *Japanese Auction*: This auction begins at a low price and increases by fixed amount. Bidders drop out at each increase and the remaining bidder wins the auction.
- *Sealed-Bid Auction*: Each and every bidder submits a single, secret bid. The bids are opened once all the bids are in or the auction is closed, whichever is earlier. The lowest bidder wins.

While exchanges and auctions suggest efficient markets, these sorts of matching mechanisms are not appropriate in all situations. Kaplan and Sawhney (2000) outline a set of conditions under which matching is likely to take place. These include situations where products are commodities or near-commodities, when demand and pricing is volatile and when trading volumes are high relative to transaction costs. Such markets assume a willingness among participants to accept dynamic pricing. Also, in certain exchanges such as those involving institutional investors, the anonymity of trading partners must be secured.

PARTICIPANT MOTIVATION

Regardless of the mechanism for B2B eCommerce, the owner of the marketplace must create an environment conducive for the commercial exchange. Crafting such a market with disparately motivated participants, with varying degrees of market power among them, is perhaps the chief challenge facing marketplace stewards. The motivation of various parties to participate in a market is strongly linked to factors related to market liquidity, exchange ownership and the value-added by the market mechanism. Key issues surrounding each of these factors are detailed below.

Liquidity

A market that cannot support an adequate number of transactions to interest both buyers and sellers is destined to fail due to a lack of trade liquidity. Matching marketplaces such as Yield Managers and Exchanges are most vulnerable to a liquidity squeeze. Market participants may be most attracted to the largest, hence most efficient markets, however only a few pioneering online marketplaces are sufficiently liquid. By Fall 2000 there were over 600 B2B exchanges, but by some estimates only 75 had any liquidity at all. The result of the scramble to lock-in participants will almost certainly lead to a B2B bloodbath. AMR Research Inc. estimates that the number of B2B exchanges in the market may fall 90% by 2002 (Copeland, 2000). Many industry exchanges are likely to exhibit monopolistic tendencies as more buyers beget more sellers and this total growth attracts more services, locking in scale advantages for those that can 'tip' an industry into mass adoption (Farrell and Saloner, 1986). The underlying economics suggest that each industry may support only one or two major exchanges. However in mid-2000 there were 40 Web marketplaces in the health care field and 50 in chemicals. Since it is hard to predict which of these exchanges will survive, most corporations are spreading their risks by playing in multiple markets, and these spread transactions further contribute to the liquidity crunch.

Electronic markets are subject to network effects (also referred to as network externalities or Metcalfe's Law). When network effects are present, a product or service becomes more attractive as its user base expands (Katz and Shapiro, 1985). This implies that all parties see value in the exchange and are motivated to participate. However, this premise is in direct conflict with the price advantages trumpeted by many exchange creators. While it is easy to see buy-side advantages for exchange participants in terms of lower cost, few suppliers are willing to see their products further commoditized by intense, price-focused competition. IndustrialVortex.com was one firm that attempted to aggregate products from thousands of suppliers, however a critical mass of suppliers refused to participate, making the exchange untenable, with the firm closing in July 2000 (Ante and Weintraub, 2000). Identifying value for all participants will be vital to generating the critical mass necessary to craft an exchange. Options for value-enhancement are detailed in a later section.

Channel Pressure

Channel pressure from competing markets or trade mechanisms can also limit trade volume and hinder liquidity (Gallaugher, forthcoming). Reluctance, or the inability of participants to migrate to the new channel, can prevent a marketplace from reaching critical mass. The inability of ECNs to route large stock trading volume to institutional matching firm Optimark has been cited as one reason that the effort has struggled. Optimark was to allow institutional investors to anonymously execute massive trading strategies, avoiding market-sensitive public moves. However due in part to channel-derived liquidity weakness, as of mid-2000 the Optimark network could only support markets in 10 of the hundreds of Nasdaq securities (Keegan, 2000).

The B2B side of consumer plays may also suffer channel pressure that can torpedo business models. The inability of the online pharmacy market to strike deals with key finance entities has devastated this once-promising sector. PlanetRx and other online pharmacies need the participation of Prescription Benefit Managers (PBMs) that control insurance reimbursement for prescriptions. Without their cooperation, there was no way online pharmacies could get consumers to come to its site and buy prescription drugs at health-plan-reduced rates. PBMs represented a vital B2B partner necessary for the execution of the pharmacy consumer play, but without their support efforts face doubtful prospects.

Price-Focused Marketplaces

The premise of price-based commoditization of supplies is in sharp contrast to the long stream of research trumpeting the advantage of tighter, more balanced relationships between buyer and suppliers (see Clemmons et al., 1993). Clearly bid-based sourcing can lower procurement costs. However, price-driven marketplaces can cause buyers harm over the long term. General Electronic has realized 15 to 20% cost savings as a result of its initial deployment of the TPN, or Trading Process Network (Rao, 2000). However, the firm has taken steps to reduce the level and severity of price competition that suppliers are subject to. Lower prices resulting from voracious competition limits supplier margins, and creates a situation where firms have fewer resources for suppliers to invest in innovation and R&D, as well as quality and service improvements. Lower margins may also prompt weaker suppliers to exit the market, ceding competition to deep-pocketed rivals. This may result in a long-term shift in power from buyers to suppliers. In order to combat such problems, GE has employed systems to scan for low-ball bidders, selecting firms that were more likely to offer competitive bids that still provided suppliers with sustainable profits. Non-price benefits of the TPN have also been emphasized. These include savings made up in cycle time and transaction cost reductions–benefits that add value to both parties in the exchange (Chronister, 1997).

First Choice vs. Last Resort Markets

The rise of Internet auctions has prompted some to suggest that dynamic pricing may be the norm rather than the exception, however this is highly unlikely in many markets given the divergent motivation of market participants. Suppliers are likely to be attracted to new markets if they feel there is a match with their product offering and the service, if they feel that more profits can be garnered than via traditional channels, and if the shift to the new channel will not result in a pre-mature weakening of the brand or other critical assets. For providers of differentiated products or services with exclusive or limited access, fluid-price markets such as auctions present a compelling alternative to traditional channels. These markets are appealing because of existing market inefficiencies. Both parties in such auctions have a strong incentive to shift their channel and participate. In fact, for many suppliers and participants, this mechanism is favored over traditional means of bringing products and services to market, so the shift to the new channel is seen as a best alternative or most favored market.

Liquidation services are likely to be less attractive and are often times viewed as markets of last resort. These auctions exist because of production, operations, forecasting and distribution inefficiencies. When such circumstances exist, the supplier's first priority is to remove the inefficiencies. Whatever is left over will then be distributed via auction format. The business model of liquidation auction services is potentially jeopardized by intense moves to squeeze excess from a firm's internal value chain (e.g., ERP and supply chain management software or self-liquidation via direct-to-buyer specials), and by more competition attracted to the space by low entry barriers (Gallaugher, forthcoming). Suppliers that feel significant price pressure brought about by liquidation auctions may seek to forward integrate and take control of the auction themselves. The airline industry provides an example of how a consortium of price-sensitive carriers have moved forward to create the Orbitz and Hotwire systems to counteract Priceline's liquidity auctions. Similar market forces are creating parallel examples in the B2B space as consortia move to take control of the channel by displacing markets run by independent third parties. Issues related to exchange ownership are detailed in the following section.

Marketplace Ownership

Online marketplaces are currently being formed by third parties, industry consortia and individual firms. While it is clear to most that new electronic market mechanisms will impact varied industries, it is not known what the optimal ownership or governance structure of such markets should be (Venkatraman, 2000). Each brings with it a series of advantages and limitations that must be considered in the context of the firm and industry.

Neutral Third Parties

Independent markets run by neutral third parties help quell the perception that an exchange is biased against a constituency of the exchange process. This may be particularly important in areas such as financial services where participants are particularly sensitive to any perception of a conflict of interest between the buy-side and sell-side. As an example, while some of the largest

Figure 1: Market Efficiency and Liquidation Auctions (Adapted in part from Gallaugher, forthcoming)

Market Efficiency Auctions: favored channel

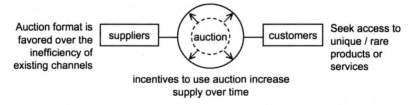

Liquidation Auctions: market of last resort

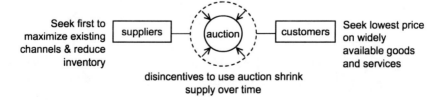

banks involved in foreign exchange have announced online networks to pool activity in this fragmented market, one of the early leaders in this space is CurreneX.com, an independent exchange unaffiliated with classic bank partners. Institutional investors and treasurers at firms such as MasterCard are now doing half of their foreign exchange over this Web-enabled system. CEO Lori Mirek claims the site's neutrality is one of its chief advantages. "Clients tell us that they don't want their counterparty also to run the platform" (Wood, 2000). Third-party marketplaces may also have an advantage in encouraging participation in a fragmented market, given that suppliers may be more likely to join an open market rather than one controlled or financed by rivals.

Despite these advantages, third-party marketplaces may suffer from limitations in key resources necessary for jump-starting the exchange, such as brand awareness, trust, profit-centers in other businesses to fuel expansion and trading partners necessary for liquidity. Also, while fragmented, disorganized markets offer great opportunities for rooting out inefficiencies and enlisting potential trading partners in a neutral, independent site, third-party marketplaces operating in industries where there are dominant rivals also face a fast-follower problem. Some participants may use the exchange as a learning tool and a gauge for the validity and interest in electronic marketplaces. Once the concept is proven and parties are comfortable with the option, then firms may seek to develop their own marketplaces independent of the third party. General Motors, for example, used FreeMarkets to procure rubber hoses, sun visors and lock systems before launching their own private exchange with consortium partners. While third parties that acquire liquidity in fragmented markets may have a more defensible position, third-party marketplaces that are reliant on large participants are extremely vulnerable. Such circumstances are apparent even in some of the most successful third-party intermediaries. As of Q2 2000, B2B Web auction firm FreeMarkets stated that two vendors (United Technologies and Visteon) accounted for 21% of the firm's revenues (Ante, 2000). Similarly, DoubleClick aggregates the sale and delivery of advertising among Web sites and advertisers. Yet despite being the industry leader, the firm's exposure was painfully evident in Spring 2000 when AltaVista, a site responsible for roughly 40 percent of the firm's revenue, announced its intention to migrate advertising to aggregators owned by parent CMGi (Fox, 2000). Fortunately for the startups, it has been estimated that some 50% of the U.S. economy is made up of industries so fragmented that these sorts of power struggles are unlikely to be an issue.

Upstarts that create marketplaces in one market may also realize scope advantages in trying to extend the concept to other markets. A firm creating an exchange in one industry may be able to reuse systems, staff, knowledge or scale in other industries. Financing, insurance, escrow, transportation, community and other services offered on one site may scale to other sites as well. VerticalNet has created 57 different marketplaces for industries as varied as energy and food. The firm reported $53.6 million in revenues for the second quarter 2000, however this means less than $1 million per marketplace, with revenues spread across transactions, ads and other eCommerce fees. Even systems that are scaleable across product categories can't compensate when there is not a critical mass of willing parties to begin transaction.

Consortia

As mentioned earlier, buyer leverage can be critical to creating demand necessary for market formation. Leverage exerted by a group of buyers can yield enormous market influence (Porter, 1985) and generate positive-sum network effects (Farrell and Saloner, 1986). Large corporations are co-investing with competitors and operating in vertical exchanges that cater to a given industry or a critical raw material. Buyers with significant leverage in a particular geographical area or industry can wield their influence to bring qualified suppliers to a given market, thereby performing the role of a market maker. It is no accident that some of the most aggressively promoted vertical exchanges not only have the major players in a given industry as buyers but also as investors. Rubbernetwork.com (Continental, Cooper, Goodyear, Groupe Michelin, Pirelli, Sumitomo and Bridgestone), Transora (50 consumer packaged-goods including Coca Cola and General Mills) and Covisint (the Big Three auto makers) are all examples of electronic markets created by the combined leverage of individual behemoths. The ability of large consortia to wield power in purchase or supply can crush even those rivals with an early lead. For example, ChemConnect began operations in 1995, however five years later the firm was hampered by the formation of three exchanges–Elemica, Omnexus and Envera–backed by Bayer, Dupont and Dow Chemical. These consortia have apparently frozen the market. Even though 11,000 buyer and sellers have joined ChemConnect, only a third of them have completed transactions (Ante and Weintraub, 2000). And exchanges that combine their resources may create even stronger network effects. The first so-called MegaHub was announced in January 2001 and would combine Transora with the retail exchange GlobalNetXchange founded by Sears, Carrefour and Oracle.

Consortia of buyers cooperating together provide an example of rivals creating a positive-sum game capable of generating benefits for all (Brandenburger and Nalebuff, 1997). However, large exchanges may suffer from a 'too many cooks' problem, and crafting exchanges among rivals presents several significant challenges. Mistrust, cultural differences, standards issues, control concern and other factors can lead to delays or even the cancellation of cooperative efforts. Consider the auto-industry exchange Covisent–the firm initially had four CEOs, took months simply to decide on a name, and as of early 2001 still hadn't named a chief executive or secured a headquarters location. An exchange created by a single entity may benefit from focus that consortia find difficult to achieve and the downside of cooperating with industry competitors has pushed many large players such as General Electric to simply act alone. GE's CEO of Global eXchange Services has stated "We spent lots of time with these industry consortia customers, and they are still trying to decide what to do" (Schonfeld, 2001).

While network effects fuel positive growth, network markets also exhibit market dominant tendencies that raise concerns among antitrust regulators. The FTC is particularly concerned about monopsony or oligopsony, where one or more purchasing companies could band together to squeeze supplier margins. The case of Covisint, a firm which may control a projected $240 billion in annual purchasing, provides an example of the scrutiny to come. The Federal Trade Commission was concerned that such cooperation among auto manufacturers could potentially result in collusion, illegal price "signaling" and other exchange of sensitive information (Wilke, 2000). The FTC and Germany's anti-trust commission categorically cleared Covisint in Fall 2000. However, the Government will continue to monitor the exchange during the implementation phase. Recognizing that monopoly is a byproduct of new-economy economics, the FTC is expected to provide specific guidelines about B2B exchanges in the near future.

Single-Party Buyer/Seller Marketplace Formation

Finally, there are situations when a single, large entity may strike out and develop its own electronic marketplace. This is an attractive option for large firms that dominate markets and that are able to single-handedly aggregate market-influencing purchasing power. From a technical perspective, such efforts are a natural extension of EDI (electronic data interchange) systems that have been developed using proprietary, closed networks. As the Internet lowers cost and increases accessibility, new tools and standards will allow these proprietary systems to be expanded and migrated to open networks.

General Electric provides an example of a large player that has been thus far been able to go it alone successfully. Since December 1999, all 500 of GE Aircraft's suppliers have been doing their delivery scheduling and billing over the Web, replacing the old paper-based system. GE Aircraft controls about 60% of the engine market, so it can already negotiate the best pricing deals with suppliers. Given its market dominance, the firm believes that opening its site to competitors such as Pratt & Whitney or Rolls-Royce would undermine its scale-based competitive advantage. The firm has also been aggressive on the supply-side, creating purchasing markets for after-market parts that support the smaller, continued purchases more likely to be made online. GEPartsEdge.com offers a growing list of more than three million parts. General Electric is involved in similar efforts across units–its size gives it the advantage of leveraging developments across the firm's deep product scope. In 2000 the volume of GE's Internet transactions produced some $5 billion in worldwide revenues. GE management believes that through Internet-derived productivity, they can save from 20 to 50% of selling, general and administrative expenses. If realized, these savings could boost GE's operating profits by nearly half (Rao, 2000).

Large entities can provide scale in aggregating buyers or sellers and can provide the liquidity jumpstart necessary to launch an exchange, however controlling firms may eventually choose to open to others if greater sum gains can be retrieved. Proctor and Gamble, for example, chose to sell its private EDI network to IBM so that other suppliers would participate, fueling adoption of mutually beneficial supply chain enhancements (Clark and McKenney, 1995). Such a move was necessary because although P&G dominated many individual product categories, the firm represented only a small percentage of total buyer purchase. Without the participation of other suppliers, buyers were not sufficiently motivated to adopt the system.

Value-Added Marketplaces

While it should be apparent that lopsided price-focused marketplaces face significant threats to ever achieving viability, few of the early pioneers have effectively extended their offerings to appeal beyond price discovery. Less than 15% of the 1,000-plus exchanges started in the last few years deliver value-added services or end-to-end electronic transactions (Seybold, 2000). Value-added services can be offered in a variety of ways that are enhanced by electronic networks. Opportunities include systems that help manage complexity, offer decision support, lower search costs, facilitate design, and foster coordination and supply chain integration.

Complexity Management

Complexity management is one reason middlemen retain their value (Andersen et al., 1997). Software-based complexity management (typically leveraged via expert systems and related AI) can facilitate product selection and add value for all participants. Milacron's Web site, Milpro.com, provides an example of such value added. The site helps small machine shops with process troubleshooting. Leveraging an online expert system, the firm's custom-developed Milpro Wizard guides customers through a set of questions about a process and related problems much as an experienced sales representative would, then it recommends a product (Byrne et al., 2000). This allows Milpro to manage goods complexity, encourages vendor participation through expertise offering and sales/support reduction, and the system can scale better than human advice since the marginal cost of repeated delivery of this expertise is effectively zero.

Decision Support

Transaction-volume itself may fuel the creation of value-added services such as decision support. Consider State Street's GlobalLink and Insight tools for institutional investors. State Street is one of the world's largest custodians of financial assets for institutional investors such as managers of pension plans and mutual funds. In Fall 2000, the firm held over $6 trillion in assets under custody. In any given day, roughly 10% of the world's assets pulse through the firm's information systems. Financial markets are highly fragmented, and institutional investors are constantly on the lookout for improved information to facilitate market moves. State Street has leveraged its huge custody volume (a market considered post-trade) to move into the pre-trade and trade markets, areas that provide an additional 74% of revenue opportunities (Melymuka, 1999). By leveraging transaction volume to provide decision support tools, the firm moves up the food chain from the commodity service of custody provision to become a value-added business partner that helps clients make better decisions. The results have been striking. Customers who use GlobalLink buy three times as many services as those who don't. Global Link is now installed on the desks of more than 200 of the world's top institutional investors. Its systems have become so pervasive that GlobalLink is now a distribution channel for competitor services–rivals have begun paying State Street to deliver their products (Cone, 2000). The platform has also become a branching off point for tools such as Insight for fund managers and BondConnect for fixed-income markets. These tools may allow the firm a head start in attempting to unify diverse and complex B2B financial markets for pension administrators, mutual fund managers and other institutional investors.

Search Cost Reduction

Search cost reduction is also recognized as a reason why participants chose electronic markets over convention systems (Malone et al., 1987; Bakos, 1991). Firms which have successfully created marketplaces aggregating a critical mass of buyers and/or sellers may leverage this asset to create a virtual distribution channel that can be re-sold to complementary or even competing efforts. Like the example of State Street above, Grainger has similarly leveraged its early lead and customer base to act as an intermediary that aggregates and sells products provided from other firms. Granger has a separate site called Orderzone.com (in addition to its own) that provides access to other distributors. FindMRO.com is another Grainger site that allows users to locate hard-to-find items not on Grainger. Grainger has also set-up a huge MRO site called TotalMRO.com. Creative intermediaries like Grainger add value by leveraging their customer base as a distribution channel, encouraging rivals to participate in a margin for volume tradeoff. As the owner of the meta-exchange, firms like Grainger and State Street see brand awareness transferred to them, as customers think of the exchange manager rather than the product supplier when making a purchase. The new middleman also gains the value of the data asset, possibly enabling it to become the architect of a tailored service that greater targets and serves customer needs (Gallaugher, forthcoming).

Design

General Electric's Polymerland shows how B2B marketplaces not only cut costs, but also provide value-added service such as support for product design. An industrial designer using Polymerland can select a plastic, enter a shape, determine what its strength or heat resistance will be and compare prices among dozens of types of plastic. The designer can also select colors from the 10,000 available with a color sample chip mailed within two days time. As in other examples, the service delivers value through process rather than price improvements.

Coordination

Many industries involve a complex chain of players and events before the product or service is delivered to the end customer. Yet suppliers of different components often communicate poorly, so electronic hubs that foster better communication among relevant players can add enormous value. While first-generation exchanges may provide value from finding and presenting information, further value can be generated by parties that create and deploy information vital to the transaction. By knowing key information from suppliers, customers and other participants in the supply chain such as R&D findings, lab reports, delivery status, scheduled capacity utilization, etc., participants can collaborate to improve processes industry-wide (Seybold, 2000).

Markets where there is significant transaction complexity can benefit by the creation of an electronic space for collaboration on things such as legal proceedings and government documentation, design, scheduling and delivery. Consider Bidcom (now Citadon), an online workplace where contracts do everything from store blueprints to order building materials to coordinate dozens of subcontractors and suppliers. The service was used to build Charles Schwab's new building, built by Swinerton & Walberg Builders. The time savings from avoiding phone calls, voice-mail tag and back-and-forth faxes got the six-month project done two weeks early–saving Schwab $880,000 in rent on its old building (Hof, 2000).

Supply Chain Integration

The increasing transparency of prices and accelerated globalization of markets brought forth by the rapid growth of electronic marketplaces expose gross inefficiencies in various distribution channels. Inefficiencies in the supply chain cannot be overcome simply by an online price-posting or auction mechanism, however most current electronic marketplaces are stand-alone systems with minimal integration with the ERP systems of the buyers and sellers. This lack of integration may affect order fulfillment and transaction costs. The next wave of B2B marketplaces and fully Internet-aware supply chain suites by vendors such as i2 and SAP are addressing these integration requirements. Such integration is bound to increase the value of the exchange and erect significant barriers to entry by increasing the switching costs for the customers of the exchange (Bakos, 1991).

Logistical visibility across the supply chain is crucial to the success of manufacturing operations. Web-based ERP systems and XML have enhanced the abilities of organizations and are positioned to deliver on the vision of integrating across entities. Electronic integration within and across corporations will add significant competitive value to long-term players in the marketplace. Collaborative demand planning, synchronized production planning and joint product development are some of the direct benefits of an integrated supply chain with value offered to all participants.

CONCLUSION

AMR has suggested that B2B eCommerce could reach $5.7 trillion by the end of 2004 with fully half of this flowing through online exchanges. Numbers like this are driving tremendous investment. In March 2000 alone, venture capitalists poured $800 million into 77 exchanges. The relative ease of entry and the "Chinese Math" being offered by firms hoping to gain a slice of this projected huge market may be offset by the reality that running an exchange may not be as lucrative as initially optimistic projections for total flow-through revenues suggest. Consider the small profits garnered by one of the oldest and highest volume exchanges, the New York Stock Exchange. In 1999, the NYSE did $8.9 trillion in transactions but earned only $75.2 million in profits, less than one-thousandth of 1%. Firms must also face the reality of marketplace competition by new rivals, existing competitors, consortia, and even a firm's buyers and/or suppliers. Additionally, problems in developing successful and compelling business-to-business marketplaces are varied and complex. Liquidity generation, participant motivation, ownership decisions, defense crafting and value generation all present significant challenges. Firms attuned to the specifics of their market, their suitability to compete with respect to other potential rivals and the sustainability of any advantages crafted are best positioned to make wise investments and avoid painful experiments.

REFERENCES

Anderson, E., Day, G. S. and Rangan, V. K. (1997). Strategic channel design. *Sloan Management Review*, 4, 59-69.

Ante, S. E. and Weintraub, A. (2000). Why B2B is a scary place to be. *BusinessWeek*. September, 34.

Ante, S. E. (2000). The big kahuna of B2B exchanges? *BusinessWeek*, October, 166.

Bakos, J. Y. (1991). A strategic analysis of electronic marketplaces. *MIS Quarterly*, 15(3), 295-311.

Brandenburger, A. M. and Nalebuff, B. J. (1997). *Co-opetition*. New York: DoubleDay.

Byrne, T., Lentz, N. and Wolin, S. (2000). Beyond the exchange. *Business 2.0*, June, 390-393.

Chronister, K. (1997). GE announces plan to move all procurement to the Internet. *Electronic Buyers' News*, July, 14.

Clark, T. and McKenney, J. (1995). Proctor & Gamble: Improving consumer value through process redesign. In *Applegate, McFarlan, McKenney Computer Information Systems: Text and Cases*, Fourth Edition. New York: Irwin McGraw Hill.

Clemmons, E. K., Reddi, S. P. and Row, M. C. (1993). The impact of information technology on the organization of economic activity: The 'move to the middle' hypothesis. *Journal of Management Information System*, 3, 9-35.

Cone, E. (2000). Cash machine. *Wired*, June, 6.

Copeland, L. (2000). Trade exchange closes virtual doors. *Computerworld*, July, 4.

Donahue, S. (2000). Plugging in the catalog. *Business 2.0*, August, 54.

Fan, M., Stallaert, J. and Whinston, A. B. (2000). The Internet and the future of financial markets. *Communications of the ACM*, 11, 83-88.

Farrell, J. and Saloner, G. (1986). Installed base and compatibility: Innovation, product preannoucements and predation. *American Economic Review*, 5, 940-955.

Fox, L. (2000). DoubleClick climbs to the top of the ad world. *Upside*, February, 58-60.

Gallaugher, J. M. (forthcoming). eCommerce and the undulating distribution channel. *Communications of the ACM*.

Gallaugher, J. M. and Auger, P. (1997). Factors affecting the adoption of an Internet-based sales presence for small businesses. *Information Society*, 1, 55-74.

Grappa, M. (2000). Promises, promises. *Business 2.0*, October, 58.

Hof, R. (2000). Who will profit from the Internet? *BusinessWeek*, June, EB56.

Hogan, M. (2000). Dynamic pricing: Everything old is new again. *ARIBA, The Magazine for Business-to-Business eCommerce*, 2, 67.

Kaplan, S. and Sawhney, M. (2000). E-hubs: The new B2B marketplaces. *Harvard Business Review*, May-June, (3), 97-104.

Keegan, J. (2000). Home from the range: Optimark founder returns to NYC and his struggling system. *Investment Dealers' Digest*, April, 3-4.

King, J. (2000). Quietly, private eMarkets rule. *ComputerWorld*, September, 1.

Malone, T. W., Yates, J. and Benjamin, R.I. (1987). Electronic markets and electronic hierarchies. *Communications of the ACM*, 6, 484-497.

Mata, F. J., Fuerst, W. L. and Barney, J. B. (1995). Information technology and sustained competitive advantage: A resource-based analysis. *MIS Quarterly*, 4, 487-505.

Porter, M. E. (1985). *Competitive Advantage*. New York: Free Press.

Rao, S. S. (2000). General Electric-software vendor. *Forbes*, January, 144-

146.

Seybold, P. (2000). Niches bring riches. *Business 2.0*, June, 135-136.

Shina, J. (2000). A Web-profit prophet spreads the word. *BusinessWeek*, September, EB68.

Schonfeld, E. (2001). Have we seen the last of the bear? *eCompany*, January, 53.

Tully, S. (2000). The B2B tool that really is changing the world. *Fortune*, March, 132.

Wildemuth, S. (1997). Aim carefully for I-net profits. *Datamation*, 7, 97-100.

Wilke, J. R. (2000). Green light is likely for auto-parts site. *The Wall Street Journal*, September, A3.

Chapter IV

Impersonal Trust in B2B Electronic Commerce: A Process View

Paul A. Pavlou
University of Southern California, USA

Although the notion of impersonal trust is not new, its significance has dramatically increased with the emergence of interorganizational eCommerce. Two types of trust are usually distinguished in interfirm exchange relations–an impersonal type created by structural arrangements, and a familiarity type arising from repeated interaction. This chapter contributes to the emerging body of knowledge regarding the role of trust in B2B eCommerce, which is primarily impersonal. The nature of trust is examined, and credibility and benevolence are defined as its distinct dimensions. Impersonal trust-primarily arising from credibility-focuses on institutional structures that B2B exchanges enable through signals and incentives to facilitate interfirm relations. Following the economic, sociological and marketing literature on the sources and processes under which trust engenders, a set of three cognitive processes that generate impersonal trust is determined. Applied to B2B exchanges, four antecedents of impersonal trust are proposed to trigger these processes: accreditation, feedback, monitoring and legal bonds. In addition, impersonal trust is proposed to increase satisfaction, reduce risk, encourage anticipated continuity and promote favorable pricing. A theoretical framework is then proposed that specifies the interrelationships between the antecedents, underlying processes and consequences of impersonal trust in B2B eCommerce. The theoretical and managerial implications of this study on B2B eCommerce are discussed, and directions for future research are proposed.

INTRODUCTION

The recent outbreak of electronic exchange activities, enabled primarily by the Internet, led to the emergence of B2B eCommerce. Interorganizational exchange relationships can provide a strategic source of efficiency, a competitive advantage and increased performance (Zaheer et al., 1998). A *B2B exchange* is a new form of structural platform that acts as a virtual intermediary enabling firms to conduct any-to-any online relations. As in traditional interfirm relations (Bromiley and Cummings, 1995), trust has also been considered crucial in online exchange relationships (Brynjolfsson and Smith, 2000), perhaps more given the impersonal nature of eCommerce (Keen, 2000). Trust in B2B eCommerce is mostly impersonal and it is created by structural arrangements through signals and incentives, whereas trust in traditional exchanges has been mostly based on familiarity, arising from repeated interaction. Impersonal trust is likely to be important where no social relations exist, relationships are episodic, there is information asymmetry and uncertainty, and there is some important delegation of authority between firms (Shapiro, 1987). Therefore, the context of B2B eCommerce resembles the characteristics where impersonal trust should be necessary. Hence, interfirm relations have been undergoing some dramatic changes, making the role of impersonal trust in B2B eCommerce of fundamental theoretical and managerial importance. Empirical evidence also suggests that B2B eCommerce moves away from basic transactions towards interfirm collaboration (Dai and Kauffman, 2000), making impersonal trust increasingly important. Therefore, this chapter attempts to shed light on the nature, antecedents and consequences of interorganizational trust[1] that is embedded in the impersonal context of B2B eCommerce.

Practically all transactions require an element of trust, especially those conducted in an uncertain environment. However, trust in B2B eCommerce does not comply with the traditional dyadic context of familiarity-based trust. The traditional setting for establishing trust based on familiarity not only may not be realistic in B2B eCommerce, but it could also limit its extent. Even if there is a rich tradition of scholarly research focused on familiarity-based trust in interfirm exchange relations (Geyskens et al., 1998), there is no agreed-upon understanding of interorganizational impersonal trust. In today's B2B exchanges, the traditional setting of establishing trust based on reputation, familiarity and length of the relationship (Doney and Cannon, 1997) may not be readily obtainable. In addition, the absence of salespeople makes trust based on the salesperson's expertise, likeability and similarity mostly unavailable. Therefore, an impersonal type of trust may be more appropriate in B2B eCommerce. There is an urgent need to go beyond traditional dyadic relationships and examine a larger context of buyer-supplier relations in B2B eCommerce. When an increasingly large number of firms conduct business with many new, even anonymous partners, the need to understand the concept of impersonal trust in B2B eCommerce becomes fundamental.

Trust is important in impersonal exchange relationships, especially where information asymmetry and uncertainty may give rise to opportunism (Akerloff, 1970), which usually leads to mistrust, agency risks and high transaction costs. B2B eCommerce takes place in an uncertain environment that allows substantial information asymmetry between firms. Opportunism creates the problems of adverse selection and moral hazard, which are described in agency theory (Jensen and Meckling, 1976). Adverse selection occurs when firms may be motivated to misrepresent their respective abilities to the other trading firm. Moral hazard occurs when firms do no put forth the level of effort agreed upon, or fail to complete the requirements of an agreement (Mishra et al., 1998). The problems of adverse selection and moral hazard could result in excessive risk associated with online transactions, eroding the foundations of B2B eCommerce, and jeopardizing its proliferation. However, according to game theory, under suitable mechanisms opportunism does not pay off in the long run (Kandori, 1992). The institutional structures of B2B exchanges can transform many single transactions into a continuous sequence of relations between organizations, preventing opportunism through cooperative signals and incentives. Drawing from agency theory and transaction costs economics (TCE), trust may be viewed as a risk-reduction mechanism, decreasing transaction and agency costs and providing flexible transactions (Beccera and Gupta, 1999). B2B exchanges provide means of building trust through a series of safeguarding mechanisms, such as accreditation, feedback, monitoring and legal bonds. Since B2B exchanges are becoming an important coordination mechanism for economic activity, this chapter attempts to provide a framework to explain the process by which their mechanisms may engender impersonal trust. Moreover, the consequences of impersonal trust in B2B eCommerce are examined.

Despite the prolific differences between the traditional view of trust and impersonal trust in B2B eCommerce, this chapter proposes that impersonal trust can still complement interfirm exchange relations. The purpose of this chapter is to provide new insights into how trust develops in the impersonal context of B2B eCommerce by drawing on trust-building cognitive processes

(Doney and Cannon, 1997). The global concept of trust is viewed as a two-dimensional construct in terms of the dimensions of credibility and benevolence. Drawing from the literature on the sources and cognitive processes through which trust engenders, I propose that impersonal trust is associated with the dimension of credibility, and four antecedents of impersonal trust are then extracted. Furthermore, I examine how impersonal trust influences satisfaction, perceived risk, anticipated continuity and favorable pricing. More specifically, I propose a conceptual framework to describe a set of interrelationships between the antecedents and consequences of impersonal trust by attempting to answer these research questions: 1) What is the nature of impersonal trust in B2B eCommerce? 2) Which are the antecedents and consequences of impersonal trust?

The chapter is structured as follows: the next section reviews the current literature on trust, describes the nature and dimensions of impersonal trust, and portrays how a set of trust-building cognitive processes engenders credibility. A conceptual framework that examines the antecedents and consequences of impersonal trust is then developed in the context of B2B exchanges. Finally, the theoretical and managerial implications of this research are discussed in terms of the future of B2B eCommerce, and recommendations for future research are proposed.

CONCEPTUAL DEVELOPMENT

Trust is important because it is a key element of social capital and has been related to desirable economic and social outcomes (Arrow, 1974; Geyskens et al., 1998; Zaheer et al., 1998) and a source of competitive advantage (Barney and Hansen, 1994). Trust has also been considered to reduce opportunistic behavior and transaction costs, resulting in more efficient governance (Bromiley and Cummings, 1995). Sociologists argue that buyer-supplier relations are embedded in a social context that modifies economic activity in important ways (Granovetter, 1985). For example, it can be intertwined with markets to produce "relational contracts" to ensure flexibility and opportunity (Macneil, 1980), and with hierarchies to produce "hierarchical contracts" to ensure stability and equity (Stinchcombe, 1985). In terms of theory building, trust-embedded economic theories provide a richer explanation of interfirm relationships than trust-absent theories, and also improve their descriptive and explanatory power (Beccera and Gupta, 1999). Even if rational analysis of risk can only study a calculative cooperation, independent of trust (Williamson, 1985), some authors did manage to merge economic and sociological theories and highlighted the role of trust in exchange relationships (Gulati 1995; Ouchi, 1980). In general, the role of trust is of fundamental importance and has an impact on all levels of buyer-supplier relationships.

There are two contextual forms of trust: impersonal created by institutional or structural arrangements through signals, incentives and rational calculation (Shapiro, 1987), or familiarity arising from long-term relationships through repeated interaction. The impersonal trust is the basis of the studies of trust from a rational cognitive perspective, often game-theoretic, mainly based on the value of keeping a reputation of honesty and competence (Dasgupta, 1988). Impersonal trust arises when no familiarity between firms is available but some structural arrangements allow subjective expectations of a firm's credibility; on the other hand, familiarity trust mainly arises from subjective anticipations of a firm's benevolence based on prior interaction. Therefore, the willingness of one firm to become vulnerable to another firm's actions depends both on the familiarity and impersonal types of trust. While there is an extensive literature on the antecedents and consequences of familiarity trust in buyer-supplier relationships (Doney and Cannon, 1997; Geyskens et al., 1998), the literature on impersonal trust is in many aspects deficient, especially at the empirical level.

Trust is formally defined as the subjective probability with which a firm assesses that another firm will perform a particular transaction according to its confident expectations in an uncertain environment. This definition captures three important attributes of trust: first, the subjective probability embraces the fact that trust is not an objective anticipation; second, the confident expectation encompasses a possibility of a (mutually) beneficial outcome; finally, the uncertain environment suggests that delegation of authority from one firm to another may have adverse (harmful) effects to the entrusting firm in case of betrayal. Therefore, trust is the subjective evaluation of the other firm's characteristics based on limited information (Beccera and Gupta, 1999). While trust could greatly improve the effectiveness of the market (Arrow, 1974), both economists and sociologists object that trust could ever become a stable coordinating mechanism because trust fails when cooperation is less profitable than cheating (Granovetter, 1985). However, given an institutional structure to encourage and safeguard cooperation, impersonal trust that is trust based on institutional arrangements through signals and incentives could perhaps be able to effectively coordinate economic activity.

The Nature of Impersonal Trust

An impersonal analysis of trust enables studying rational and contextual cooperation, independent of familiarity trust that is usually irrational. The literature on interorganizational relations provides two general characteristics of trust: confidence or predictability in a firm's expectations about the other firm's behavior, and confidence in another firm's goodwill (Ring and Van de Ven, 1992). Moreover, trust has been viewed as the expectation that a firm can be relied on to fulfill obligations (Anderson and Weitz, 1989), behave in a predictable manner, act fairly and not take unfair advantage of another firm, even given the chance (Anderson and Narus, 1990). Credibility arises from the belief that the other firm is honest and competent (Anderson and Narus, 1990), whereas benevolence arises from the belief that a firm is genuinely interested in the other firm's welfare and would seek mutual gains. Therefore, there is a broad consensus that there are two distinct dimensions of trust: credibility and benevolence (Ganesan, 1994), who investigated them independently and concluded that they did demonstrate different relationships with other variables. Credibility deals with predictability, acknowledging contracts and fulfilling the requirements of an agreement, while benevolence deals with expectations that a firm will not act opportunistically, even given the chance. Therefore, this research views two distinct trust dimensions: impersonal trust or credibility, which is based on the extent to which a firm believes that the other firm has the honesty and expertise to perform a transaction reliably, and familiarity trust or benevolence, which is based on the extent to which a firm believes that the other firm has intentions beneficial to both firms, even when new conditions without prior commitments arise.

The proposed view of trust readily corresponds to extant conceptualizations of trust. For example, Zaheer et al. (1998) viewed interfirm trust as three components–predictability, reliability and fairness. Impersonal trust encompasses predictability and reliability, while familiarity trust is equivalent to fairness. In addition, the two-dimensional view of trust is comparable to the three forms of trust defined by Sako and Helper (1998). First, contractual trust, which refers to the other firm being honest and fulfilling the explicit and implicit requirements of the contractual agreement, and second, competence trust, which pertains to whether the other firm is capable of fulfilling the contract, encompass impersonal trust. According to Sako and Helper, competence and contractual trust are often indistinguishable since contract default might be due to either dishonesty or mere inability. On the other side, goodwill trust, which relates to a firm's open commitment to take initiatives for mutual benefit while withholding from opportunistic behavior refers to familiarity trust. In sum, there is a hierarchy of trust, where fulfilling a minimal set of obligations constitutes credibility (impersonal trust), and honoring a broader set constitutes benevolence (familiarity trust).

B2B exchanges reduce the need for familiarity trust by structuring the transactional context in such a way that opportunism becomes irrational, while cooperation becomes a mutually beneficial solution. In this context, B2B exchanges compensate for the low levels of familiarity trust, which is difficult to accomplish among a great number of firms, by promoting impersonal trust based on credibility. In addition, transactional arrangements aim to predict most probable unforeseen contingencies to avoid relying on another firm's benevolent motives. Hence, B2B exchanges provide a set of trust-building functions such as accreditation, feedback, monitoring and legal bonds that make opportunism irrational, thus promoting a trustworthy environment. The fact that many real-life anonymous B2B exchanges function without familiarity trust (e.g., Altra.com, Chemconnect.com) suggests that impersonal trust is at least sufficient for basic market transactions. Credibility can be regarded as the dimension of trust that governs economic activity along with the price mechanism in B2B eCommerce. Following Ganesan (1994) and the recommendations of Geyskens et al. (1998), I propose that trust has two theoretically and empirically distinct dimensions, credibility and benevolence. Impersonal trust based on credibility mostly applies to B2B eCommerce, which focuses on institutionalized structures and arrangements that B2B exchanges provide to create a stable context within which interfirm cooperation could develop.

A Process View of Impersonal Trust

Doney and Cannon (1997) drew on several theories developed in social psychology, sociology, economics and marketing to isolate five cognitive processes through which trust engenders. These distinct processes by which trust can develop are the capability, the transference, the calculative, the intentionality, and the prediction process. These processes suggest a trust-building attempt, followed by a favorable outcome towards actually engendering trust. Therefore, these processes assume both an attempt towards developing trust, followed by a positive outcome. For example, the calculative process does not solely generate trust; the outcome of the calculation may generate trust given a favorable assessment of the calculation. In general, these five processes engender the global construct of trust. However, only the capability, transference and calculative processes are able to generate trust in an impersonal context. The processes of intentionality and prediction necessitate interaction and familiarity-learning from contact. Therefore, only capability, transference and calculative are proposed to act as mediating variables connecting the antecedents of impersonal trust in B2B eCommerce with credibility. For a more exhaustive view of all five impersonal and familiarity trust-building cognitive processes, see Pavlou (2001).

Capability Process

Can I trust a firm to have the competence to perform as expected? According to Sako and Helper (1998), competence is the source of capability trust, which assesses whether a firm is able to carry out its promises. Doney and Cannon (1997) argued that trust can be developed from evaluating a firm's competence. The capability process is unavoidable in all aspects of B2B exchange relations, and as long as there is adequate information to perceive competence, this impersonal trust-building process can become the groundwork of a trustworthy relationship. Therefore, the capability process of engendering trust may develop in eCommerce to promote trust in a firm's credibility.

Transference Process

Can I trust a firm based on its performance in prior transactions with others? The institutional source of trust is associated with structural arrangements that build trust through incentive mechanisms (Shapiro, 1987). Trust can be gained based on reliable information received from a trusted network of firms, suggesting that trust can be transferred from one buyer to another, even if the trustor has no other experience. A firm may employ the cognitive transference process (Doney and Cannon, 1997) to analyze information from other firms to form its trust perceptions. Therefore, given a trustworthy network of firms, the transference process of engendering trust can become another element of impersonal trust and build trust in a firm's credibility.

Calculative Process

Can I trust a firm based on a calculation of its costs and benefits of cooperating? The economics literature suggests that the primary source of trust is based on a buyer's sober calculation of the other firm's cost and benefits of cheating (Dasgupta, 1988). Hence, trust involves a calculative process that a buyer assesses the potential losses compared to the short-term gains of a firm's non-cooperative behavior (Doney and Cannon, 1997). This process suggests that as long as it is irrational for a firm to cheat, it can be trusted since it is to its advantage to cooperate. Therefore, the calculative process can become another constituent of trustworthy transactions. This subjective calculation has different implications for the two dimensions of trust. While a firm's credibility can be trusted, benevolence cannot be generated based on the calculative process. According to the definition of benevolence, the other firm is expected to cooperate, even given the chance (greater benefits) of cheating; hence, the calculative process will always suggest that a firm's benevolence cannot be trusted because the benefits of cheating given the chance would always be greater. Therefore, the trust-building calculative process can build trust in a firm's credibility.

Antecedents of Impersonal Trust in B2B eCommerce

An increasingly important application of interfirm eCommerce is the B2B exchange, which is an interorganizational information system (IOIS) through which multiple firms interact to identify and select partners, negotiate and execute transactions. Most IOIS support the following market-making functions: identification, selection, execution and integration (Choudhury et al., 1998). Moreover, B2B exchanges provide some trust-building mechanisms that are proposed to act as antecedents of impersonal trust. Some antecedents can invoke multiple trust-building processes, and each antecedent represents a different method of developing impersonal trust through these basic processes.

Accreditation

Accreditation or prequalification is defined as efforts undertaken *ex ante* to verify a firm's capability to perform as expected (Heide and John, 1990). The idea of accreditation makes sense only in a world with uncertainty and risk; in this sense, accreditation is a type of market signaling activity. Adverse selection problems can be managed by implementing qualifications processes that identify potential trading firms *ex ante* that have the skills necessary to transact in a B2B exchange (Bergen, Dutta and Walker, 1992). Accreditation may also take the form of screening by known track records; for example, e-steel.com (www.e-steel.com), a B2B exchange for trading steel, requires all potential participants to have prior trading experience and letters of reference from previous trading partners in order to register in its marketplace. Accreditation could be ascertained by a third-party B2B exchange, which may become a reliable means of characterizing firms. Accreditation triggers the capability process to assess a firm's capability to fulfill its promises, since qualification efforts can screen out incompetent firms. In this regard, accreditation is a signal that reduces adverse selection problems. Moreover, if a firm has information whether organizations are accredited, trust could be granted based on a firm's history and reputation. Accreditation is used as a surrogate of reputation for competence, which is transferable to other firms in a B2B exchange. Therefore, the transference process is also triggered by accreditation efforts. In sum, impersonal trust is associated with accreditation through inducing the capability and transference processes.

Feedback

Research in game theory has shown that a properly designed third-party system can be an effective for assuring cooperation (Kandori, 1992). By introducing an appropriate feedback mechanism, each firm is transformed into a long-term player who conducts repeated transactions, constraining them into cooperative behavior. If there is a repeated play and an indeterminate ending point, formal analysis shows that organizations may arrive at a stable cooperative outcome (Radner, 1986). The feedback mechanism in many B2B exchanges is similar in nature to the suitable mechanism of trust presented by Lahno (1995). Given such mechanism, firms are informed about other firm's past behavior and they are able to choose them. Hence, the probability of finding partners depends on their past behavior. On the basis of this dependency, only cooperative conduct pays in the long run; hence, rational firms tend to act trustworthy. This dependency engenders trust by triggering the calculative process, following a sober assessment that a firm's benefits of cheating are greater than the costs of lost transactions.

Feedback may also be regarded as a surrogate (signal) of good reputation (Pavlou and Ba, 2000), which is an important antecedent of trust in buyer-seller relationships (Anderson and Weitz, 1989). Therefore, reputable firms would have greater incentives to cooperate since they have a better feedback to protect than non-reputable firms do, and they are more likely to act ethically (Telser, 1980). Following the same argument, firms would eminently value long and unblemished history, since more organizations are more unlikely to destroy a good name to exploit a single transaction. Therefore, feedback triggers the transference process of engendering trust, where firms infer trustworthiness through feedback from other firms participating in a B2B exchange. Feedback mechanisms provide both signals of past experience, and also incentives for cooperation. Consequently, feedback is associated with impersonal trust by triggering both the calculative and transference processes.

Monitoring

In B2B exchanges, monitoring may have two aspects. First, a third-party authority monitors all interfirm transactions and assures that everything is performed in accordance with the agreed terms. In case of a problem, a neutral authority attempts to solve the issue to the satisfaction of both firms, or in accordance with the prearranged agreement. Second, a third-party authority can assure that the quality of all products exchanged is in agreement with the preapproved specifications. For example, independent contractors offer quality-assurance services to the B2B exchange of Chemconnect.com (www.chemconnect.com). Therefore, agency risks of moral hazard are minimized by monitoring that discourages opportunistic behavior. B2B exchanges may continually monitor the trading activity, convey sanctions to inappropriate trading behavior and punish any wrongdoing. Third-party monitoring provides the incentives for firms to engage in cooperative and honest practices. Therefore, the calculative process suggests that trust can be built when a B2B exchange monitors the transaction if the costs of opportunistic behavior will be higher than the benefits from cheating. Given proper government, monitoring provides the incentives for firms to engage in cooperative practices since simple calculation would suggest that the costs of opportunistic behavior would exceed potential short-term benefits. Hence, the calculative process can be invoked by monitoring, which is proposed to be associated with impersonal trust.

Legal Bonds

Written contracts are also proposed as a mechanism to reduce opportunistic behavior and moral hazard. However, contracts are only partial safeguards against opportunism since they are almost always incomplete due to unforeseen circumstances, since firms are considered boundedly rational and cannot foresee all possible states of nature (Williamson, 1985). Nevertheless, impersonal trust based on legal bonds can be built on the basis of the calculative process since it is rational to cooperate given a legal contract that increases the costs of opportunism. Therefore, legal bonds provide protection and can promote trust in a firm's credibility.

Consequences of Impersonal Trust

Satisfaction

According to Anderson and Narus (1990), satisfaction is conceptualized as a very important consequence of exchange relationships, showing that satisfaction is an outcome of trust-based relationships. Mutual trust indicates equity in the exchange and promotes satisfaction. Moreover, trust enhances channel member satisfaction by reducing conflict (Anderson and Narus, 1990; Geyskens et al., 1998). In summary, satisfaction represents an important outcome of business exchange relations and a global evaluation of fulfillment exchanges relationships (Dwyer et al., 1987), in which both dimensions of trust should contribute. Following Ganesan (1994), there should be a positive relationship between satisfaction and impersonal trust.

Perceived Risk

Most buyer-supplier relationships are characterized by information asymmetry since one firm usually possesses uneven information regarding the transaction compared to the other firm (Mishra et al., 1998). The general problem faced by organizations is the inability to foresee and control the actions of the other firm, leading to delegation of some authority to the other party. This problem creates a double-sided agency relationship between the buyer and the supplier (Jensen and Meckling, 1976). According to Shapiro (1987), agency relationships are present in all types of social relationships from simply familiarity interactions to complex forms of a firm. Although risk is inevitable in every transaction, trust reduces the expectations of opportunistic behavior (Sako and Helper, 1998) and risk perceptions (Ganesan, 1994). Trust has been shown to reduce the perceived risk of being taken advantage of from the other firm (Anderson and Weitz, 1989) and improves favorable impressions for the other firm (Anderson and Narus, 1990). Since signals and incentives were shown to build trust and reduce fears of moral hazard and adverse selection, trust should also reduce perceived risks. Consequently, trust in a firm's credibility should diminish risk perceptions, predicting a negative relationship between impersonal trust and perceived risk.

Anticipated Continuity

Anticipated continuity is defined as the perception of a firm's expectation of future transactions in a B2B exchange. There is significant evidence to suggest a strong association between trust and a propensity to continue a relationship (Morgan and Hunt, 1994). According to Ganesan (1994) trust is a necessary ingredient for long-term orientation because it shifts the focus to future conditions. Similarly, Morgan and Hunt found a negative relationship between trust and propensity to leave, and also Anderson and Weitz (1989) showed that trust is key to maintaining continuity in buyer-supplier relationships. Therefore, trust should be associated with a firm's intention to continue participating in a B2B exchange. Firms participating in impersonal B2B exchanges usually make decisions based on objective, calculative evidence (credibility), rather than subjective evaluations (benevolence) since familiarity trust is rarely present. Nevertheless, anticipated continuity should be affected by trust in a firm's credibility, predict a positive relationship between impersonal trust and anticipated continuity.

Pricing

A major reason for the existence of different prices is the need to compensate some firms for reducing agency risks and transactions costs (Rao and Monroe, 1996). Therefore, in an efficient or dynamic pricing mechanism, firms need to reward reputable firms with better prices to assure safe transactions, since reputable firms are more likely to reduce transaction and agency costs. Similarly, in B2B exchanges, trustworthy firms are likely to reduce such costs and receive more favorable pricing. This phenomenon could be explained by the notion of returns to reputation (Shapiro, 1983), where reputable agents tend to receive more favorable terms. On the contrary, organizations tend to mandate compensation for the risk they are exposed to when they transact with less reputable firms. Consequently, differences in trust may cause different prices given a dynamic pricing scheme. Pavlou and Ba (2000) empirically showed that differences in trust perceptions affect price premiums and discounts in eCommerce auctions. Similarly, in B2B exchanges with dynamic pricing schemes, impersonal trust is viewed as a risk-reduction mechanism, allowing trustworthy firms to obtain more favorable pricing terms for reducing transaction-specific risks. The complete set of antecedents, trust-building processes and consequences of impersonal trust is shown in Figure 1.

DISCUSSION

The primary contribution of this research is that a set of interrelationships between constructs that tend to be associated with impersonal trust in B2B eCommerce are specified. First, the nature and dimensions of trust in eCommerce are described, and it is proposed that impersonal trust is mostly

Figure 1: Conceptual Framework

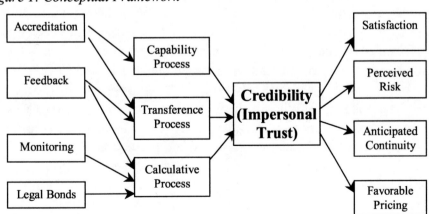

applicable in this context, primarily arising from the dimension of credibility. Second, the conceptual development provides the trust-building cognitive processes that may engender impersonal trust. Third, four trust-building mechanisms usually present in B2B exchanges are proposed to act as antecedents of impersonal trust by triggering the trust-building cognitive processes. Finally, four consequences of impersonal trust on key aspects of interfirm exchange relations are proposed. Although this study does not empirically examine the interrelationships among these variables, the theoretical foundation provides a comprehensive view of the role of impersonal trust in B2B eCommerce; an empirical validation of the proposed framework can be seen in Pavlou (2001). Another contribution of this research is the examination of the two distinct dimensions of trust–independently, proposing that each dimension would have different underlying cognitive processes, antecedents and consequences. While the extant literature paid particular attention to benevolence as the most important aspect of interfirm trust and viewed trust as a global construct, this research showed that in B2B eCommerce, impersonal trust arising from the dimension of credibility could be studied as an independent concept in its own right. Viewing trust as a unidimensional construct may be a valid simplification when analyzing long-term relationships (Doney and Cannon, 1997). However, given the impersonal context of B2B eCommerce, this simplification underscores the importance of credibility on vital outcomes of interfirm exchange relations (Ganesan, 1994).

Key Findings

This research is one of the first to address the importance of impersonal trust in B2B eCommerce. In online interfirm exchange relations where familiarity trust in not readily applicable, impersonal trust can still have beneficial outcomes, primarily based on the dimension of credibility. The two dimensions of trust-credibility and benevolence–are related constructs, although theoretically distinctive from each other. While there is rich scholarly literature on the antecedents of familiarity trust, no research has investigated the effect of an extensive set of antecedents of impersonal trust. Not only does this study propose some precursors of impersonal trust in B2B eCommerce, these antecedents are theoretically grounded in the cognitive processes by which trust engenders. Whereas it may appear that impersonal processes-competence, transference and calculative-are only weak complements of the familiarity-based processes-intentionality and prediction, the proposed impersonal processes seem to be critical in establishing trust and generating favorable social and economic outcomes. Therefore, even if the notion of studying impersonal trust independently is novel, its antecedents and consequences are established based on solid ground.

Theoretical Implications

This research proposes that firms tend to make many decisions based on objective evidence of competence, reliability and honesty (credibility). This finding is in line with Williamson (1993) who argued that familiarity trust only exists at the individual level, whereas business relations require institutional safeguards against opportunism. Also, Ganesan (1994) showed that even in long-term interfirm relationships, credibility was the sole determinant of long-term orientation. Therefore, these findings call for reconceptualization of the role of interfirm trust and more exhaustive research on the antecedents and consequences of the impersonal concept of trust. Nevertheless, whereas the dimension of credibility is proposed to induce favorable outcomes in interfirm exchange relations, it is not the purpose of this chapter to undermine the importance of familiarity trust. However, while other researchers argued that benevolence is the only stable form of trust (Granovetter, 1985), I argue that credibility is also a robust form that is increasingly important in the impersonal environment of B2B eCommerce.

Many authors argued that trust is only embedded in repetitive transactions and ongoing relationships, essentially arguing that impersonal trust is not a true form of trust but a functional substitute for it (Granovetter, 1985; Williamson, 1993). Sitkin and Roth (1993) argued that 'legalistic remedies' are not effective in creating trust, while Granovetter (1985) maintained that institutional processes are 'functional substitutes' of trust. On the contrary, Shapiro (1987) argued that institutional practices and norms could provide a very strong level of trust. In sum, the role of impersonal trust in the literature has been controversial; however, given the importance of impersonal trust in today's B2B eCommerce, this chapter attempts to disentangle the complex notion of trust and encourage research on the antecedents, underlying trust-building cognitive processes and consequences of each distinct dimension. By examining the two types of trust independently, research could validly conclude which type is robust, easy to build and maintain, and consequential.

Lewicki and Bunker (1995) argued that there are different levels of trusting relationships with impersonal processes as the most fragile and familiarity ones as the most robust. However, the impersonal processes are fragile if the underlying institutional structure is fragile, and the signals and incentives are weak. Given strong and well-accepted institutional rules, practices and norms to guide B2B eCommerce, impersonal trust can also become a robust mechanism to govern interfirm economic activity. Even if familiarity trust is indeed more robust, familiarity may not always be possible in eCommerce, since it may be physically or socially difficult to personalize all interfirm relationships, and it might also have negative economic consequences (Helper, 1991). Therefore, impersonal trust can be encouraged in B2B exchanges without significant costs, and provide substantial benefits to the participating firms without forcing them into repetitive transactions.

Managerial Implications

This study has practical implications for the ways B2B exchanges might increase the general level of interorganizational trust. Heightening the extent of firm accreditation, improving feedback mechanisms, and ensuring an effective monitoring and legal system promotes a trustworthy environment. Failure to provide these antecedents of trust might reduce the general level of credibility in the marketplace, which would eventually force firms to seek other alternatives. Moreover, this study proposes that impersonal trust is an important determinant of satisfaction, reduced perceived risks, anticipated continuity and favorable pricing. These associations set new standards for B2B exchanges; an important consideration should be to develop the appropriate mechanisms to build and sustain interfirm trust. Since the future of most B2B exchanges relies on many participating firms, high liquidity and trade volume, impersonal trust would probably become an important determinant of the future of many B2B exchanges. This research not only proposes the antecedents of impersonal trust, but it also indicates the cognitive sequences by which trust develops.

In considering their participation in B2B exchanges, firms should appreciate the role of impersonal trust that is based on functional mechanisms, institutional structures and regulations instituted in the marketplace. Since these structures provide the secure context in which interfirm exchange relations can develop, companies should either depend on these structures to trust other firms, or rely on exchange relations with familiar partners. Managers should decide which exchange relations should be based on impersonal trust, and which on familiarity trust. For more extensive managerial recommendations on how the proposed framework could be useful, see Pavlou (2000).

Limitations and Suggestions for Future Research

This research attempts to make theoretical contributions to the academic and managerial literature on the role of impersonal trust in B2B eCommerce. The purpose is to stimulate empirical research in the area towards validating the proposed framework and shedding some light on the pragmatic nature of impersonal trust in B2B eCommerce. It should be clear that this framework proposes only a subset of the many possible relationships between trust and its antecedents, cognitive processes, consequences and other moderating variables. Hence, other important constructs could have been neglected. Future research should take a more extensive approach to cover other variables related to impersonal trust in B2B eCommerce. Therefore, future research should identify other factors that complement the proposed conceptual model, and empirically test a more complete framework.

The proposed framework may not be generalizable to other dissimilar cultures. Governance by familiarity trust is prevalent in Japanese markets; hence, impersonal B2B eCommerce might be an infeasible solution in this culture. For example, Sako (1992) compared Japanese and British companies and showed that Japanese firms exhibit higher levels of familiarity trust towards their trading partners. Therefore, the notion of worldwide B2B eCommerce may be restricted by the cultural norms of some nations that rely on familiarity relations. Future research should examine the role of ethnic culture in interfirm relations and predict the boundaries of global B2B exchanges.

REFERENCES

Akerlof, G. (1970). The market for 'lemons': Quality under uncertainty and the market mechanism. *Quarterly Journal of Economics*, August (84), 488-500.

Anderson, E. and Weitz, B. (1989). Determinants of continuity in conventional firm working partnership. *Journal of Marketing*, 54(1), 42-58.

Arrow, K. J. (1974). *The Limits of Firms*, New York: Norton.

Barney, J. B. and Hansen, M. H. (1994). Trustworthiness as a source of competitive advantage. *Strategic Management Journal*, Special Issue (15), 175-190.

Beccera, M. and Gupta, A. K. (1999). Trust within the firm: Integrating the trust literature with agency theory and transaction cost economics. *Public Administration Quarterly*, 177-203.

Bergen, M. E., Dutta, S. and Walker, Jr., O. C. (1992). Agency relationships as marketing: A review of the implications and applications of agency-related theories. *Journal of Marketing*, 56, 1-24.

Bromiley, P. and Cummings, L. L. (1995). Transaction costs in firms with trust. In Bies, R., Sheppard, B. and Lewicki, R. (Eds.), *Research on Negotiation in Firms*. Greenwich, CT: JAI Press.

Brynjolfsson, E. and Smith, M. D. (2000). Frictionless commerce? A comparison of Internet and conventional retailers. *Management*

Science, 46(4), 563-585.

Choudhury V., Hartzel, K. S. and Konsynski, B. R. (1998). Uses and consequences of electronic exchanges: An empirical investigation in the aircraft parts industry. *MIS Quarterly*, 471-507.

Dai, Q. and Kauffman, R. J. (2000). Business models for Internet-based eProcurement systems and B2B electronic markets: An exploratory assessment. *34ᵗʰ Hawaii International Conference on Systems Science*, January 2001.

Dasgupta, P. (1988). Trust as a commodity. In Gambetta, D. (Ed.), *Trust: Making and Breaking Cooperative Relations*. New York: Basil Blackwell, Inc.

Doney, P. M. and Cannon, J. P. (1997). An examination of the nature of trust in buyer-seller relationships. *Journal of Marketing*, April (61), 35-51.

Dwyer, F. R., Schurr, P. J. and Oh, S. (1987). Developing buyer-seller relationships. *Journal of Marketing*, 52(1), 21-34.

Ganesan, S. (1994), Determinants of long-term orientation in buyer-seller relationships. *Journal of Marketing*, 58, 1-19.

Geyskens, I., Steenkamp, J. B. and Kumar, N. (1998). Generalizations about trust in marketing channel relationships using meta-analysis. *International Journal in Marketing*, 15, 223-248.

Granovetter, M. (1985). Economic action and social structure: The problem of embeddedness. *American Journal of Sociology*, 91(3), 481-510.

Gulati, R. (1995). Does familiarity breed trust? The implications of repeated ties for contractual choice of alliances. *Academy of Management Journal*, 38, 85-112.

Heide, J. B. and John, G. (1990). Alliances in industrial purchasing, the determinants of joint action in buyer-supplier relationships. *Journal of Marketing Research*, 37, 24-36.

Helper, S. (1991). How much has really changed between U.S. automakers and their suppliers? *Sloan Management Review*, Summer (32), 15-28.

Jensen, M. C. and Meckling, W. H. (1976). Theory of the firm: Managerial behavior, agency costs and ownership structure. *Journal of Financial Economics*, 3, 305-360.

Kandori, M. (1992). Social norms and community enforcement. *Review of Economic Studies*, 59, 63-80.

Keen, P. G. W. (2000). Ensuring eTrust. *Computerworld*, March, 34(11), 13, 46.

Lahno, B. (1995). Trust, reputation, and exit in exchange relationships. *Journal of Conflict Resolution*, 39(3), 495-510.

Lewicki, R. J. and Bunker, B. B. (1995). Trust in relationships: A model of development and decline. In Bunker, B. B. and Rubin, J. Z. (Eds.), *Conflict, Cooperation and Justice*. San Francisco: Jossey-Bass.

Macneil, I. R. (1980). *The New Social Contract*. New Haven, CT: Yale University Press.

Mishra, D. P., Heide, J. B. and Cort, S. G. (1998). Information asymmetry and levels of agency relationships. *Journal of Marketing Research*, 35, 277-295.

Morgan, R. M. and Hunt, S. D. (1994). The commitment-trust theory of relationship marketing. *Journal of Marketing*, July (58), 20-38.

Ouchi, W. G. (1980). Market, bureaucracies and clans. *Administrative Science Quarterly*, 25, 129-141.

Pavlou, P. A. (2001). The role of trust in electronic commerce: Evidence from business-to-business and business-to-consumer electronic intermediaries. *Working Paper*, Marshall School of Business, University of Southern California.

Pavlou, P. A. (2000). Building trust in B2B relationships through electronic commerce intermediaries. *Working Paper*, Marshall School of Business, University of Southern California.

Pavlou, P. A. and Ba, S. (2000). Does online reputation matter? An empirical investigation of reputation and trust in online auction markets. *Proceedings of the 6th Americas Conference in Information Systems*, Long Beach, CA.

Radner, R. (1986). Repeated partnership games with imperfect monitoring and no discounting. *Review of Economic Studies*, 111, 43-57.

Ring, P. S. and Van de Ven, A. H. (1992). Structuring cooperative relationships between firms. *Strategic Management Journal*, 13, 483-498.

Sako, M. (1992). *Trust in Exchange Relations*. Cambridge, MA: University Press.

Sako, M. and Helper, S. (1998). Determinants of trust in supplier relations: Evidence from the automotive industry in Japan and the United States. *Journal of Economic Behavior and Firm*, 34, 387-417.

Shapiro, S. P. (1987). The social control of impersonal trust. *American Journal of Sociology*, 93, 623-658.

Sitkin S. B. and Roth, N. L. (1993). Explaining the limited effectiveness of 'legalistic remedies' for trust/distrust. *Firm Science*, 4, 367-392.

Stinchcombe, A. L. (1985). Stratification and firms. *Selected Papers*, Cambridge, MA: Cambridge University Press.

Telser, L. G. (1980). A theory of self-enforcing contracts. *Journal of Business*, 53(1), 27-44.

Williamson, O. E. (1975). *Exchanges and Hierarchies: Analysis and Anti-*

trust Implications. New York: The Free Press.

Williamson, O. E. (1985). *The Economic Institutions of Capitalism*. New York: The Free Press.

Williamson, O. E. (1993). Calculativeness, trust and economic firm. *Journal of Law and Economics*, 26, 453-486.

Zaheer, A., McEvily, B. and Perrone, V. (1998). Does trust matter? Exploring the effects of interfirm and interpersonal trust on performance. *Organization Science*, 9(2), 141-159.

Section II

Supply Chain Management Issues in B2B eCommerce

Chapter V

From EDI to Internet Commerce in Supply Chain Management: The Singapore Experience

Seng Kwong Gwee
Singapore Productivity and Standards Board, Singapore

Albert Wee Kwan Tan
Institute of Systems Science, Singapore

This chapter provides an overview on the use of business-to-business (B2B) eCommerce by Singapore companies as a means of streamlining their procurement and transportation activities. Specifically, it addresses how Electronic Data Interchange (EDI) and Internet have proliferated in Singapore from 1990 to the present, and the efforts needed to sustain its growth. Challenges in implementing B2B eCommerce in procurement and transportation are also discussed, so that companies can avoid similar pitfalls when planning to implement these technologies with their business partners.

INTRODUCTION TO SINGAPORE'S ECONOMY

According to the Economic Development Board of Singapore (EDB), manufacturing is one of the key drivers of the Singapore economy with a contribution of 25% to the country's Gross Domestic Product (GDP). The largest contributor to Singapore's total manufacturing output is the electronics industry, comprising four key sectors namely computer, semiconductors, data storage and consumer products, which have been growing rapidly since the 1960s. In 1997, the electronics industry produced an output of SGD70 billion, accounting for 53% of total manufacturing output. The second largest contribution came from the chemical industry, which is made up of the petroleum, petrochemical, specialty chemical and pharmaceutical sectors. This industry has attracted investments of nearly SGD3.0 billion, with an output of SGD33 billion in 1997.

The electronics and chemical industries import large quantities of raw materials from overseas, process them adding value in Singapore and export the finished goods to overseas markets. Thus, transportation costs in and out of Singapore are high for these companies. By optimizing their supply chain networks, these companies will be able to reduce their overhead costs and achieve faster turnaround time. This will allow them to be more competitive and boost the national output for Singapore. In 1997, the total output generated by these two industries was about 75% of the total national output of SGD131 billion.

Given the trend towards global manufacturing, just-in-time (JIT) production and a very short time-to-market, conventional ways of managing supply and distribution chains are changing. Logistics providers are no longer just managing warehouses or offering isolated transport services. Instead, logistics companies here offer integrated solutions with regional coverage and new value-added services such as reverse logistics, product configuration and international procurement. With the increased demand on outsourcing from manufacturers, more third-party logistics services are expanding their businesses to meet this demand.

Total trade between Singapore and the rest of the world has been expanding steadily over the years. In 1998, Singapore's external trade amounted to SGD354 billion which is almost three times the nation's Gross Domestic Product (GDP), according to the Trade Development Board of Singapore (TDB). As a result, Singapore's logistics industry has been expanding in tandem with development in external trade and new ways of doing business, both in terms of volume and the range and level of services offered. Recognizing the robust prospects ahead, the Singapore Government has continually developed and strengthened the country's trade logistics capabilities. This has helped Singapore become one of the busiest seaports and airports in the world.

Strategically located at the heart of the Asia Pacific, Singapore serves as a gateway to the world's most dynamic growth region. With the continual development of its trade infrastructure, Singapore aims to be an international hub, linking the region with the rest of the world. Several major international logistics companies (e.g., FedEx, AEI, DHL, Nippon Express and Schenker International) have already set up their regional logistics operations in Singapore to better serve their global clients like Apple Computer, AT&T, Caterpillar, DuPont and General Motors.

THE EVOLUTION OF SUPPLY CHAIN MANAGEMENT

Supply chain management is an integrated approach in managing business processes across organizations. Rather than just coordinating traditional functions, companies are identifying and managing core processes that cut across all of the organizations involved in delivering a product to the customer.

In a traditional channel of distribution, even if logistics activities are well managed, there is still a lack of coordination and integration between organizations which may lead to increased costs and a decreased level of service. The traditional channel is normally managed by a push inventory control system in which pre-set safety stock levels and re-order points determine what will be produced, and each channel member tends to keep relatively large safety stocks to guard against demand variability. Operating the channel under these conditions tends to result in what is called the "bullwhip" effect, where order variability is magnified throughout the channel such that a small increase in demand at the consumer level results in a disproportionately large increase in demand elsewhere (Lee et al., 1997). The consequences of such an effect are increased inventory, increased transportation costs and inefficient allocation of resources.

Leading-edge companies are using information to integrate the activi-

Figure 1: Information-Based Supply Chain

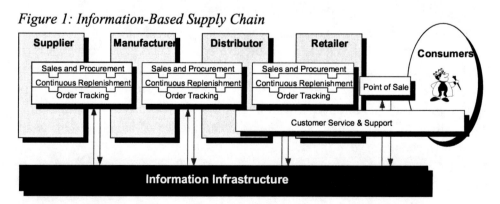

ties and processes of supply chain members in a way that creates a seamless flow of products synchronized with actual demand. In information-based supply chains, actual demand drives the activities of all supply chain members and "pulls" the product through the supply chain (Figure 1).

Production at all levels is synchronized to the actual consumption or demand at the consumer or final customer level. This means that all members of the supply chain have real-time visibility to actual demand and that activities can be integrated and coordinated. This not only eliminates the bullwhip effect by reducing uncertainty and lead times, it also ensures that the final product is what consumers want.

The key element of such integration is the free flowing and sharing of information. Companies realize that while today's competition is among companies, tomorrow's competition will be among supply chains.

This inter-company integration was made possible with the use of Electronic Data Interchange (EDI) in the mid 1990s. However, the use of EDI was only prevalent between big manufacturers and their big trading partners. It was not cost-effective for smaller players to utilize this technology, as it was expensive, difficult to implement and maintain.

The introduction of the Internet has changed the landscape, and created many opportunities for companies to exploit the use of web-based EDI to complement the traditional EDI currently being used to integrate the entire supply chain. In fact, we are seeing a new wave of innovation and the emergence of B2B eCommerce as we continue our move into the new millennium (Figure 2).

Figure 2: Evolution of B2B eCommerce from EDI to Internet Technologies

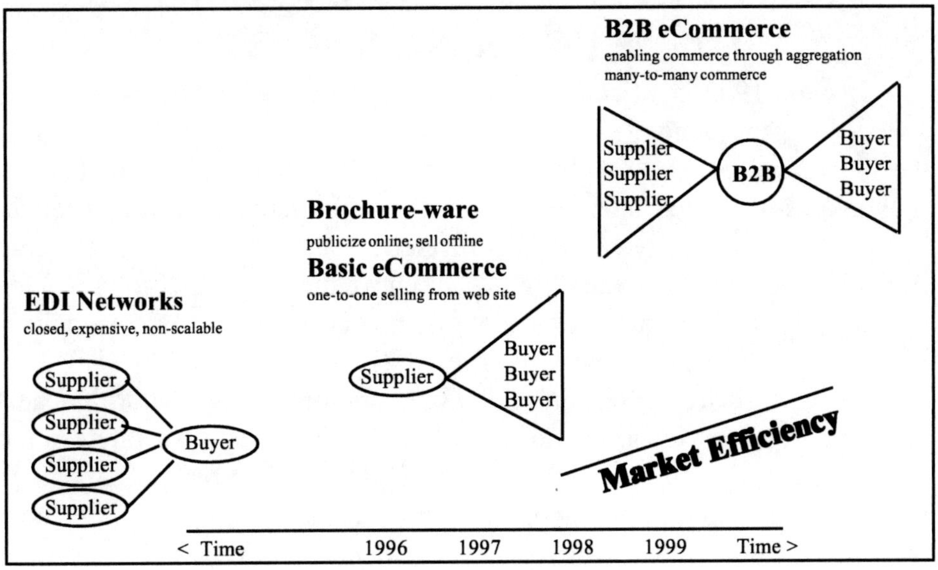

BUSINESS-TO-BUSINESS ECOMMERCE IN SINGAPORE

Based on a recent survey by Singapore's Department of Statistics (Wong and Lam, 1999), the number of Singapore's eCommerce transactions, including B2B and B2C, is still very small, accounting for only 0.1% of total turnover of the overall economy. For companies already selling over the Internet, eCommerce transactions made up 6% of their total turnover. eCommerce transactions leaped from SGD958 million in 1997 to SGD1.6 billion in 1998, and the figures were expected to increase further in 2000 to SGD2.0 billion.

The survey also revealed a shift of B2B transactions from closed EDI networks (for example Value Added Network) to the Internet. In 1997, almost all sales were conducted over closed networks, whereas in 1998, 16% of sales were conducted over the Internet and is likely to increase to 24% in 1999. eCommerce sales to overseas markets are still relatively small, contributing less than 5% of total eCommerce transactions in 1998. Some of the reasons for this could be the limited range of products offered online, security concerns as well as the problems in clearing payments in foreign currencies.

Numerous efforts and initiatives to exploit B2B eCommerce for the electronic, chemical and logistics industries in Singapore are discussed in the following sections. The goal is to make Singapore a vibrant eCommerce hub linking information with major hubs in the U.S. and Europe.

EFFORTS TO PROMOTE B2B ECOMMERCE THE ELECTRONICS SECTOR

In early 1993, the Economic Development Board of Singapore (EDB) conducted a study among multinational manufacturing companies (MNCs) in the electronics industry and confirmed that many MNCs were keen to have EDI linkages with their suppliers. However, as each supplier serves more than one MNC, it would have to handle different formats of similar documents from different MNCs as each MNC could have their own EDI format. This would lead to a proliferation of standards and duplication, causing suppliers to incur heavy costs in supporting different EDI formats.

The need to develop a unify EDI standard for the manufacturing sector in Singapore has led to the creation of EDIMAN (Electronic Data Interchange for Manufacturing) messaging guidelines. EDIMAN messages have been developed specially for Singapore's manufacturing sector to facilitate electronic transactions between buyers and suppliers in the procurement process.

Figure 3: EDIMAN messages for Electronics sector

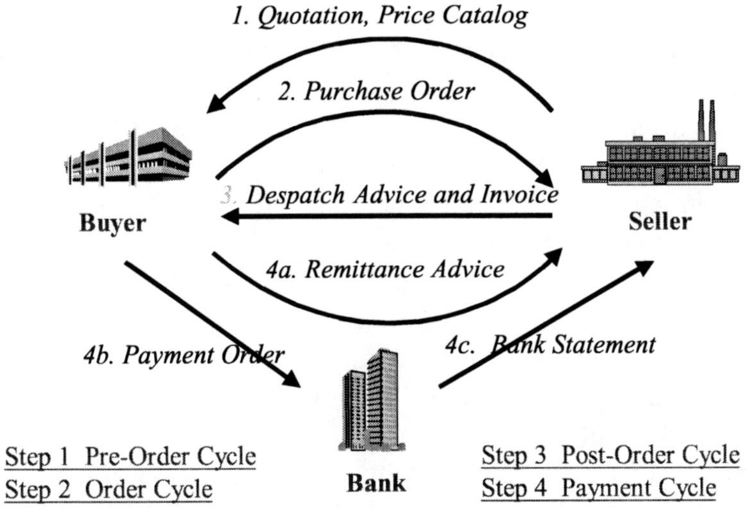

1. Quotation, Price Catalog

2. Purchase Order

3. Despatch Advice and Invoice

4a. Remittance Advice

Buyer

Seller

4b. Payment Order

4c. Bank Statement

Bank

Step 1 Pre-Order Cycle
Step 2 Order Cycle

Step 3 Post-Order Cycle
Step 4 Payment Cycle

It specifies the data elements and formats contained in business documents (Figure 3).

Currently, the major international messaging standards for EDI are those that comply with the UN/EDIFACT (United Nations EDI for Administration, Commerce and Transport) standard. Formed in 1986, the UN/EDIFACT has since played a key role in standardizing EDI messages for various economic sectors. As most companies do not need the full set of messages, EDIMAN messages are subsets of UN/EDIFACT, customized to suit the needs of Singapore manufacturers and their suppliers.

A survey conducted in 1997 on the use of IT in enhancing supply chain management (Tan, 1999) confirmed that most of the companies were using the EDIFACT standard to communicate with their trading partners as compared to other messaging standards. However, proprietary standards were used extensively in sectors, such as the financial and logistics sectors and for intra-company communication (Figure 4).

The initial usage of EDIMAN was low but had been increasing steadily since 1996 with 40 MNCs such as Hewlett-Packard, Texas Instruments, Baxter Healthcare, Philips Singapore, Motorola, Murata Electronics, Hitachi Asia and AT&T actively involved in implementing EDI for their suppliers and customers. Most of these companies started to implement B2B eCommerce for their procurement and forecasting needs, but none were interested in electronic payment at that point in time.

Most respondents from the 1997 survey indicated that purchase order, sales orders and inventory status were common key information exchanged with their suppliers and customers (Figure 5). In contrast, marketing and promotion information were not commonly exchanged among trading partners, as the Internet was seen to be a better platform for publishing such information.

In order to encourage more companies to implement EDI, a standard EDI agreement called Singapore EDI Agreement (SEDIA) was drafted to assist companies in setting up a trusted environment for B2B eCommerce between buyers and suppliers. SEDIA has helped to alleviate some fear among the trading partners in case of a dispute. However, most MNCs do not use the complete version of the original SEDIA; instead it is used as a template to incorporate their head office legal requirements to suit Singapore's needs. This has helped to expedite the adoption by many Japanese, American and European MNCs with their suppliers.

By the end of 1998, approximately 950 companies in the electronics industry had either implemented EDIMAN or were in the midst of implementing EDIMAN with their trading partners (Figure 6). The EDIMAN standard has enabled suppliers to transact easily with multiple buyers without having to worry about proprietary procurement systems used by different buyers.

With increased Internet penetration and the need to facilitate global business requirements, a new XML-based standard for the electronics and semi-conductor industries is emerging. Currently, members of the EDIMAN community have started to pursue their interest in RosettaNet (www.rosettanet.org), which is a consortium actively setting global standards

Figure 4: Number of companies using different EDI standards to communicate with external parties

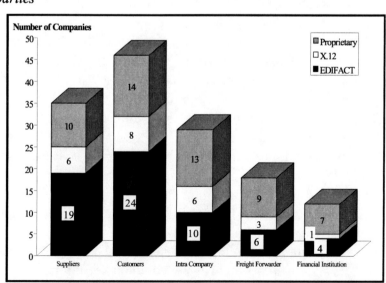

Figure 5: The use of EDI for information exchange with customers and suppliers

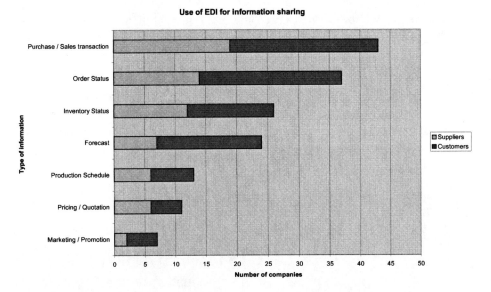

Figure 6: Adoption of EDI by the Electronic companies

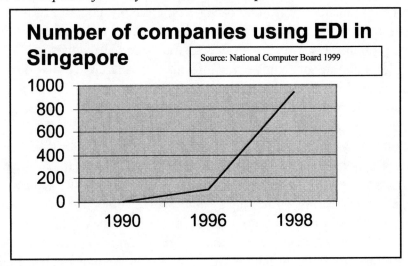

for the exchange of information via the Internet among the computer and semi-conductor industries. RosettaNet has set up an office in Singapore to assist EDIMAN users in their migration to leverage on the global standard as most of MNCs' suppliers are from overseas. With the experience gained from implementing EDIMAN, most users are aware of the benefits of B2B eCommerce and are therefore willing to embrace the new standard.

This is a significant milestone for RosettaNet in creating a truly global standards-based organization," said Jennifer Hamilton, CEO, RosettaNet. "RosettaNet began as a multinational-based initiative, and we continue to expand the global operations with local and regional offices that will participate in ensuring the development of truly global standards and implementation of RosettaNet eBusiness processes" (CMPnetAsia, 2000).

The RosettaNet consortium in Singapore will consist of a steering committee, supply chain partners, solutions partners and coalition partners, and is facilitated by the Infocomm Development Authority (IDA) of Singapore. Representatives from 10 MNCs are also involved and include Agilent Technologies, Chartered Semiconductor Manufacturing, Compaq, Hewlett-Packard, Intel and Motorola.

EFFORTS TO PROMOTE B2B ECOMMERCE FOR THE LOGISTICS SECTOR

In 1986, Singapore pioneered the introduction of a nation-wide electronic data interchange (EDI) system called TradeNet (Siong et al., 1995). It was set up to link traders, freight forwarders, shipping agents and government organizations for the processing of trade documents as well as airway bills and shipping orders. Users can also access trade-related databases like flight schedules, shipping schedules, cargo information and freight tariffs. TradeNet, which is now Internet enabled (www.tradenet.gov.sg), has helped to reduce trade documentation processing time from three days to 10 minutes, thereby increasing productivity.

PortNet (www.portnet.com), migrated from EDI to Internet technology recently, is linked to major ports like Rotterdam and Seattle to facilitate trade document processing for sea cargoes, while SPECTRUM (www.ccn.com.sg), a specialized air cargo community system, was developed to allow paperless cargo-related information exchange among members of the community. Continual investments in state-of-the-art telecommunications and a nation-wide EDI are all aimed at Singapore an intelligent logistics hub to meet the demands of globalization.

With increasing demand from shippers, logistics companies in Singapore are increasingly implementing and exploring state-of-the-art technology to raise productivity and competitiveness. Many new warehousing and distribution centers are equipped with automated storage and retrieval systems (ASRSs) and warehouse management systems to enhance their operations.

To facilitate electronic linkages between shippers, consignees, buyers and suppliers with their freight forwarders or transportation companies, EDI for Transportation System (EDITRANS) standard was launched in Novem-

Figure 7: Information flows between shippers and the logistics companies

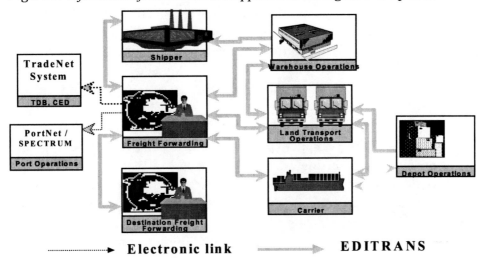

ber, 1996 (Figure 7). Seven EDI messages standards were developed in compliance with UN/EDIFACT in the initial phase.

The intention of EDITRANS was to enable freight forwarders to respond faster to shipper's needs and thus tighten the supply chain, resulting in better customer service. However, after more than a year of promotion and marketing to the shippers and logistics providers, the number of companies using EDITRANS was still relatively small. A closer look into the low penetration rate of EDITRANS revealed several causes:

a. Shippers did not engage logistics companies in the same proportion of buyers to suppliers. For example, shippers could use only one logistics company to manage their full logistics requirements.

b. Some shippers have the luxury of having order processing clerks from the logistics providers stationed at their premises to manage their export and import documentation. Therefore, EDI was not crucial in this context.

With a limited number of shippers interested in using EDITRANS, few logistics providers were keen to implement EDI, as cost savings were low without a critical mass. Eventually, the EDITRANS group was disbanded, showing clearly that B2B eCommerce would prevail only when there is sufficient critical mass to warrant sustainability.

In 1998, a study was conducted by Accenture (formerly known as Andersen Consulting) to map out the essential IT functionality to support the logistics industry. The main objectives of this study were to:

establish an industry-wide logistics best practice using IT that could be

adopted by the industry upon completion;
- conduct an industry-wide analysis of the logistics sector to determine IT gaps and the functional requirements to narrow those gaps;
- identify new EDI and Internet message standards that could be deployed to existing EDI networks (PortNet, TradeNet and SPECTRUM); and
- propose an IT implementation methodology as a guide for the logistics industry.

Eight companies from the logistics industry were selected for this study with the majority of them providing more than two types of logistics services (e.g., warehousing, transportation, etc). A focus group interview was conducted for each of these companies at their premises. Each interview lasted about one day and involved a site visit and software demonstration. The interviewees were mainly senior executives and operational managers. Accenture examined the internal processes of the eight companies, and the interactions between them and the other entities (such as the shippers, consignees, carriers and government agencies). The internal processes of the other entities (e.g., the procurement process of consignees and shipping process of shippers) were outside the scope of this study.

Within each of the eight companies, key operational processes were relatively straightforward. The management of the eight companies had correctly focused their attention on the need to reduce the cycle time of each process. However, the lack of integrated IT systems to support these processes had resulted in:
- duplication of work, and

Figure 8: IT Functional Framework for Logistics industry

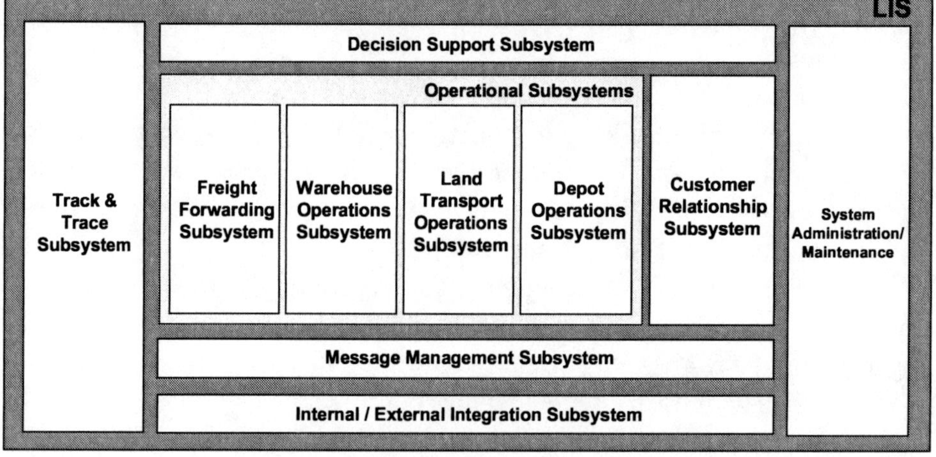

- an absence of performance measurements to monitor overall process effectiveness.

Within this industry, there is a large number of interactions between the logistics companies and external entities. While most interactions with the government agencies are electronically linked, interactions between the companies and with commercial entities are still mainly paper-based. This had resulted in duplication of effort, increased chances of data errors and longer cycle times. Linking the entities electronically within the supply chain would help to reduce the overall cycle time and achieve higher standards, such as:

- a cycle time reduction from five hours to less than two hours to deliver goods from the manufacturers' premises to the airport, and
- a cycle time reduction from eight hours to less than four hours to deliver goods from port to consignee.

An IT functional framework describing functional models needed to support the industry was developed after the study by Accenture, within the aim of facilitating information sharing and exchange. This frameowrk is shown in Figure 8.

The core of this functional requirement framework consists of the Customer Relationship Subsystem and the Operational Subsystems. The Customer Relationship Subsystem will help logistics providers to provide integrated logistics services by maintaining contracts spanning all services, delivering a single bill to the customer, tracking performance and managing customer contacts. The Operational Subsystems–Freight Forwarding, Warehouse Operations, Land Transportation Operations and Container Depot Operations–will enable end-to-end processing of the key business processes. The implementation of the Customer Relationship Subsystem and the Operational Subsystems will enable the logistics providers to improve customer service and process performance, and provide them with the means to monitor the efficiency of their operations.

To support the demand for value-added logistics services and increasing volume of business, a Decision Support Subsystem to model and simulate facilities, networks and customers' requirements are recommended to help logistics providers utilize their assets more effectively and be more responsive to their customers. The Track and Trace Subsystem will help monitor shipments at the level of detail needed by the customer and by selected milestones.

The logistics industry is characterized by numerous interactions between the entities and within each entity. The Internal/External Integration Subsystem and the Message Management Subsystem are thus required to manage the flow of information into and out of the core modules using specific integration methods (e.g., API, Servlet) and direct the requests to the appropriate subsystems. With these subsystems in place, there will be a reduction in the overall cycle time across logistics providers and the external entities, and Singapore will be better positioned to conduct business electronically as eCommerce gathers momentum.

Accenture recommended that government agencies should consider the following four recommendations to improve the flow of information within the logistics industry:

1) The EDITRANS Working Group should consider including additional EDI messages to facilitate information interchange between the logistics companies and other commercial entities. Currently, such information flows are paper-based with a standard format and thus can be automated.

2) Encourage shippers, consignees and carriers to increase their electronic linkages so that the overall processing cycle times can be improved and data errors reduced.

3) Assist logistics companies to develop an Internet presence so that they will be well-positioned to provide logistics service within the region using Singapore as an eCommerce hub.

4) Provide financial assistance for logistics companies to acquire some of the subsystems identified in the IT functional framework, in particular, those that are common across service providers such as the External/Internal Integration Subsystem and the Message Management Subsystem.

Some of Accenture's recommendations to exploit eCommerce for information and document exchange were implemented by the respective parties to cut down the overall cycle time. For example, the Singapore Trade Development Board (TDB) and Infocomm Development Authority (IDA) of Singapore have initiated an IT Action Plan to identify key programs and deliverables to prepare the logistics industry in the face of new opportunities and challenges. The overall goal of this Action Plan is to provide an IT framework for the deployment and integration of information and technologies across the logistics industry (Figure 9).

The action plan needs to be robust to meet the needs of the various logistics players with varying capabilities, and this resulted in a three-pronged thrust in advancing the IT-readiness of the logistics industry. The three key thrusts are:

i) Facilitate intra-company integration to enhance logistics competencies.

ii) Enhance inter-company connectivity to foster business collaboration.

iii) Establish international linkages to position Singapore as the Asia Logis-

Figure 9: IT Action Plan for the logistics industry

Goal

To provide an IT framework for the integration of information and technologies across the logistics industry

Thrust 1

Facilitate intra-company integration to enhance logistics competencies

Thrust 2

Enhance inter-company connectivity to foster business collaboration

Thrust 3

Establish international linkages to position Singapore as the Asia Logistics Hub

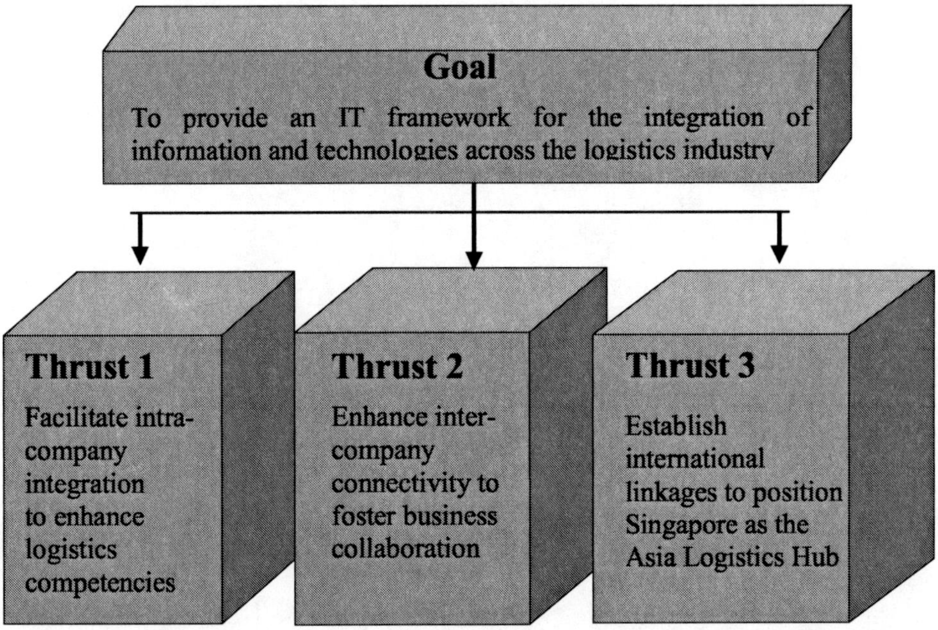

tics Hub.

David Chin, Deputy Chief Executive Officer, TDB, said, "In the 'new electronic economy,' opportunities for logistics and supply chain management companies are abundant. Against the backdrop of rapid growth of business-to-business eCommerce, it is pertinent that the Singapore logistics industry continues to be adaptive to changing business trends, by adopting changed mindsets, tapping on new business concepts and progressing in line with the Internet revolution. The IT Action Plan was developed with these opportunities in mind" (TDB Press Release, 2000).

The implementation will evolve in stages, namely internal integration, external integration and international linkages. Each stage will involve different sets of IT requirements, and it is important for companies to migrate progressively from stage to stage to ensure that information from each earlier stage will form the foundation for the next stage.

For other areas of development, a few EDI providers had started to refocus their efforts to target shipping lines to use EDITRANS for exchanging Bill of Lading information between these shipping lines and freight forwarders. This shift in direction was logical since a single shipping line could be serving many freight forwarders. The outcome of this new move could only be determined later.

Figure 10: Home page of PRISMS

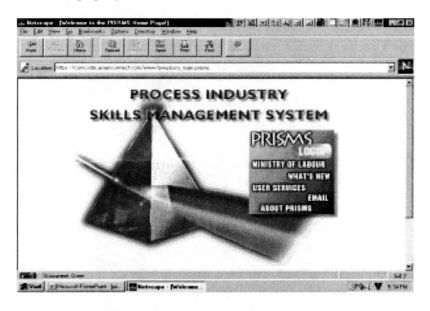

EFFORTS TO PROMOTE B2B ECOMMERCE FOR THE CHEMICAL SECTOR

The chemical sector is the most recent sector to use eCommerce capabilities on an industry-wide basis. However, being last was a blessing in disguise, as it was able to learn from the experience of the electronics and logistics sectors. Instead of many proprietary and legacy network systems, it was able to utilize Internet solutions quickly.

Singapore's process industry, a sub-sector in the chemical sector, launched its Internet-based system for efficient skills management in 1998. Called Process Industry Skills Management System (PRISMS), it allows contractors to pre-qualify welders online, and allocate them to worksites throughout the country quickly and efficiently, as skilled workers are scarce in Singapore (Figure 10).

The first module in PRISMS (www.prisms.com.sg) incorporated the Common Welder Qualification Scheme (CWQS) that ensures consistent work quality by using skilled welders. It resulted in better utilization of welders and led to annual cost savings of over SGD2 million for the next few years. The system uses Internet technology to facilitate certifying and testing of welders before they are recruited into the process industry.

Chong Pak Yuen, Chairman of the Process Industry Steering Committee, said: "PRISMS has a lot more potential in that it is a skills management system to be used by our oil and petrochemical industry to manage the various skills and workforce needed to guarantee work quality through the use of trained and competent craftsmen. Over the next three to four years, we expect 4,000 to 5,000 craftsmen to be trained, certified and managed electronically" (EDB Press Release, 1998).

The next project was an ambitious effort to transform Singapore's chemical sector into a world-class chemical hub. The Jurong Island, an amalgamation of seven smaller islands south of Singapore into a world-class integration petroleum and petrochemical complex at an estimated cost of SGD7 billion (www.jurongisland.com). Currently, 50 companies operate on Jurong Island with a workforce of 6,000. When fully completed in 2003, the Island will house 150 companies with 30,000 workers. Its output was SGD27 billion in 1997 and is expected to post an annual growth of 12%.

A Jurong Island IT Masterplan was also conceptualized with the vision of leveraging IT to enhance the hub competitiveness of Jurong Island. It was envisaged that the application of eCommerce on an industry-wide basis would offer opportunities to achieve the next level of integration beyond the current physical integration. In fact, Chevron, which has its regional head-quarters on the Jurong Island, has also announced ambitious plans to integrate its upstream and downstream supply chain using eCommerce. Likewise, Shell Chemical, which also has significant investments on the Island, has established an electronic procurement system, linking it to its customers and suppliers worldwide.

George Yeo, Minister for Trade and Industry, at the official opening of the Jurongisland.com Internet portal in November 1999 commented: "Jurong Island is being prepared for the new age of IT. A broadband optical fiber network has already been installed on the Island. Building the network

Figure 11: Proposed IT applications for Jurong Island

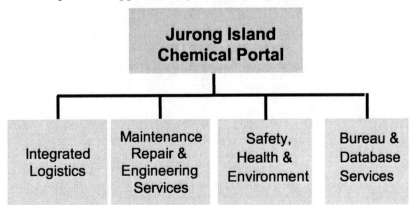

hardware is the easy part. We need the applications and services to make Jurong Island an even more competitive location to operate from in the future. To spearhead this effort, a Jurong Island IT Masterplan Taskforce has been formed" (EDB Press Release, 1999).

The taskforce comprising chemical companies (Exxon, Dupont, Sumitomo, Philip Petroleum, Chevron, Eastman and others) and government bodies, was formed in 1998 to assess the IT requirements for companies operating on Jurong Island. The taskforce's main tasks included:

a. outlining functional requirements identified during the detailed study,
b. presenting potential benefits and estimated costs of implementation,
c. recommending the scope and approach of implementation, and
d. examining challenges in implementation.

A detailed requirement study was conducted between May and June 1998. The taskforce invited companies on Jurong Island to participate in the definition of the functional requirements and four IT applications were considered critical for the chemical community (Figure 11).

The first module, Integrated Logistics System, was recommended to enable B2B integration within the supply chain via a central server with a common access point for exchange of different types of information (Figure 12). A workflow management function was incorporated in the system to monitor each step in the logistics cycle to ensure completeness of jobs assigned, and a business intelligence tool was added to optimize and analyze data for use in decision-making.

The main objective of this module was to cut down the order-to-cash

Figure 12: Integrated Logistics System

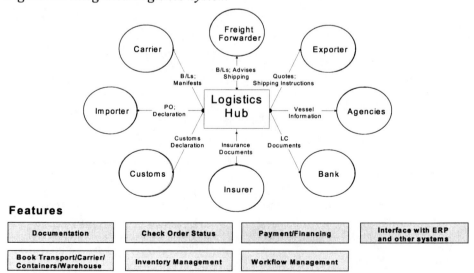

cycle from the current two weeks to three days. This will allow the chemical companies to reduce their safety stock level without affecting their turnaround time. The project was awarded to an IT vendor and the site has now gone "live" (http://www.chemxlog.com).

An Integrated Maintenance Exchange Center (IMEC) was the second proposed module to serve companies' procurement requirements in maintenance, repair and overhaul (MRO) supplies and services (Figure 13). Maintenance suppliers and service providers would post their MRO spare parts and offer MRO services, including management of MRO spare parts inventory via the Internet, while IMEC would store fast-moving parts centrally for the companies. (www.sesami.net/chemx).

Alfred A. Voskian, President and Managing Director of Eastman Chemical Asia Pacific Private Limited, said: "The e-MRO portal creates value for Eastman by reducing search and information transfer costs and enhance matching for buyers and sellers. It is a win-win for both buyers and suppliers as they have more choices, and these value drivers will grow and increase as more players enter the portal." The e-MRO solution will streamline and automate the purchasing processes at Eastman's plants in Malaysia, Hong Kong and Singapore, and items to be purchased through this system include gaskets, pipes, fittings, motors, valves, uniforms and compressors. With the implementation of e-procurement at its plants across Asia, Eastman will conduct all procurement tasks from the desktop and in real-time, with improved turnaround in service and delivery from its suppliers. This solution

Figure 13: Maintenance and Repair Operations System

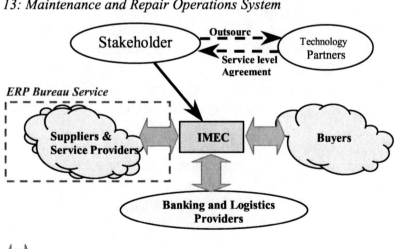

Figure 14: Proportion of transaction volumes and values for purchase items from chemical companies

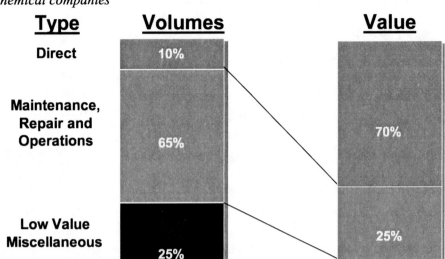

will enable Eastman's procurement personnel to concentrate on higher value-added activities such as contract negotiation, inventory optimization and strategic sourcing resulting in lower costs, improved productivity and re-duced procurement cycle time.

Detailed analysis of chemical companies' data confirmed that the trans-action volume for MRO purchases is about 65% of their total transaction volume, even though these purchases contribute to only 25% of the total purchase value (Figure 14). Furthermore, companies on Jurong Island usually deal with about 300 to 500 MRO suppliers, of which 80% are local suppliers; this electronic system is anticipated to help companies better manage their supplier base. In fact, some companies interviewed are currently spending two-thirds of their total time sourcing for suppliers and service providers.

However, some challenges were identified during the requirement study by the taskforce:

a. Most companies (especially MNCs) interviewed have their IT require-ments supported by their corporate offices overseas. This reduced their flexibility in adopting new software and systems, as the central system at their headquarter catered to the needs of its global operations.

b. Companies are at different stages of implementation of their Enterprise Resource Planning (ERP) systems. Thus, some companies may need more IT features to support their eCommerce, while others are content with their existing ERP systems.

c. Most companies were concerned about data security and confidentiality in electronic transaction and asked for assurance that the issue had been given ample consideration in the development of such systems.

d. Linkages to overseas business partners could be hampered, as certain parts of Asia have not acquired a high level of Internet connectivity.

The taskforce had to consider these challenges while evaluating and choosing IT applications. Eventually, a few vendors were awarded to build the chemical portal to support B2B electronics. This is expected to be completed by end of 2001.

The other two modules were delayed as the taskforce felt that they were not commercially viable to warrant business sustainability.

CONCLUSION

Based on the experience gained in implementing B2B eCommerce for the three economic sectors, the following factors should be taken into consideration for higher success.

First, most companies are interested in doing eCommerce based on the 80/20 rule, regardless of the technology used, whether EDI or Internet. They are keen to connect with 20% of their trading partners that contribute to 80% of their transaction value or volume according to EDIMAN users. This will help to justify their investment in eCommerce.

Second, procurement and transportation functions seem to be the most common B2B integration in eCommerce, while payment is deferred to a later stage due to security issues. Apparently, procurement can generate substantial immediate savings through economies of scales for the companies and thus are given higher priority than other functions. This fact was confirmed by EDIMAN users.

Third, the greatest barrier in B2B eCommerce is security and as long as this barrier is not lowered, the benefits of eCommerce will not be fully realized. The Singapore government is setting up a taskforce to ensure a trust environment for electronic trading to take place.

Fourth, all companies are at different stages of their ERP implementation and thus, B2B eCommerce solutions should be flexible enough to cater to various degrees of integration to be effective. This fact was borne out by findings from the chemical sector. Those companies who had fully implemented their ERP system would need minimum features from the eCommerce solutions, as most of the features would have been provided by the ERP system.

Fifth, for B2B eCommerce to be successful, both the sellers and buyers need to establish a win-win situation. Lessons learned from the EDITRANS example have confirmed that shippers are not keen in using the standard, as cost savings were not substantial enough to warrant their investment and effort.

Sixth, companies that have implemented EDI before are more ready to migrate to Internet commerce. These companies know about the processes involved in implementing EDI and understand that successful transition to Internet technology will require similar processes.

As a whole, it is apparent that some industrial sectors are more ready to adopt eCommerce than others due to a number of factors (e.g., product lifecycle, competition, government policies and directions, etc. Electronics companies tend to be more proactive in adopting new technologies to streamline their supply chain as compared to the logistics and chemical industries as their product life cycle tends to be shorter and profit margin is relatively lean. Therefore, it is unlikely to have a "one size fits all" eCommerce strategy for all industrial sectors. What would be more appropriate and attractive would be a customized strategy to suit the technology needs of each sector as well as individual companies within each sector.

REFERENCE

Albert Tan (1999). The use of Information Technology to enhance Supply Chain Management, *Production and Inventory Management Journal*, Volume 40, 7-15.

CMPnetAsia, (2000). *RosettaNet Establishes Singapore Chapter*, October.

Infocomm Development Authority of Singapore website: http://www.ida.gov.sg.

Lee, H., Padmanabhan, V. and Whang, S. (1997). The Bullwhip Effect in Supply Chains, Sloan Management Review, Spring, 93-102.

Singapore Economic Development Board website: http://www.sedb.com.sg.

Singapore Trade Development Board website: http://www.tdb.gov.sg.

Siong, N. B., King, J. and Applegate, L. M. (1995). Singapore TradeNet: "Beyond TradeNet to the Intelligent Island, Harvard Business Case Studies."

TDB Press Release, (2000). TDB and IDA introduce S$20m IT Action Plan for Logistics Aim to elevate Singapore as a premier e-logistics hub, http://www.tdb.gov.sg/newsroom/press/pr_01200.shtml. March 2000.

Wong, J. and Lam, E. (1999). Measuring eCommerce in Singapore-Methodological issues and survey findings, *Conference on the Measurement of eCommerce in Singapore*. Available on the World Wide Web at: http://www.singstat.gov.sg/EC/papers.html. Accessed in December 1999.

Chapter VI

Manufacturing Connectedness: Managerial Challenges and Solutions

Darren Meister
Queen's University, Canada

INTRODUCTION

As B2B eCommerce becomes more important to the daily operations of manufacturing firms, the scope of activities will broaden to a large set of data exchange activities (Davies and Garcia Sierra, 1999; Threlkel and Kavan, 1999; Unitt and Jones, 1999). Electronic Data Interchange (EDI) has been investigated for a significant period of time (e.g., Iacovou et al., 1995; Massetti and Zmud, 1996), but other forms of interfirm exchanges such as design and manufacturing data have not received much attention. This is in spite of the fact that there is extremely strong industry interest in these activities (e.g., automotive, aerospace and other online exchanges) as well as the identification of its necessity for factories that are part of extended virtual organizations (Upton and McAfee, 1996).

Manufacturing connectedness (simply "connectedness" for the remainder of this chapter) is the sharing of business and technical data through electronic linkages. It includes business transaction-based EDI as well as the exchange of manufacturing information, design transfer and collaboration. Standards-based data exchange is a key element in effectively sharing data in digital formats. Standards that have been used for EDI include ANSI X.12 and EDIFACT. Other standards include STEP (Standard for the Exchange of

Product Model Data), SGML (Standard Generalized Markup Language) and IGES (Initial Graphics Exchange Standard). Developing standards include XML (eXtensible Markup Language). The role of standards is essential in connectedness as it reduces the need for companies to have separate exchange for each partner to more similar formats for all partners.

In 1999, the Manufacturing and Processing Technologies (MPT) Branch of Industry Canada (IC) and the Integrated Manufacturing Technologies Institute (IMTI) of the National Research Council Canada (NRC) collaborated to survey Canadian manufacturing companies about current practices in connectedness. The survey collected data on general levels of connectedness, the usage of certain standards, the barriers and benefits associated with these standards, aids to implementation and lessons learned (Industry Canada, 2000). Many respondents provided brief lessons learned, indicating that manufacturers have a significant amount of interesting and useful experience worthy of further investigation. Four themes were identified: standards development and definition, standards implementation, internal commitment to change and interorganizational relationships. The survey reported on in this chapter was based on the lessons learned submitted in response to the initial survey.

The aim of this chapter is to enable managers in manufacturing organizations to recognize and anticipate common concerns in implementing connectedness as well as to prepare to take action to minimize negative outcomes. While it does not offer all of the solutions that will be necessary for every situation, it does provide a building block for the improvement of a company's connectedness capabilities.

METHODOLOGY

The goal of this research was to further our understanding of what concerns influence managers in adopting connectedness and what actions they take to address these concerns. An open-ended survey technique was selected for two reasons. First, we wanted to allow managers to provide more contextual information than might be attained through a scale-based survey. Second, the respondents were senior managers in manufacturing facilities. It is extremely difficult to schedule these people for telephone or face-to-face interviews, especially as we were drawing from a wide geographic area. This was confirmed in some survey pilot testing. However, the managers were willing to respond to a written survey, in return for a report compiling the results. Therefore, in order to maintain consistency and to facilitate data collection, a written survey was used for all respondents. It was based on the four categories of lessons learned initially identified.

The author as well as expert staff from Industry Canada and National Research Council developed individual questions to elicit a wide range of responses based on the initial four categories. An additional question on the greatest concern was introduced to obtain information not requested elsewhere. Two hundred and seventy-eight (278) surveys were distributed to each company in the previous survey that indicated prior experience with connectedness, of which 29 were returned as undeliverable. Reminders were sent at 10-day and three-week intervals. After four weeks, data collection ended. While the 12.5% return (31/249) was disappointing, it was not surprising given the schedules of the target audience and the effort required to complete the survey.

The respondents included firms from almost every major discrete manufacturing category but were concentrated in three areas: aerospace, automotive and equipment manufacturers. The firms ranged from small, local firms to large, well-known global organizations.

A coding system based on the initial four categories was first applied to the data. The data was captured as a set of text files and analyzed using the text analysis software, N*Vivo. From this data, common concerns and possible counteractions were identified. Some comments were not covered and additional coding schemes were developed. Over three iterations, the coding resulted in the set of concerns and actions presented in the following sections.

SEVEN COMMON CONCERNS

The respondents' concerns about connectedness can be broadly placed into seven main groupings. The first concern is that it is difficult to get buy-in for the initiative throughout the organization. A second pair of concerns revolves around supply chain issues. Of this pair, the first concern revolves around the fact that often, especially for standards such as IGES or ANSI X.12, each customer seems to want its own slight variation of the 'standard' implemented. The second concern is that standards implementations do not get planned in advance but occur as a rapid response to a customer demand. The supply chain-oriented concerns add significant complexity to connectedness.

Finally, four concerns focus on more operational issues. Respondents were concerned about security holes connectedness may cause. They were also concerned about the reliability of the networks used for exchange.

Implementing connectedness often subtly changes a company's operations and some respondents expressed concern that it was difficult to make sure the process integrity was maintained. Finally, resources for connectedness projects seem to be scarce, partially attributable to the frequently reactive nature of the implementations.

Together these concerns provide a watch list for managers as they implement connectedness. The following sections outline the concerns in more detail.

Difficult to Get Buy-In

Standards are not being adopted in a broadly accepted manner in these manufacturing organizations. Throughout the organization, executives, managers and staff personnel do not perceive standards as a source of value or a critical success factor. Consequently, support is less than enthusiastic. One reason given is that many executives towards the end of their careers are not comfortable with technology. One respondent explains: "We have executives who don't even use a computer. Data exchange standards don't mean anything to these individuals. Trying to explain the benefits and needs are lost on them. I don't believe this is unique [to our company]."

Additionally, the fact that there are often extreme time pressures to implement solutions creates specific challenges for Information Technology (IT) departments which therefore have further reasons to be reluctant to change. Often the IT department is charged with implementing a standard as quickly as possible. In order to complete the project, IT departments may charge ahead using "a ramrod approach" to complete the task. Unfortunately, this "often leaves major gaps in the execution of projects," requiring rework, additional resources and creates other management problems.

Data standards adoption affects numerous departments in the organization through production, engineering change or customer support. It seems to be challenging and time-consuming to get buy-in from all the relevant parts of the organization. Identifying the parts of the organization from which buy-in is required seems to be quite straightforward and does not present a challenge. In organizations with multiple locations, it is perhaps not surprising that it is more difficult to get alignment.

Customer-Specific Implementations

A very common and significant problem in the implementation of standards is the variety of ways in which standards are implemented in different organizations. Many standards allow flexibility to deal with changing business needs, however this flexibility can also be detrimental as it contributes to standards incompatibility. One explanation for this is that companies see the benefit in "improving" a standard to better fit their needs but not the drawback. As one survey respondent explains, companies "are often required to implement in a manner that is complimentary to our customer's implementation, or our customer's interpretation of the standard...the standards are open to interpretation, and to continue a business relationship we must conform to our customer's interpretation of the standard and/or procedure."

Another respondent suggests that cutting supply chain costs may be a more important concern in the future among the OEMs. As data exchange increases so do the problems that come along with it. The respondent explains "big customers tend to want things done their way but I sense that big customers would be willing to follow standards if it meant reduced cost."

Many companies find that trying to support multiple formats, such as doing EDI using ANSI X.12, EDIFACT, proprietary formats or the Web is becoming unmanageable. However difficult it may be, for many smaller companies, dealing with individual customer requirements is viewed simply as a cost of doing business and keeping that business. However, when included, standards incompatibility costs arise that must come out of the company's product margins or be compensated for through increased costs to customers. The following is a list of the kinds of costs incurred in situations with multiple standards for each customer which were mentioned frequently by survey respondents:

·   different software training,
·   multiple software updates,
·   multiple hardware and network updates,
·   different starter files.

Given the scope of these costs, it is likely that at least some of these costs are being passed on to customers.

Given unique customer requirements, often each new customer acquired forces the development of a custom exchange solution with that customer. In general, suppliers have been smaller companies than their customers, with less resources and power in the relationship. This results in the companies with the fewest resources handling the bulk of the data exchange problems. Some large companies have recognized this and are assisting smaller suppliers in developing their capabilities through direct assistance or offering instructional courses. This is accompanied by the fact that "big" customers were viewed as being more aggressive about forcing certain standards interpretations.

To date, there does not seem to be an efficient work-around for this problem. Every company stated that the way this issue is currently managed is to have multiple translators for multiple customers. The multiple file formats are managed internally. Effectively, brute force is used rather than an elegant standards-based solution.

Reactive Implementation

The adoption of data exchange standards is not a well-planned activity in most companies. Most frequently, implementation occurs as a response to customer demand and a company must react quickly.

For example, several companies mentioned that the Internet was going to change how they exchange data in the coming years. However, none were able to discuss how these changes would impact their business, e.g., what standards might become more common, will private VANs disappear, etc. There does not seem to be much long-term planning. This in turn leads to problems in getting resources, as the projects only coincide with regular budget and planning cycles by happenstance. Several companies identified lack of resources as a barrier to implementation, and this might be one cause.

Security and Intellectual Property

A commonly stated concern that companies held about the adoption of data exchange standards related to security and potential loss of intellectual property. There does not seem to be any evidence, even anecdotal, to support this concern. However, there is still some trepidation, especially at executive levels. It also appears that IT managers are not comfortable in guaranteeing the security of data transmitted.

These concerns mirror common societal worries about privacy, identity theft and Internet security and it is unlikely that there is a quick fix here. Hacker attacks on popular consumer sites, such as ones that happened in early 2000 at yahoo.com and Amazon.com, will exacerbate these concerns. These issues need to be considered when implementing standards, and require that the entire system including network security being implemented be explained.

Reliability

There is a drive to use the Internet to exchange data, either directly or through virtual private networks (VPNs). The reliability of the Internet to do this however is not well accepted. Several respondents voiced concerns as reflected by the following comments:

While the costs are lower, the reliability is not consistent. We must know that the data has been transmitted accurately and in a timely manner while reducing the costs of data exchange.

I am more concerned about being assured the data has been exchanged completely and unchanged and in a timely manner.

You do not blindly accept EDI data...you should cross-reference received data with your customer to verify data integrity.

There are two dimensions to reliability: did the transmission actually arrive at the intended destination unaltered and does it convey the intended meaning? Technological solutions such as public key infrastructure (PKI), VPNs or electronic courier services should address the first question. However, as long as companies deviate from a standard or the standards are not adequately specific, the risk of varying meanings will exist.

Finally, there are bandwidth issues for many companies. As was pointed out, the "time to transfer CAD files over 2 MB in size is still time consuming." Companies may not have invested in the network infrastructure to support these activities making data exchange tedious and unreliable.

Process Integrity

A topic of concern is process integrity and reliability. Some respondents felt that the implementation of data exchange standards will limit the "flexibility to adapt to changing requirements." Standards should improve process flexibility by creating a common vocabulary and providing a defined interface. However, given the variety of ways in which a standard is implemented, the implementation is often 'hard-wired' into the company's process and, in turn, reduces flexibility.

Another "significant reason to adopt standards is to ensure that the correct information is available throughout all elements of a process." However, one concern "learned as a result of experience, is that interconnectedness allows bypassing of checks and approvals." This might lead to knock-on problems in assembly or simply substandard work. The company's engineering change process can be comprised by the ease with which data can be exchanged.

A related concern is that of version control, ensuring that employees had the right information in the right place in the process. There was concern that electronic drawings could be out of date or incorrectly tagged. However, whether this differs from physical drawings is not clear.

Indeed, most companies felt that standards could help with checks and approvals. However, these benefits failed to be realized as, in general, companies have not revised their process to take advantage of easier data exchange.

Resource Scarcity

Whether resource scarcity is the cause of or the result of barriers already discussed, it undoubtedly prohibits effective and efficient implementation of connectedness standards and is a common problem. Several companies described their resources for connectedness-related projects as extremely constrained. This creates several types of problems. In a resource-poor circumstance, implementation is often done on an ad-hoc basis where little planning is done and projects are rushed. This means that there is less time to get buy-in at operational or executive levels.

IT personnel are often required to gather data themselves from various Internet sites rather than having comprehensive training. Another problem that arises from the lack of resources is that when the consultants have completed the job, "there is no one to pick it." Everyone is too busy. This means that there is no one to whom the knowledge can be transferred. Consequently, these project hand-offs are often rough and post-project reviews that could be used to build future business cases do not exist.

Synopsis

To summarize, seven common concerns have been identified. The concerns stem from the organization's motivations, cooperation along the supply chain and operational issues. The listed concerns are not inclusive of every problem a manager may experience in a connectedness project. However, in this survey, they were the most commonly raised issues and seem to fit well with anecdotal evidence. By recognizing these seven common concerns, a manager can take proactive action to prevent major difficulties. The next section outlines some useful actions that mitigate these concerns.

EIGHT USEFUL ACTIONS

Definite themes emerged from the respondents about useful actions in establishing manufacturing connectedness: setting the stage, getting the right resources and implementing the standard.

When setting the stage, the goal is to bring the organization's focus towards connectedness. This is accomplished in three ways. First, executive support for the initiative must be secured, primarily by stressing the importance of customer service and the economic benefits. Second, the role of standards in an organization's plans must be considered. Third, the organization must work closely with its supply chain partners in developing its strategic and implementation plans.

After the organization has made a commitment to connectedness, getting the right resources becomes most important. One way to secure these resources is to ensure that organizational bottlenecks do not occur by first securing broad internal commitment. This is different than securing executive commitment as it means that personnel throughout the organization in middle management and operational positions are also supportive of the initiative. Another way to get the right resources and to solidify the internal commitment is to use cross-functional teams in the implementation process. Finally, an organization is unlikely to have all the required resources readily available internally. It needs a resource network consisting of internal and consulting personnel. Through these three actions, an organization will increase its odds of securing the correct resources for a connectedness project.

Finally, the rubber must hit the road. The surveys resulted in two common project-based recommendations. Pilot projects and formal project management techniques were often mentioned. Formal project management seems not to be done due to some of the common concerns, primarily a lack of resources and reactive implementation demands.

Together, this set of eight useful actions would help companies in putting connectedness into operation. The actions are not mutually exclusive and in reality would often occur together. For example, gaining executive support and working with supply chain partners are likely to mutually reinforce one another. Similarly, executives who are supportive of connectedness initiatives are key players in developing the requisite broad internal commitment. The set of eight actions provided here will help managers plan and implement connectedness in their organization.

Secure Executive Support

In almost every Information Technology Management textbook, it says that one of the most important predictors of success is executive support. Therefore, it is not surprising that several respondents mentioned this requirement. Earlier, some of the difficulties in getting buy-in were introduced. From the surveys, there seem to be two main ways in which to convince executives that connectedness projects are important: "Hard financial numbers and customer service are the most compelling, in that order."

On the financial side, there is a belief that the data does not yet support good financial business cases. While costs are relatively straightforward to identify, it is not true that the financial benefits are as straightforward. In some areas, such as "letting customers confirm shipments or place orders," the financial benefits are obvious.

However, it is not clear to most companies that design and manufacturing data exchange yields similar financial returns. Therefore, one action that firms can take towards improving the climate for standards adoption is to track ongoing implementations to develop "hard financial numbers" for future business cases. This is not happening now because many of the implementations are occurring in order to fulfill customer demands. The decision in this situation is based on whether or not the company wishes to keep the customer. In many sectors, this is not really a choice.

However, relying on a cost-based business case has its limitations. In the words of one respondent, "financial methods (NPV, IRR, etc.) do not do a full justice to the benefits" of connectedness. For these companies, formulating the strategic rationale has been difficult.

Executive support was gained by outlining the importance of standards to our customers. However, it took a lot of work to get the message through.

It is clear that executive support is required for adoption and that the awareness of executives towards these issues is low in many companies. This awareness must be raised. One respondent suggested that an executive or accountable representative be included in meetings about standards. Another way to increase awareness is to make sure that executives know customers' long-term data exchange plans. Additionally, business cases with financial numbers from prior implementations internally or external benchmarking studies should be developed, even if the implementation was done to fulfill a specific customer requirement. While approaches beyond customer support and financial return may be listened to, these would appear secondary.

Plan the Role of Standards

Most companies articulate their corporate strategy but do not align the role of standards with this strategy. No responding organization reported application of their corporate strategy to data standards management or planning. Practically, this means that when funding for strategic projects is made available, that standards projects are relatively low priority. For example, a company might plan a sales expansion into Europe, but it does not allocate any resources that enable EDI using EDIFACT in addition to ANSI X.12.

Another reason given by companies for the lack of planning was the "lack of a multi-departmental champion of the standards. There is no clear owner of standards." Therefore, it might be helpful to make a person responsible for managing standards. Often, it seems that this role falls to an IT person, which may not be the best place, given that need often arises in one of the business functions such as manufacturing or customer support. There was no clear best answer to this problem. The only consensus emerged around the idea that it would be important to have someone responsible, likely with cross-functional experience. Such a person would also need the time and resources to attend industry conferences and to stay aware of ongoing initiatives.

Respondents were asked whether they worked together with customers in this process. The question was asked because it is often customer requests that drive standards adoption decisions. The most common answer was "no," "not really" or "keep an eye." One company did state: "We have managers that are responsible for the long-term view, who keep up to date with [...] customer implementation plans." Another company was involved in "long-term teams for projects." This is good advice for other companies in that it might add months to the time available for project implementation, especially in the important early stages.

Work with Supply Chain Partners

While most companies do not involve their suppliers or customers in data exchange planning, they also seem to implement the standards in isolation. Many companies do not work with supply chain partners, either customers or suppliers. This may be partly because "the issue is just now emerging in many parts of the market." However, even for those companies in aerospace and automotive where the issues are relatively advanced, little consultation goes on.

Several respondents mentioned that they would like to know: "What works? What are the savings? What are the benefits?" Nevertheless, these respondents typically did not share information along the supply chain. In some cases, this was a fear of intellectual property loss because "[some companies] feel that sharing too much information is giving away your product ideas." Therefore, companies would need Non-Disclosure Agreements and other IP protection before proceeding to exchange data electronically.

In other cases, there is a reluctance to open up business processes and systems and potentially reveal weaknesses to key customers and suppliers. In order to improve information sharing in these circumstances, the supply chain partners need to develop a program of mutual continuous improvement. This attitudinal shift would be similar to that undergone in many organizations through employee empowerment programs, quality circles and other initiatives. It is likely that companies that have not made such changes with its own workforce would have difficulty implementing partnerships at the organizational level.

In some cases, companies do work closely with customers to articulate their business and standards plans. There are some real benefits of working together. For example, some of the problems of differing standards implementations can also be addressed. One company "works with [its] customers, because of their specific interpretations of standards and procedures." It is more important to work closely with your customers if their business is not likely to fit existing standards well. Further, supply chain partners can interact through an industry association or government-sponsored body. This would enable a broader consensus within the industry about the implementation of a standard. Additionally, it would raise the issue at the level of executive managers, as mentioned earlier.

Not much attention seems to have been paid to alliance or other forms of interorganizational management. "It is much harder to work with external companies than it is to work internally!" Since data exchange is inherently an interorganizational activity, companies should develop these skills.

Gain Broad Internal Commitment

A consensus point about standards implementation is that it requires an organizational effort. This is important for at least three reasons. First, initial consensus lessens the chance that an individual or small group will be able to derail implementation. Second, areas or issues requiring special attention may be uncovered through a broad consultative process. Third, more resources may be brought to bear on the project.

There are several challenges in bringing internal stakeholders on board. One respondent stated, "It is challenging to get everyone to the same level of understanding. Explaining the technical details and cost benefits are difficult. Many departments do not understand how they fit in the process." While the education and awareness process may be slow and laborious, if it is rushed, internal parties may become resistors.

The consensus was that the commitment to change needs to be broadly held, including customer support, sales, marketing, engineering and manufacturing, as "the degree of integration of information management requires all parties to participate."

Some organizations are able to benefit from their size. From example, "[in] a relatively small company, with a unified IT strategy, [lack of consensus] has not been a big challenge." A key action here for companies, regardless of size, is the importance of having an IT strategy.

Change management literature (e.g., Kotter, 1996) suggests that it is important to get middle managers on board. This is because they communicate directly and influentially to executives and line personnel. One company subscribed to that by obtaining "consensus among the managers first-they must agree that the change is necessary." This avoids the issue of gaining cooperation. There must be a clear reason for the change and one that is communicated throughout the organization.

One backhanded benefit of being forced to adopt standards in a fast implementation is that there does not seem to be as much resistance. "Cooperation is forced on us by clients" brings the organization together. If an organization were to try a proactive implementation, it would be well served to find out if a competitor that had already undertaken a similar project. While the competitor would be unlikely to provide detailed information, it would likely be possible to find out what suppliers and consultants were used and some of the business effects.

Finally, the attitude towards change in the organization in general is important, i. e., regular communication such as "in our quarterly all-employee meetings, we stress the importance of change to stay competitive and save our jobs." Additionally, some companies invest in training before it is required as part of a professional development program.

In conclusion, if a company wants to gain buy-in to a standards implementation project, it needs to build a compelling reason for change and provide employees with the required tools.

Use Cross-Functional Teams

One way to improve the chances for buy-in is to use cross-functional teams. Such teams can be used to structure steering committees or actual implementation teams. For example, one company that had trouble getting buy-in developed a "steering committee made up from a cross-section of [their] organization that will make the decision with [their] strategic plan in mind."

Cross-functional teams are not a panacea. For example, the fact that there are "different backgrounds makes [coordination] hard." Using a cross-functional team will likely increase the amount of time up-front required to educate and train people. One company described its approach as "primarily IT department driven. The primary advantage is that IT can quickly implement the new standards and deploy them to the organization. The main disadvantage is that the users of the systems based on these standards don't understand the importance if they haven't been involved from the start."

Some companies included outside consultants as part of their implementation team. Consultants are beneficial in that they bring experience and specific skills to the team. However, they are often not able to articulate organizational needs as well as an internal person.

Overall, it seems that the most consistent appropriate use of a cross-functional team is to define and coordinate the project. Then, a variety of resources, from inside or outside the company, can be brought to the realization process.

Develop a Resource Network

Consultants seem to be an important resource in standards implementation for most companies. The role of the consultant takes three forms. In some cases, the consultant develops and implements the application and then trains the appropriate personnel. In other cases, the consultant leads the company's implementation team. Finally, the consultant may form a technical role in the organization. For almost all companies, consultants are part of the company's implementation plan.

Companies not in close proximity with major urban centers seemed to have more difficulty in acquiring good resources. Not surprisingly, experienced consultants seem centered in large cities. Companies outside these areas reported difficulty in accessing consultants with, most significantly, experience. The added travel expenses for out-of-town consultants are a burden on the companies.

Companies also rely on vendors, sometimes with mixed feelings. Understandably, the impartiality of vendors is questionable. Companies had positive feelings about the vendors, but were uncomfortable with their reliance on the vendors.

One of the most common resources required are training resources. Consultants and industry associations have been useful pools for training resources, even if difficult to access in some small towns not close to major cities.

Overall, companies reported good success with consultants. Therefore, it is important for companies and industry associations to develop good resource networks in order to minimize the amount of time that it takes for a company to find an appropriate consultant. As consultants become more familiar with a specific company or industry, the quality of their advice will improve further. Companies that are not in urban centers may wish to develop consultants and resource networks in conjunction with other local firms, even if they are not in the same industry.

Use Pilot Projects

One of the approaches that several companies used to learn more about standards and to prepare for general implementation was a pilot project. The purpose of the pilot projects may include verifying feasibility, providing information for cost information and developing project plans. They might be used "like R&D projects, to verify feasibility. Once accomplished successfully, they can be implemented on a wider scale."

At least one company sets up "dummy separate companies" in order to execute the pilot projects. One of the other comments is that companies do not need to conduct the pilot themselves, but need access to the results of the pilot. This opens the possibility for companies to form collaborative alliances, with customers, suppliers and even potentially competitors, to implement and record pilot studies.

Pilot studies are certainly not used for every project. If the initiative is relatively minor, they are not used. If implementation is inevitable, they are used not to evaluate the standards but to develop implementation plans, as pilots "can dictate the details." Usually, one location in the company is selected to lead the implementation and to provide the lessons learned for the rest of the company.

Pilot projects are an effective tool to ensure the appropriateness of a connectedness project and to develop project-planning and implementation details.

Manage as a Project

One of the points of strong agreement was that a standards implementation had to be managed as a project, with a definite start, finish and deliverables. This might seem obvious but it is not how many standards are implemented. At this time, a customer demands its implementation and the company responds without a project-planning exercise. Often, the responsibility is given to the IT department, which may not understand the context in which the standard will be deployed. It then becomes difficult to coordinate different groups and implement a cross-functional team due to time constraints.

The first piece of advice to improve the implementation process would be to "appoint a formal project manager." A project manager could coordinate the many resources required and manage the relationships with executives, other internal parties and, usually, relevant customers and suppliers. Further, experienced project managers are usually good at estimating implementation requirements as well as anticipating the need for new or different resources. Defining the requirements up-front for the projects was a common problem.

In practice, I think you are only able to estimate 80% of the implementation requirements or even perhaps less. This is because there is generally little time to fully plan infrastructure projects in competition with revenue projects.

While good project management is perhaps an obvious action companies can take, it is important to include it here. The reactive manner in which many connectedness projects are undertaken pushes good project practices away. Consistent use of project management principles would likely improve connectedness initiatives.

Synopsis of Actions

The actions outlined in this section can be used in concert. Indeed, to address the common concerns, many, if not all, should be applied. However, in order to do this, standards implementations must be planned. To be useful planning must also be conducted in conjunction with supply chain partners. In turn, to get the time and resources to do the planning correctly, executive support must be secured. Therefore, while each of the actions is important to achieve success in implementing connectedness, the first three are likely precursors for success. Fortunately, these actions are helpful for many initiatives. By acting on these options, an organization will start to lay the foundation for enhanced connectedness capabilities.

SUMMARY

The findings of this report are in some ways not that surprising. For example, many of the concerns reflect frequent concerns in change management such as senior executive support and organizational buy-in (e.g., Kotter, 1996). The increased complexity of managing interorganizational systems (Kumar and Cook, 1999) has been recognized by these managers, as it affects multi-partner complexity and the time available for execution. Connectedness issues need to be addressed by senior executives working proactively and with supply chain partners.

For each of the common concerns, several actions are available to reduce its effects. For example, an organization in which it is difficult to get buy-in would find it efficacious to implement some of the suggestions towards securing executive support, planning the role of standards and gaining internal commitment. Some of the other actions would of course be helpful, but perhaps not as efficacious. Therefore, a suite of actions is necessary and perhaps the actions outlined form the basis of that set. The concerns lay out a number of issues to be kept in mind. For example, Trent and Monczka (1994) reported that cross-functional sourcing teams required the availability of key organizational resources, supply chain cooperation, senior executive support and organizational buy-in. Table 1 provides some possible relationships between concerns and actions. These relationships are proposed through comments in this study or through the research literature but need to be validated through a separate research project.

Table 1: Proposed Relationships Between Concerns and Actions

Concerns	Actions							
	Secure Exec. Support	Plan Standards	Work with Supply Chain	Gain Internal Commitment	Use Cross-Func. Teams	Develop a Resource Network	Use Pilot Project	Manage as a Project
Difficult to Get Buy-In	***	*	*	***	***			
Customer-Specific Implementation		*	***				*	
Reactive Implementation	*	***	***				*	
Security & IP			*			*	***	
Reliability						*	***	***
Process Integrity			***	*				***
Resource Scarcity	***		*	***	*	***		*

*** *Significant potential influence;* * *Minor influence*

It is entirely likely that taking certain actions will lead to increased prominence for different concerns that in turn require additional actions. Perhaps what is most obvious is that there is no silver bullet and it is important that companies realize that implementing connectedness will be an iterative process.

Connectedness is likely to become more important to manufacturers as eCommerce moves from relatively simple order placement and tracking to virtual organizations. Given trends in globalization and technology proliferation, companies in all countries will be affected by these changes. From the lessons provided herein by other manufacturers, companies should be able to accelerate the development of connectedness capabilities in their company. While a connectedness approach based on standards may be difficult to implement, the alternative is the development of separate methods with every partner, an action that will likely lead to a reduction in the number of interfirm partnerships. However, managers recognizing these concerns and actions will improve their organization's ability to compete in an eCommerce world leading to greater future success.

ACKNOWLEDGMENT

This work was supported by the Integrated Manufacturing Technologies Institute, National Research Council of Canada and the Manufacturing and Processing Technologies Branch, Industry Canada. The assistance of Susan Gillies, Mia Yen and Leighann Neilson is appreciated.

REFERENCES

Davies, A. J. and Garcia Sierra, A. J. (1999). Implementing electronic commerce in SMEs-Three case studies. *BT Technology Journal*, 17(3), 97-111.

Iacovou, C. L., Benbasat, I. and Dexter, A. S. (1995). Electronic data interchange and small organizations: Adoption and impact of technology. *MIS Quarterly*, 19(4), 465-485.

Industry Canada. (2000). *Maufacturing Connectedness*. Available on the World Wide Web at: http:/strategis.ic.gc.ca/manufacturing_connectedness.

Kotter, J.(1996). *Leading Change*. Cambridge, MA: Harvard Business School Press.

Kumar, R. L. and Crook, C. W. (1999). A multi-disciplinary framework of the management of interorganizational systems. *Database for Advances in Information Systems*, 30(1), 22-37.

Massetti, B. and Zmud, R. W. (1996). Measuring the extent of EDI usage in complex organizations: Strategies and illustrative examples. *MIS Quarterly*, 20(3), 331-345.

Threlkel, M. S. and Kavan, C. B. (1999). From traditional EDI to Internet-based EDI: Managerial considerations. *Journal of Information Technology*, 14(4), 347-360.

Trent, R. J. and Monczka, R. M. (1994). Effective cross-functional sourcing teams: Critical success factors. *International Journal of Purchasing and Materials Management*, 30(4), 3.

Unitt, M. and Jones, I. C. (1999). EDI: The grand daddy of electronic commerce. *BT Technology Journal*, 17(3), 17-23.

Upton, D. M. and McAfee, A. (1996). The real virtual factory. *Harvard Business Review*, 74(4), 123-133.

Chapter VII

Supply-Chain Challenges for B2B eCommerce with Examples from the Chemical Industry

ManMohan S. Sodhi
Gandiva, USA

INTRODUCTION

In this chapter, I examine supply-chain-related challenges that eMarketplaces and existing companies face as business-to-business eCommerce increases. Although the Internet is increasingly attractive for B2B commerce and for supply-chain management, eCommerce is more likely to reveal the inefficiencies in supply chain and to increase customer expectations relative to offline trade. Therefore, managers must understand the supply-chain management challenges associated with B2B eCommerce, especially in light of the fulfillment failures already experienced in business-to-consumer eCommerce.

Although many businesses have developed new business models, the impact of the Internet on supply-chain management has been evolutionary rather than revolutionary. The Internet has made possible new ways to buy and sell products, for instance, auctions and reverse auctions in electronic marketplaces. And it has facilitated the creation of new markets for many manufacturers and decreased procurement costs for others. For physical goods that cannot be translated into bytes and sent over the Internet, however, the manufacturer's supply chain itself has not fundamentally changed, and therefore, supply-chain management is not fundamentally affected. The supply chains of fertilizer or television-set manufacturers will continue to have brick-and-mortar components for material flows even as they increasingly use the Internet for information flows. Parts and products must be bought, manufactured, moved, and delivered, just as they were before commercial use of the Internet. For supply-chain management, information exchange across companies predates the Internet. Large companies and their major suppliers, customers, and carriers send order-related information by electronic data interchange (EDI) links, faxes, phones, and mail. Information transmission via the Internet, though cheaper, ubiquitous, and close to real time, fills existing business needs and merely extends the existing solutions.

To understand supply-chain management in the online B2B world, we should start with the supply chain predating B2B eCommerce and understand its operation and challenges as they are carried into the new context. Supply-chain management can be viewed as comprising (1) *execution*, i.e., synchronizing the cash, inventory, and order status associated with any transaction; (2) *planning*, i.e., creating a plan covering what products to produce where, against a forecast and how to distribute for the next, say, six months; and (3) *monitoring*, i.e., tracking orders and shipments to confirm delivery against orders. We can categorize supply-chain challenges in the same manner:

·   transacting and executing orders;
·   planning, both within and across companies; and
·   monitoring and tracking orders and shipments.

To illustrate these challenges, I give examples from the $1.6 trillion chemical industry, which already has a significant investment in B2B eCommerce.

LITERATURE SURVEY

The growing importance of supply-chain management in B2B eCommerce is readily apparent in such trade journals as *Business 2.0* and *e-Company*, and from analysts' reports, including those from AMR Research and the Gartner Group. For instance, Christie (2000) reports on recent projections by Jupiter Research asserting that Internet marketplaces "will drive a significant shift in supply-chain management for several core industries," such as aerospace and defense, chemicals, computer and telecommunications equipment, electronics, and motor vehicles and parts, with more than half of these industries' sales being online by 2004. Mougayar (2000) highlights the growing importance of supply-chain management, provides a historical context, and outlines the potential of online supply-chain management. Dell (2000) and Mougayar also discuss Internet-related change in supply-chain models. An example, provided by Donahue (2000), is the collaborative planning at Sun Microelectronics, a division of Sun. Donahue reports that Sun is using i2 software to enable its "suppliers to share product-demand forecasts and manufacturing schedules." Donahue also describes the division's vision of becoming an "aircraft controller," directing its various contract manufacturers through the Internet and Internet-hosted i2 software.

The academic and top-tier management literature so far includes only a handful of articles directly concerning eBusiness, but many articles discussing strategic issues in supply-chain management are equally relevant to online and offline commerce. For instance, Lee and Billington (1992) describe 14 pitfalls of supply-chain management and identify corresponding opportunities. Fisher (1997) suggests the need for supply chains to respond to innovative products early in their lifecycles, and to operate efficiently for mature products, thus matching the demand characteristics for the products to the supply chain.

Articles in the top-tier management practice literature about eCommerce include the following: instead of discussing the appropriate supply chain for eBusiness as is usual, Chopra and Van Miegham (2000) recommend that a firm seek the right eBusiness for its supply chain based on how the eBusiness enhances value or decreases costs. Kaplan and Sawhney (2000) propose a framework for categorizing eMarketplaces and online B2B purchasing based on (1) whether the purchased materials are direct (components used in manufacturing finished goods) or indirect (all others, including office-supplies and uniforms), and (2) whether the purchasing is spot based (e.g., through auctions) or contract based (through long-term contracts typically ranging from six months to two years). Currently most commercial transactions are conducted offline and in the direct and contract-based quadrant. So most of the challenges I discuss concern that quadrant as well.

Given the value of the Internet in facilitating information flow, articles in the academic literature concerning modeling the value of information are relevant. The Beer Game, developed by John Sterman (1987), has highlighted the value of sharing actual or forecasted demand and inventory information by demonstrating the bullwhip effect, i.e., the amplification of demand fluctuations as the demand signal travels upstream from the customer to the plant. Lee et al. (1994) analyzed the bullwhip effect's four sources–demand signal processing, the rationing game, order batching, and price variations. Lee et al. (2000) take the analysis further for a two-level supply "chain" by quantifying the benefits of information-sharing between retailers and their suppliers. Finally, Cachon and Fisher (2000) use a model and simulations to show how information-sharing decreases supply-chain costs.

Modeling is beneficial for supply-chain planning as well, and existing supply-chain models will carry over to B2B eCommerce. Geoffrion and Powers (1995) provide an overview of the previous 20 years of modeling and supply-chain planning, predating the packaged technologies from i2 and other advanced planning and scheduling vendors. Sodhi (2000) presents a modeling-based framework that permits a company to understand supply-chain planning before attempting to implement it. Specifically for B2B eCommerce, Sodhi (2001) discusses existing uses and potential uses of operations research in supply-chain management. Lee and Billington (1993) report on the initial development of a model of material flows and its application at Hewlett-Packard to study the effect of postponing product-differentiation; such postponement can be effective regardless of eCommerce.

THE CHEMICAL INDUSTRY AS A CASE STUDY

The chemical industry provides a good case study in discussing B2B eCommerce and supply-chain challenges because it stands to benefit greatly from B2B eCommerce and has begun to do so. Companies within the industry often use enterprise resource planning (ERP) systems for supply-chain management and are hungry to leverage their huge ERP investments for eBusiness. Furthermore, they have embraced planning solutions as a way to improve their use of manufacturing capacity given its high cost. In 1999 in the U.S., chemical industry assets worth $593 billion produced only $43 billion in net income, and capacity utilization ranged from 74.9% to 79.1% (O'Reilly, 2000). The industry is large, approximately $1.6 trillion in revenues worldwide, about a quarter of which is the U.S. share at $431 billion. The industry is global. The U.S. exported $68 billion in goods in 1999 and imported $60 billion worth, mostly from western Europe. Trade in the chemical industry is primarily between businesses, and hence B2B eCommerce is important. About half of U.S. production goes to other manufacturing companies, including other chemical companies, as raw material. Finally, the chemical industry has many commodity products suitable for auctions and spot markets, precisely in the form of the early eMarketplaces corresponding to the direct- and spot-purchasing quadrant in the Kaplan-Sawhney framework.

The industry, therefore, moved early toward B2B eCommerce. Such large players as DuPont and BP backed the startups, for example, of ChemConnect and CheMatch. They also hedged their bets by investing in technology startups, such as WebMethods, in bilateral links or private exchanges, and in Web-based services, such as ShipChem and WWTesting. B2B eCommerce activity in the chemical industry falls into five categories:

1. *Direct-contract-based sales among major business partners*: In terms of volume, most commercial activity is conducted through direct-contract-based sales and only a little through eCommerce. SAP and 20 German chemical and pharmaceutical firms, including BASF AG, Degussa-Huls AG, Henkel KgaA, and Metellgesellshaft, launched an independent venture using mySAP in 2000 to enable contract-based sales (AMR, 2000). Chemical companies can link their ERP systems with their major suppliers' systems for seamless online ordering using XML-based technologies; PolyOne is an example. Two newly announced eMarketplaces, Envera and Elemica, promise to support contract-based direct purchases by linking the ERP systems of business partners (Table 1). Chemical companies can also join other industries' eMarketplaces, such as the auto industry's Covisint, as suppliers.

2. *Direct and indirect spot-based sales for small orders for laboratory, sample, experimental or emergency shipments*: Such specialized marketplaces as SciQuest are usually best suited for such orders. A company may also obtain small orders through its own extranet (Table 2) and then pass on these orders to dealers for fulfillment.

3. *Spot and contract-based sales to dealers and customers via extranets*: Chemical companies have created their own extranets for selling products to their dealers and customers. Such a Web site is Dow's MyAccount@Dow where customers can configure their orders and purchase (Table 2). Sites such as Dow's can either fill all orders or divert small orders to dealers or distributors, avoiding the cost of filling small orders while still capturing customer order information without competing with their dealers and distributors. Finally, companies can serve their customers via extranets by using vendor-managed inventory (VMI) solutions like Simon, the hybrid Web/Lotus Notes solution that Shell Chemicals created and that it uses to monitor its customers' inventories and generate orders.

4. *Direct spot-based sales of commodities, excess inventory, second-grade material, and scrap*: Companies can purchase commodities through spot-based exchanges, such as ChemConnect (for the commodity-chemicals market) or PetroChemNet (for petrochemicals) (Table 3).

Table 1: eMarketplaces Offering ERP Integration Want to Provide Contract-Based Sales in the Chemical Industry

Example	Description
Envera	Aids the integration of partners' applications to allow machine-to-machine transactions between trading partners without human intervention. Offers browser-level integration for small companies who cannot afford integration but do contractual work for larger companies.
Elemica	Helps buyers and sellers of all sizes by providing electronic connections for order-to-cash processing and logistics, a hub for ERP connectivity enabling many-to-many rather than one-to-one connections.

Table 2: Large Chemical Companies Offer Online Purchases for Their Customers and Dealers Through Extranets Allowing Customers to Configure Their Orders and Purchase

Example	Description
MyAccount @Dow	Dow's extranet that provides registered customers with order status, account history, repeat orders, and payment information
BPChoice	BP Chemical's extranet for its customers
OneSource Coatings	PPG Industries' extranet that provides small customers who are ordering between 50-500 gallons of liquid coatings and less than 2,000 lbs/month with product information, expertise, and the means to order online.

Table 3: Many "Vertical" eMarketplaces that Specialize in Chemical Companies Selling to Other Chemical Companies Do So through Spot-Based Sales, Through Auctions and Reverse Auctions, and Through Anonymous Buyer-Seller Matching

Example	Description
PaintAndCoatings	Marketplace for paints and coatings
CheMatch	Bulk commodities exchange – mainly benzene, P-X, styrene, and methanol – to match buyers and sellers anonymously
ChemConnect	eMarketplace for chemical and plastics manufacturers, buyers, and intermediaries; offers private-auction service as well
E-Chemicals	eMarketplace for supply-chain functionality
Omnexus	eMarketplace for thermoplastics with products and services from participating resin manufacturers, other plastic-related materials, molding equipment, tooling, maintenance supplies, and packaging materials. It allows buyers to aggregate orders with a single invoice covering all suppliers.
Rooster	eMarketplace where farmers can market crops as well as buy fertilizer, crop protection products, farm supplies, and equipment
Shell Chemicals global online exchange	Global online eMarketplace, yet unnamed, to ensure liquidity for key commodity chemical products using standard trading instruments and contracts. Will develop a market for financial derivatives based on these standard contracts.

Table 4: Some eMarketplaces Offer Services other than Direct Buying and Selling to the Chemical Industry

Example	Description
Industria-solutions	Procurement in the $75 billion worldwide fluid processing market, including chemicals, oil and gas, paper, power generation, pharma
ShipChem	A virtual logistics provider for the chemical industry
WWTesting	A network of industry partners who provide sampling, inspection, and testing services
Yet2	A global technology exchange forum for companies and other institutions that buy, sell, license, exchange, and research technology
Trade-Ranger	Procurement for petrochemical companies and upstream (exploration and refining) and downstream (distribution and sales) firms
Shell Chemicals global online exchange	Provides financial instruments with which to manage risk; for instance, Shell already offers 3-6-12 month futures for polymers, olefins, and aromatics

They can sell unwanted inventory, including excess inventory, second-grade material, and scrap through the company Web-site (Table 2) or through such spot-exchanges.

5. *Indirect purchasing of goods and services that is typically spot based but could also be contract based*: A dominant service is transportation, and large companies can already move orders by using EDI or Web-based (XML) messaging to carriers. Companies can use transportation exchanges directly, but third-party logistics companies usually coordinate transportation for them. Chemical transportation costs are estimated at $37 billion (Elemica, 2000). ShipChem, created by Eastman, is a transportation marketplace for the chemical industry. Elemica also wants to help companies to coordinate transportation. eMarketplaces also exist for other services including testing, knowledge management, and indirect procurement (Table 4).

Tables 1-4 show some of the better-known existing or announced eMarketplaces offering products and services in the chemical industry. The information in the tables is taken mostly from Vasnetsov and Kennedy (2000).

Existing eMarketplaces do not offer supply-chain planning solutions for the chemical industry, but other efforts have been announced. Planning is important to the industry because the use of longer decision horizons with collaborative forecasting can improve firms' efficiency in planning production and help them to reduce inventory. SAP and 20 German chemical and pharmaceutical firms, including BASF AG, Degussa-Huls AG, Henkel KgaA, and Metellgesellshaft, launched an independent venture using mySAP and SAP's planning solution, APO, to design and run eMarketplaces (AMR, 2000). Aspen Technologies has partnered with E-Chemicals to use the MIMI toolkit in the chemical industry for scheduling and supply planning and has announced its own eMarketplace technology offering, Process City. Still, like other industries, the chemical industry is still waiting for supply-chain planning solutions for B2B eCommerce.

I return to supply chain challenges for B2B commerce and shall refer to examples from the chemical industry to illustrate these challenges.

TRANSACTIONS AND ORDER EXECUTION

In the early 1990s, companies instituted large-scale implementations of ERP, partly out of fear that their legacy systems would collapse in 2000, and partly because they expected ERP systems to improve supply-chain management by providing better visibility of order status and available inventory and through rudimentary production planning. However, the difficulties of technology and process-change associated with implementing ERP systems imply that implementation of systems to enable B2B eCommerce will not be easy. This is because B2B eCommerce, especially for direct sales based on contracts, will attempt to coordinate orders, inventory, and cash across companies just as ERP systems do within the enterprise. Still, the incentive to conduct online transactions is huge as the average cost to order online is a fraction of that for a paper- or phone-based order. Indeed, in the chemical industry with an estimated 90 million transactions per year, a paper-based order costs a company an average of $150 for an order while ordering online costs only a tenth to a third of that (Elemica, 2000). B2B eCommerce faces at least three problems in handling orders:

1. *The complexity of B2B transactions*: The first challenge in enabling online transactions for B2B eCommerce is, just like ERP implementations, integrating systems and changing processes. These are difficult because business-to-business transactions are complex, especially for direct sales based on contracts. These transactions are complex to handle online (a) through eMarketplaces with many buyers and many sellers, (b) through hubs with a single buyer (seller) and many sellers (buyers), or (c) through bilateral links between a single buyer and a single seller. According to Phillips and Meeker (2000), enabling these transactions through the Internet is difficult because "many systems and business processes have to be restructured" and because procurement and fulfillment processes are inherently complex. Procurement requires requisitioning, obtaining approval, generating a purchase order, receiving and checking against the purchase order, and paying. The challenges go beyond implementing the necessary technology and encompass prevent-

ing maverick purchasing within the firm and fostering acceptance by purchase managers, who may view an automated purchasing system as usurping their authority. Integrating disparate systems also presents enormous problems.

2. *Integrating the order-to-cash cycle*: Integrating the entire order-to-cash process via the Internet is more difficult than enabling online transactions. Companies expect this integration because if all the trading partners—buyer, seller, logistics provider, and common carrier—are online, they can share information in near-real time. The subprocesses for a buyer include ordering (possibly against an existing contract), approving the purchase, arranging transportation, accepting delivery, and paying the seller and the transportation provider. It is easy to see why the existing eMarketplaces mostly offer spot-based sales instead of contract-based sales and require buyers and sellers to arrange for everything else.

3. *Export restrictions*: To conduct global eCommerce, the seller must comply with government export requirements. Companies expect that the Internet will make global trade easier, but they find conducting global transactions challenging now, and conducting these via the Internet will only exacerbate compliance problems. For example, the U.S. maintains three types of license requirements based on (1) the nature of the item, (2) the possible end use of the item, and (3) the end user (who could be an individual, a company, or even an entire country on any of the black lists maintained by different departments) (Christensen, 2000). The Departments of Commerce, State, Energy, Treasury, and the Nuclear Regulatory Commission all maintain separate lists, making it difficult for a company to track and comply with export requirements. This gets harder with Internet commerce. Equally problematic is that the definition of "export" in the U.S. includes releasing information residing on a U.S.-based server to one that is outside the U.S. Therefore, an eMarketplace based in the U.S. could be non-compliant with U.S. export laws by facilitating an automated transaction between two parties, even though neither party is based in the U.S. and the product does not originate in the U.S; Syntra and Vastera have created software solutions for exporting firms, and their solutions will extend to online marketplaces, but responsibility for compliance with government requirements will rest with sellers and eMarketplace operators.

The chemical industry faces all three of these challenges. The absence of any B2B solutions for contract-based sales testifies to the difficulties of integrating technologies and processes. Recently, new ventures, for example

Envera and Elemica, have announced efforts in this direction (Table 1). Companies are also making their own efforts through private exchanges and through bilateral links with their trading partners. Automating the entire order-to-cash cycle is still a pipedream, and may be further for the chemical industry than some others industries such as the high-tech industry. These problems are reflected in the state of the existing eMarketplaces. CheMatch and ChemConnect, for example, still do not having a critical mass of buyers and sellers, and PlasticsNet and Chemdex have ceased operations. The third problem is of particular concern in the chemical industry given its products and global nature. While exports of chemicals have always been restricted, the inclusion of information under export regulations, at least in the U.S., creates a difficult hurdle for eMarketplaces.

SUPPLY-CHAIN PLANNING

Companies began to implement enterprise resource planning (ERP) during the 1990s partly to improve the operation of their supply chains. Because ERP systems provided little planning capability, in the mid-1990s companies began to implement advanced planning and scheduling (APS) systems offered by such vendors as Chesapeake, i2, and Manugistics. In 1999, B2B eMarketplaces attracted media and managerial attention because they promised to lower procurement costs for buyers and increase revenues for sellers. The existing marketplaces are transaction-based so the APS and ERP vendors offer planning and planning-related collaboration. These vendors include i2 (tradeMatrix), Manugistics (bStreamz), Oracle (OracleExchange), and SAP (mySAP.com). Also, such industry efforts as collaborative planning for forecasting and replenishment (CPFR) have reported success (Ireland and Bruce, 2000) and will likely expand beyond retail by helping firms understand the benefits and changes needed in business processes and technology. Achieving planning capability in online marketplaces may still take time, partly because the current focus is tackling the complexity of B2B transactions that go beyond spot-based sales. So far companies have not implemented ERP and APS systems widely, so I expect companies will continue to implement these systems in the near future.

B2B eCommerce implies at least two planning-related challenges:

1. *Training and reengineering*: Planning is conceptually difficult, and operations personnel and planners have developed a variety of rules, which they must revise to implement a new planning process or technology. Planning within the firm is difficult enough, but collaborative

planning across firms via marketplaces, hubs, or direct links is even harder because the firms' planning systems and processes may be different. For a company to change its planning processes as it is changing execution processes by adopting B2B eCommerce is doubly challenging.

2. *System architecture*: An architecture that is appropriate for planning—local, hosted by an application service provider (ASP), or provided by a marketplace—is neither obvious nor easily standardized for all marketplace participants. For instance, near-term planning requires transactions data that may be in the firm's ERP system or in the marketplace. Forecasting requires historical data on orders over an extended period of time, and preferably in a data warehouse local to the company. Collaborative planning by trading partners requires sharing information so the eMarketplace would be appropriate for that.

The chemical industry was a leader in operations research and planning technologies during the 1970s and 1980s, but its heavy ERP investment and ongoing implementations make training and reengineering truly daunting. As to developing a system architecture appropriate for collaborative planning, vendors have announced that they will provide such systems. Several German chemical companies have adopted mySAP and SAP's planning solution, and e-Chemicals promises planning functionality, possibly through its partnership with Aspen Technologies, but it is not yet clear what the architecture is or will be.

TRACKING AND MONITORING

ERP systems provide adequate information for monitoring order status and fulfillment within the company. During the 1990s, tracking was therefore not emphasized. However, B2B eCommerce increases the importance of tracking orders and shipments across companies. Not surprisingly, a chemical company that conducted a survey of its customers found that their top online needs were "notification of pending delay" and "immediate order confirmation." Current tracking systems are piecemeal. The "glass pipeline" notion of providing complete transparency for order status and inventories remains unrealized. Companies (or eMarketplaces) must decide how much visibility they can reasonably provide. Five piecemeal solutions exist for tracking orders and shipments across companies, each with problems:

1. *EDI*: Large firms have used EDI to share information with their large suppliers, customers, and carriers. Vendors of transportation planning software, such as Manugistics, sell software that uses EDI for carrier-shipper

communication, but EDI is too expensive and inflexible for most small companies. Hybrid EDI and XML (eXtensible Markup Language) solutions are expected to broaden the use of EDI and extend its life. However, for both EDI and XML new standards specific to different industries are appearing, which may help within an industry but not trading between companies in different industries.

2. *Integrated carriers*: Such carriers such as FedEx and UPS can provide tracking information because their transportation and tracking information systems are integrated within their companies. On the other hand, most common carriers—trucking companies, railroads, airlines, ships, and even pipelines—are not integrated in the same sense, and they cannot provide detailed tracking information, nor do they always provide it electronically. The lack of a single standard among common carriers and warehouses hinders tracking as shipments change hands en route to the destination. For instance, airlines and freight-forwarders have struggled for almost a decade to build common processes and technology with which to track packages all the way from shippers to consignees. Integrated carriers cannot possibly transport all freight for eMarketplaces; they will have to rely on a multitude of transportation providers using collaborative information systems, but these provides may not be able to provide detailed real-time shipment information as the integrated carriers do. Some eMarketplaces may choose to work with one specific carrier for all shipments who can provide good tracking information; however, no single carrier can transport all freight for a marketplace that serves a large or global market.

3. *Linking ERP systems*: Trading companies may also link their ERP systems to provide visibility into inventory and order status. Many companies establish bilateral links to do this. However, linking more than two companies' ERP systems is technologically daunting. Moreover, it does not help the firms to track shipments.

4. *Internet-based services or software*: During the 1990s, some vendors offered Internet-based solutions for tracking shipments through a company's supply chain. Internet-based solutions allowed companies to track shipments from suppliers through the inbound distribution network to the company's plants and their finished goods through the outbound distribution network all the way to the customers. These vendors included the British firm M-Star, acquired by i2 in 1998, and the Dutch firm Calixon, acquired by the Canadian firm Descartes in 1999. Such solutions could be useful additions to B2B commerce, although it is not yet clear how i2 will leverage the M-Star product for its B2B

marketplace technology, tradeMatrix. Similarly, even though Descartes has created a Web-based tracking solution, it is not clear how eMarketplaces will use it.

5. *Vendor-managed inventory (VMI)*: Vendors (suppliers) in some industries (chemical and retail, for example) may monitor inventory at their customers' sites for automatic replenishment. Wal-Mart has used this idea successfully with its major suppliers, albeit with heavy IT investment, by transmitting point-of-sale data to the suppliers who then replenish the shelves. Inventory at the customer site may be owned by the supplier and bought by the customer only when used, or owned by the customer and simply monitored by the supplier for replacement. The idea is attractive for many companies, but there are no standard solutions. ERP vendors, such as SAP, support VMI for various industries, but ERP systems by themselves cannot monitor inventory. On the other hand, many tank-monitoring technologies in the petroleum industry use ordinary telephone-modem-based connections, but, not being linked to ordering systems or ERP, these monitoring technologies do not yet trigger orders automatically.

The chemical industry has tried or is trying these piecemeal solutions but faces challenges, perhaps even more so than other industries. It is developing its own XML standard, but it is not clear how this will work with sales to other industries or whether everyone within the industry will follow the same standard. Integrated carriers for this industry are almost unthinkable given the volumes shipped and the global reach required. Moreover, tracking shipments is especially challenging for the chemical industry because a gallon of benzene or a pound of polymer resin cannot be bar-coded for tracking in storage and transit. Some companies are trying to devise Web-based monitoring solutions: one company is building a Web-based solution to monitor inventories in its petroleum and chemical tanks so it can bill customers in real-time as they withdraw inventory from its tanks. The chemical transportation eMarketplace ShipChem is promising shipment-tracking functionality in the future, but it will likely be quite rudimentary for several years. Linking ERP systems through such marketplaces as Envera or Elemica or via bilateral links like PolyOne is an attractive option for the industry because of its large ERP investment. Finally, regarding VMI, Shell Chemicals has created a hybrid Web- and Lotus-Notes-based solution to replenish its customers' inventories, but no standards have emerged from this solution for widespread use within the industry.

CONCLUSION

The advent of the Internet in commerce and the attendant hype created false hopes about its capabilities to plan and execute orders in the supply chain and to monitor them, but substantial supply-chain challenges remain for B2B eCommerce, many of which carry over from before the Internet became so important. Although eMarketplaces have grabbed a lot of media attention, thus far they have provided very little supply-chain functionality. Companies must first address the existing problems they have in managing their supply chains while they wait for better B2B eCommerce channels or attempt to create them. By solving their long-term deficiencies in supply-chain management, they will be prepared for B2B eCommerce as it matures.

The lesson applies to the chemical industry. For any chemical company to do well in the world of eBusiness, it must set its own house in order first. If succeeding in eBusiness requires integrating deeply with other companies' ERP systems bilaterally or through eMarketplaces, the company must have its own ERP system in order. If a company wishes to go from available-to-promise to capable-to-promise functionality via the Internet, it must be able to plan production in near real-time. If the company wishes its favorite eMarketplace to provide order-status and shipment-tracking information to customers, it must be able to provide its share of that information. The hardest, yet most crucial task that lies before any company is to determine what supply-chain functionality it must develop itself and what it can leverage from the eMarketplaces it will join. Looking within is a good start.

REFERENCES

AMR. (2000). mySAP.com gets a boost from German chemical companies. *AMR Research*, March. Available on the World Wide Web at: http://www.amrresearch.com. Accessed September 15, 2000.

Cachon G. P. and Fisher, M. (2000). Supply chain inventory management and the value of shared information. *Management Science*, 46(8), 1032-1048.

Chopra, S. and Van Miegham, J. A. (2000). Which eBusiness is right for your supply chain? *Supply Chain Management Review*, 4(3), 32-40.

Christensen, L. (2000). Compliance at Internet speed. *Supply-Chain Management Review*, 4(4), 17-18.

Christie, J. (2000). Supply chains latch on to B2B commerce. RedHerring.com. Available on the World Wide Web at: http://www.redherring.com/industries/2000/1003/ind-supplychain100300.html. Accessed on February 19, 2001.

Dell, A. (2000). Meeting supplier demand. *Business 2.0*, March. Available on the

World Wide Web at: http://www.business2.com/content/magazine/ebusiness/2000/03/01/20666. Accessed on February 19, 2001.

Donahue, S. (2000). Supply traffic control: How i2 keeps Sun's global supply chain in its backyard. *Business 2.0*, February. Available on the World Wide Web at: http://www.business2.com/content/magazine/indepth/2000/02/01/12472. Accessed on February 19, 2001.

Elemica. (2000). Available on the World Wide Web at: http://www.elemica.com. Accessed on November 12, 2000.

Fisher, M. L. (1997). What is the right supply chain for your products? *Harvard Business Review*, March-April, 105-116.

Geoffrion, A. M. and Powers, R. F. (1995). Twenty years of strategic distribution system design: An evolutionary perspective. *Interfaces*, 25(5), 105-127.

Ireland, R. and Bruce, R. (2000). CPFR: Only the beginning of collaboration. *Supply-Chain Management Review*, 4(4), 80-88.

Kaplan S. and Sawhney, M. (2000). E-hubs: The new B2B marketplaces. *Harvard Business Review*, May-June, 97-103.

Lee, H. L. and Billington, C. (1992). Managing supply chain inventory: Pitfalls and opportunities. *Sloan Management Review*, 33.

Lee, H. L. and Billington, C. (1993). Material management in decentralized supply chains. *Operations Research*, 43(4), 546-558.

Lee, H. L., Padmanabhan, V. and Whang, S. J. (1997). Information distortion in a supply chain: The bullwhip effect. *Management Science*, 43(4), 546-558.

Mougayar, W. (2000). High times on the back end. *Business 2.0*, January. Available on the World Wide Web at: http://www.business2.com/content/magazine/indepth/2000/01/01/12549. Accessed on February 19, 2001.

O'Reilly, R. (2000). Chemicals: Basic. *Industry Surveys Report*, January. New York, NY: Standard & Poors.

Phillips, C. and Meeker, M. (2000). The B2B Internet report: Collaborative commerce, Morgan Stanley Dean Witter, Equity Research, North America. Available on the World Wide Web at: http://www.msdw.com/techresearch/B2B/info.html. Accessed on April 5, 2000.

Sodhi, M. (2000). Getting the most from planning technologies. *Supply Chain Management Review: Global Supplement*, 4(1), 19-23.

Sodhi, M. (2001). Applications and opportunities for operations research in Internet-enabled supply chains and electronic marketplaces. *Interfaces*, 31(2), 56-69.

Sterman, J. D. (1987). Testing behavioral simulation models by direct experiment. *Management Science*, 33(12),1572-1592.

Vasnetsov, S. and Kennedy, B. (2000). Chemical eCommerce 2.0. *Global Equity Research Report*, April. New York, NY: Lehman Brothers.

Chapter VIII

Business-to-Business Electronic Commerce: Electronic Tendering

Ahmad Kayed and Robert M. Colomb
University of Queensland, Australia

While there are many proposals to automate the buying and selling process, there has been no actual attempt to automate the tendering process (sealed auction). This chapter contributes toward the steps to move in this direction. In this chapter, the benefits of an on-line tendering system are clarified, the tendering process is analyzed, the current attempts are surveyed, the competency of EDI and on-line auctions approach is criticized, and a framework solution is proposed.

INTRODUCTION

The number of businesses and individuals through the world who are discovering and exploring the Internet is growing dramatically. The Internet is a cheap, open, distributed, and easy-to-use environment which provides an easy way to set up shop and conduct commerce at any place in the world (Lim et al., 1998).

Technology development represents a powerful driving force for the establishment of new methods of managing and organizing public procurement processes. Future development will make it possible to automate the tender process (Blomberg and Lennartsson, 1997; Slone, 1992). Electronic tendering may contribute to increase efficiency and effectiveness of the procurement process in terms of costs, quality, performance, and time for both buyers and sellers. The sellers' efficiency and effectiveness will be increased by applying electronic tendering techniques in terms of cuts to manpower costs, reduced administrative and transaction costs, improvements in tender quality, strengthened tender preparation capacity, simplified public market access, competitiveness, and high integration capability with internal and external systems (Blomberg and Lennartsson, 1997).

The use of electronic tendering reduces the processing time and cost of RFQ (request for quotes) (Madden and Shein, 1998; Shein, 1998). It allows analyzing the company's purchase activities, selecting the sellers more competitively, and reducing the time to get the best price. Since the Internet is open for all, buyers can order at any time and reach out to an array of qualified small and large businesses (Madden and Shein, 1998; Shein, 1998).

The development of an electronic infrastructure will create excellent opportunities for buyers to establish closer cooperation in many areas of great importance to them, such as coordinate tendering in order to increase their purchasing power and to minimize distribution and stock-keeping costs, exchange of supplier information, procurement plans, tender enquiry samples and technical specifications, legal and procedural aspects, etc. This cooperation between buyers may take place at any level in the community: locally, regionally, nationally, and even globally (Blomberg and Lennartsson, 1997).

This chapter is organized as following: Section 2 reviews the current efforts to facilitate on-line tendering. Section 3 analyzes the tendering process and reviews current related protocols. Section 4 discusses the related problems and points out what are still missing in electronic tendering. Section 5 discusses our framework for automating the tendering process, and Section 6 concludes the chapter.

ELECTRONIC TENDERING

Automating the tender process is a major goal for many international and governmental bodies. Many countries such as the USA, Canada, Europe, Australia, Mexico, etc. are adopting legislation to contend with some technological issues, mainly bonding and signatures. This will facilitate business on the Internet. Some examples are:

In the USA, General Electric Information Services Inc. produced Trading Process Network (TPN)(GEIS, Inc., 1999). TPN lets buyers prepare bids, select suppliers, and post orders to its Web site. Commerce One Inc. (1999b) allows the employees to access the Seller's Web catalogs, select items, and order them. Gateway (Business Gateway, 1999) is a mediator matching sellers and buyers. Suppliers and buyers go to the Business Gateway Web site (*www.businessgateway.com*) and fill out forms indicating what they have to buy or sell plus other information. Business Gateway then matches buyers and sellers (Madden and Shein, 1998). Ariba Technologies Inc. (1999) produces the Operating Resource Management System ORMS. ORMS lets a user open e-catalog for specific companies, create a purchase request, then it sends automatically for sign-off approval. ORMS lets a user create business rules that define the workflow and routing of the requests. SmartProcurement is developed by the National Institute for Standards and Technology and Enterprise Integration Technologies as a prototype to automate the tender process, mainly the RFQ (Smart Procurement, 1996; EIT Inc., 1996; Cutkosky et al., 1993). The system is initiated by RFQ, then a buyer agent acquires a list of registered vender agents for that item. Finally the buyer agent collects the bids submitted before the deadline and selects the best bid (O'Leary et al., 1997). The SmartProcurement system uses two evolving computer technologies: the World Wide Web (WWW) and software agents.

The Mexican Government started a plan for on-line tendering, in a project called Compranet (Noriega, 1997; *Compranet*, 1999). The main aim is to incorporate IT into small and medium companies. The Mexican Government regulates the procurement process in such a way that most acquisitions are made through a form of sealed bid auction. The call for tenders is announced via the Internet through Compranet. It is possible to submit tenders by Internet (Noriega, 1997).

SIMAP (Simaptests Projects, 1999) is a European project whose objective is to develop the information systems infrastructure needed to support the delivery of an effective public procurement policy in Europe, by providing contracting entities and suppliers with the information they need to manage the procurement process effectively (Simaptests Projects, 1999). Eventually, the project will address the whole procurement process, including bids, award of contracts, delivery, invoicing, and payment (Simaptests Projects, 1999). SIMAP depends on EDIFACT specification in building up their information system. They collect samples of different EU tender documents and try to make mapping between the common elements in these documents and EDIFACT 850 (EDFACT Purchase Order Message) to facilitate on-line tendering. The full specification of this project can be found in Blomberg and Lennartsson (1997).

Tenders on the Web (1999) is produced by Context Ltd., an electronic publishing company based in the UK. Context is a gateway provider for Tenders Electronic Daily (TED), the database hosted by the European Commission Host Organization (ECHO). All public sector purchasing in the EU over a certain value has to be advertised and tenders invited. TED provides information about public sector purchasing in the EU (*Tenders on the Web*,

1999).

In Canada anyone can connect to a bulletin board called New Brunswick Opportunities Network to view tender information (1999). MERX (1999) is Canada's Electronic Tendering Service which aims to provide access to procurement opportunities from the federal, provincial, and municipal governments across Canada. BIDS (1999) is another Canada's company which plays the role of mediator. The sellers tell BIDS what products or services they sell. When tenders are issued from any buying agencies, BIDS notifies the relevant sellers.

In Australia, TenderSearch (1999) is a company providing Australian businesses with a tender information service. TenderSearch use the Internet to provide this information. This helps them to provide a timely, accurate, and up–to–date service to many businesses (TenderSearch, 1999).

The main difference among these applications is which party will control the other. As we see it, we have three parties: the buyer, the seller, and the mediator; and we have four approaches to deal with this issue: (1) buyer puts his own tender and forces sellers to fill in the blanks, (2) the sellers put the standard and the buyer follows, (3) all must follow the pre-agreed standards, or (4) no one forces anyone. In the last case the mediator matches between sellers and buyers.

These systems were not designed to inter-operate in complementary stages to provide a full electronic tendering system. They support only buying or selling one item at a time. No system supports multiple items from multiple sellers. They focus in how to choose the lower price, and little attention has been given to manipulate the conditions or item specifications. In an agent-mediated system, they used a simple and direct agent communication to avoid the network overhead and ontology problems (Ong and Ng, 1998).

ELECTRONIC TENDERING PROCESS ANALYSIS

To automate any business process, we have to define the specification and execution of the process. General definitions include activities to be performed, their control flow and data exchange, organizational roles of persons and software components that are to perform activities, and policies that describe the organizational environment (Merz et al., 1996; Workflow Management Coalition, 1996).

To automate the tender process, we need to subdivide the process into atomic tasks, define each task, the interactions among these tasks, control flow and data exchange, the interrelated problems among these tasks, and determine which task should be or not be automated. Moreover we need to define the roles, and the interactions among these roles. In the following section we will define the main actors and activities of the tendering process.

There are two types of business models, transactional and non-transactional business models. The non-transactional business models include searching the Web for an item but completing the transaction via other means like fax or phone; advertising on the Web; and intermediaries. There are three different transactional business models on the Web (Stark et al., 1997):

- Browse, select, and purchase model: This is the most popular on the Web. Internet Shopper Web site (www.internetshopper.com) lists more than 25,000 on-line stores, this popularity gained from its simplicity.
- The Auction Model: In this model, the customers bid for individual items.
- The Bid Model: This is a business–to–business application. Instead of going out to find suppliers, businesses use the WEB as a channel to post their Request for Tender.

To analyze the process, we review the scope of the process, define the main actors and activities, point out to the system(s) that try to automate these activities, and indicate the missing issues needed to put the tendering on-line.

Tendering Activities and Actors:

The tendering process involves three actors:

- Buyers who are looking to purchase a service from sellers.
- Sellers or the suppliers who offer the services.
- Mediators (Brokers) who facilitate communication between buyers and sellers.

Tendering activities can be categorized into interaction and non-interaction activities. Interaction activities are the activities that contain more than one actor. Tender document interchange, tender invitation, tender return, tender advertising, negotiation, communication, collaboration, and matching between the sellers and buyers can be considered as this type. Non-interaction activities are activities which involve only one participant. Forming and evaluating the tender, forming the bid, data maintenance, and templates repository are considered in this category.

In the following, we will describe each actor's activity and point out to the system(s) that are needed to automate this activity. Table 1 summarizes these activities.

The Buyer Activities

Table1. The Roles and Activities of Tendering Process

Buyer	Seller	Mediator
-Non Interaction Activities-		
Workflow Management	Catalogs Building	Templates Repository
Tender Forming	Bid or not to bid (DSS)	Data Maintenance
Bids Evaluation	Bid Forming	
-Interaction Activities-		
Tender Invitation	Information Collection	Advertising
Tender Advertising	Bid Submission	Reputation Building
Buyers' Collaboration	Catalogs Interoperability	Auction App.
		Standardized App.
		Buyer-Seller Matching

Although the buyer is a cornerstone for any procurement process, little attention has been given to automate the buyer's activities. The main non-interaction buyer's activities are forming the tender and evaluating the bids. The well-known examples that support the automation of these activities are word processing and spreadsheet. The main buyer's interaction activities are: tender invitation and tender advertising, tender document interchange, collecting the return bids, negotiation, communication and collaboration. In the following we will discuss some of these activities.

Tender Forming: Forming the tender is an important step in the tendering process. King and Mercer (1988) argue that less detailed specification may mean the buyer has to evaluate different design features. Modelling this can be very difficult for both buyers and sellers. Gabb and Henderson (1996) also state that a poor specification will make the development of the evaluation model very difficult.

In a survey (Department of Defence, 1994), which encompasses 80 firms, among the reasons for unsuccessful tenders were that the actual users don't participate in preparing the tenders. Any system should provide mechanisms for the end users to participate in forming the tender.

In forming the tender, we have two situations: one off tenders and frequent tenders. An example of the former is a tender to buy establishment equipment. The key issue here is how to collect the actual users' needs and how to convert these needs to formal specifications. In other words, how to reduce the gap between the buyer's need and the sellers' offers to form a detailed specified tender. In this situation, attention must be given to automate the communications among parties, clustering the user's needs, converting needs to sellers' specifications, and facilitate negotiation among all parties.

Usually the tendering or sealed auction is used by governmental or large organizations to purchase or sell valuable things. In general, the buyer forms two committees to deal with tenders: one dealing with legal issues and the other dealing with specification and technical issues and providing recommendation to the first one. A system is needed here to support these activities and to coordinate the interactions between committees.

Generally, in the one off situation, the buyer consults someone else to write the tender, so the process will be repeated but with different items and/ or different parties. Construction contracts and oil exploration rights are examples of frequent tenders. In this situation, problems like how to learn from experience and how to extract knowledge form experience should be given more attention.

Bid Evaluation Activity: The main activity on the buyer side is how to choose the best bid. A formal economic mechanism to perform this activity is the auction. Auction theory is a complex economics subject. Auction is an economic mechanism in which the buyers bid for an item following a predetermined set of rules (McAfee and McMillan, 1987; Wurman et al., 1998b). In the sealed-bid auction (*tendering*), the participants do not learn the status of an auction until the end of the auction.

Usually the lower price determines the rule of selecting the best bid. Vickery (1961) proved that using the second lowest price policy (Vickery mechanism) will reduce counter-speculation. Some of the on-line auctions (Tsvetovatyy et al., 1997) used Vickery mechanisms as a policy to chose among bids. In some countries the lowest price is selected with some restrictions, as in Saudi Arabia the bid should be not less than 70 percent of the cost estimate (Hatush, 1996).

Hatush et. al. (Hatush and Skitmore, 1998; Hatush, 1996) use Multi-Attribute Utility Theory (MAUT) to build a model for bid evaluation. In their model, the main criteria besides the price were financial soundness, technical ability, management capabilities, safety performance, and reputation. King and Phythian (1992) proposed repertory grids to elicit the knowledge from expert managers involved in bids evaluation. Using statistical techniques, they determined the key factors in evaluating bids.

In automating bid evaluation activity, we should not think in forms of one-to-one correspondence to the manual work. Usually sellers provide many documents to prove their abilities to win the tender. An electronic certificate issued from a legal body can measure the ability of sellers. Moreover buyers could register terms of qualification at this legal body, and the electronic certification issued only for the sellers that meet these terms.

The Seller Activities

The seller side in the tendering process is well discussed in economics, knowledge-based, knowledge extracting, expert system, decision support systems, information management systems, security, and other disciplines.

Stark and Rothkope (1979) gave 500 titles which deal with models related to competitive bidding. These titles include ad hoc advice to bidders, analytical models and evaluations of auctions. Many of these titles discussed the construction contract, oil exploration rights, and securities.

The main non-interaction activities for the seller are done to develop catalogs, bid or not to bid, and form the bids to win. The seller interaction activities are: know about the tenders, submit the bid, and tender document interchange. In the following we will discuss some of these activities.

To bid or not to bid. This activity is related to many disciplines. It is normally discussed in the form of competitive bidding. There are many approaches treating this activity. King and Mercer (1988) categorized these approaches into four topics. These are:

- The basic probabilistic approaches
- The probabilistic strategy approaches
- The game theoretic approaches
- The non-price approaches

King and Phythian (1992) proposed a repertory grid to elicit knowledge from expert managers involved in bid evaluation. Using statistical techniques, they determined the key factors in evaluating bids. These factors were used to build an expert system to support the decision to bid or not to bid. Ward and Chapman (1988) proposed an informational framework procedure to support sellers in preparing their bids. Vanwelkenhuysen (1998) proposed a tender support system to improve the tender-to-order-to-production process for a pump company.

Dawood (1996) surveyed bidding approaches. He criticizes the mathematical approach (game and probabilistic models) for the lack of managerial knowledge of such models, and that these models are incomplete and model only a tiny part of the situation. He summarized his opinion in the following points:

- Probability theories alone are not sufficient to model bidding problems.
- Expert systems offer a good base for building bidding models, but the user should verify the knowledge rules and the inference engine, and this can be very time consuming.
- Neural Networks (NNs) are relatively simple to develop and require less time and effort. However, the black box nature of NNs make them less popular.
- The integration between information systems and expert systems can provide advice and information to aid the management in the bidding problem.

Franklin and Reiter (1996) proposed a secure sealed-auction protocol to solve traditional sealed-auction problems. McAfee and McMillan (1987) and Guttman and Kasbah (1998) raised the winner's curse problem where the winning bid value is greater than the product's market valuation.

Mediators' Activities

The electronic broker plays an important role in cyberspace. A broker is a party which mediates between buyers and sellers in a marketplace. Brokers play an integral part in some procurement transactions. Brokers are often useful when a marketspace has a large number of buyers and sellers, when the search costs are relatively high, or when trust services are necessary (Bichler et al., 1998). Mediators or intermediaries provide automated assistance for electronic tendering through knowledge of the market and the requirements of these markets. Mediators with their knowledge help the buyers inspect the goods electronically (Lee, 1997). More specifically, mediators provide knowledge of the market, requirements analysis, and negotiation (Robinson, 1997). Tendering process needs to combine disparate information sources. A possible approach is through the use of *mediators*, which can perform a customized integration. A mediator can reduce the gap between the buyer specification (which is general) and the seller specification (which is more technical). Another typical role of a mediator is to provide value-added services. In summary, mediators provide mediation, coordination, integration, negotiation, matching, and searching services.

There are two mechanisms to cope with the mediator's roles: auctioning and standardization mechanisms. In the following we will review the two approaches.

Auction Mechanism. Auction acts as a mediator among buyers and sellers (Lee, 1997). Yahoo (Wurman et al., 1998a) lists 95 on-line auctions. There are several prototypes and protocols for on-line auctions (Smith, 1980; Sandholm and Lesser, 1995; Wurman et al., 1998a; Michigan Internet AuctionBot, 1998; Moukas et al., 1998; Onsale Auction, 1998; Tsvetovatyy et al., 1997; Wurman et al., 1998b; Mullen and Wellman, 1998; Chavez and Kasbah, 1996; Lee, 1997; Rodríguez-Aguilar et al., 1998; Noriega, 1997; Collins et al., 1997; Sun and Weld, 1995). In the following we state some significant examples.

Smith (1980) pioneered research in communication among distributed agents with the Contract Net Protocol (CNP) (Collins et al., 1998). Smith's model is based on the sealed bid auction which works in a cooperative agent environment. In this model, each contractor is allowed to make only one bid, and the bids of the other contractors are not revealed to him (Smith, 1980).

Sandholm et. al. (Sandholm, 1993; Sandholm and Lesser, 1995; Sandholm,

1996) extended the CNP. In this model, each agent accepts deals which are profitable to it, based on marginal cost computations. They negotiate only the marginal cost within the announce-bid-award cycle. The agents are self-interested, and each agent negotiates directly with each other.

Kasbah (Guttman and Kasbah, 1998; Chavez and Kasbah, 1996) is a Web-Based multi-agent classified ad system where users create agents to buy and sell on their behalf. A user wanting to buy or sell a good creates an agent, gives it some strategic direction, and sends it off into a centralized agent marketplace. Kasbah agents seek out potential buyers or sellers and negotiate with them on behalf of their owners. Each agent's goal is to complete an acceptable deal, subject to a set of user-specified constraints such as desired price, a highest or lowest acceptable price, and a date by which to complete the transaction.

Rodríguez-Aguilar et al. (1998) and Noriega (1997) built an agent-mediated auction house for a fish market which was based on the Dutch auction bidding protocol. Bichler et al. (1998) proposed a prototype called OFFER which is CORBA-based and uses the auction mechanisms to buy and sell. The AUCNET system is a centralized, on-line wholesale market in which cars are sold using video images, character-based data, and a standardized inspector rating (Lee, 1997). Cathay Pacific (www.cathaypacific.com) used an electronic sealed-bid to sell airline tickets.

MAGMA (Tsvetovatyy et al., 1997; Collins et al., 1998) is a generalized multi-agent architecture that supports complex agent interaction. Examples of such interactions are: negotiation protocols, automated contracting, sealed-bid auction, and open-bid or advertised-price buying and selling. In this model, the agent negotiates with other agents through market sessions. A session is a mediator through which services are delivered to participating agents. A market's registry is used to find an agent willing to bid in call-for-bids request.

AuctionBot (Michigan Internet AuctionBot, 1998) is a general purpose auction server at the University of Michigan. A user creates an auction from a list of auction types and enters its parameters (e.g., the number of sellers, clearing time, etc.). The buyers and sellers can bid according to the negotiation protocol of the created auction.

Lim et al. (1998) proposed communication architecture for a commerce system. They proposed three types of agents: buyers, sellers and a directory agent. The agent could deal with user interface, thread manager, price manager, communication module, and log manager. Agent communication protocol is partitioned into four phases: specify the product, search for relevant sellers, choose the best seller (negotiation phase), and make payment.

Standardization Mechanism. The other main role of a mediator is to provide a common view between the buyers and sellers so they can understand each other, i.e., standards. Mediators provide standards to facilitate integration, cooperation, and communication among different actors, mainly buyers and sellers. Also the standard provides a mechanism so all the parties can understand the structure of the tender documents. A standard helps to solve the interaction problems among actors, and this will facilitate the automation of the non-interaction activities.

The well-known standard protocol for interbusiness transactions is Electronic Data Interchange (EDI). EDI has two standard protocols: private (ANSI X12) and public (UN EDIFACT ISO 9735) (Kalakota and Whinston, 1996). EDI transfers structured data by agreed message standard between computer applications. EDI has been extensively and successfully implemented, and is growing in popularity. EDI is also inflexible, insufficient, ambiguous, closed, expensive, slow, and supports only one-to-many relationships (Kimbrough and Moore, 1997; Wing, 1998; Kalakota and Whinston, 1996).

Lee and Dewitz (1992) proposed AI extensions to EDI to facilitate international contracting. Slone (1992) suggests adding functionality to the current EDI standards to automate the tendering process. Blomberg and Lennartsson (1997) proposed new functionality to the current EDIFACT 850 (EDFACT Purchase Order Message) to facilitate on-line tendering.

The trend now is to use XML as a basis to standardize the procurement process (Glushko et al., 1999). Examples of these are EDI/XML, ICE (Information and Content Exchanges), OPT (open trading protocol), OBI (open buying on the Internet), OFI (Open Financial Exchange), etc.

Other protocols that encourage corporations to initiate payments through the Internet and other public networks by increasing system security are: Secure Sockets Layer (SSL), Secure Electronic Transactions (SET), Bank Internet Payment System (BIPS), Joint Electronic Payments Initiative (JEPI), and Open Financial Exchange (OFX).

An example of a system that tries to integrate the current standard protocols and provides an interoperability framework is eCo system (Glushko et al., 1999). eCo began as an architectural vision for open Internet commerce (Tenenbaum et al., 1997). eCo system is led by CommerceNet Consortium (1999) which was considered as a CORBA-based interoperability framework. In 1997, eCo systems adopted the XML framework. eCo tries to integrate the current standards by providing the Business Interface Definitions (BIDs) through the Common Business Library (CBL) (Glushko et al., 1999). CBL includes XML templates for EDI X12, OPT, ICE, OFX, and OBI.

These templates can be customized and are easily understood by agents as well as people (Glushko et al., 1999). A company can define its business interface and communicate with another company even when the other company subscribes to different standards.

Keller (1995), presents an architecture for smart and virtual catalogs to solve interoperability problems between heterogeneous e-catalogs. In his approach, companies create smart catalogs of searchable, machine-sensible product information. Retailers and distributors create virtual catalogs that provide customers with product information dynamically requested from manufacturers' smart catalogs. Product data is stored in a database which communicates with a catalog agent which communicates with a facilitator agent broker. Facilitators identify the agents that support a user request.

ELECTRONIC TENDERING–RELATED PROBLEMS

The Internet is an open environment, widely distributed, and relatively cheap. Business transactions usually run under closed environments. To conduct business on the Internet, many problems must be solved. Examples of these problems are: security, authentication, heterogeneity, interoperability, and ontology problems.

In a large-scale and dynamic environment, the matching between the buyer's request and the seller's offer is nontrivial (Mullen and Wellman, 1998). EU uses a tendering mechanism to purchase about 480 billion Pounds with 150,000 procurement notices a year dealing with 600 to 800 procurement documents every morning. It is worth notifying the sellers only with relevant tenders instead of dealing with 600 documents (Tenders on the Web, 1999).

Current EC applications require users to search or locate relevant Web sites for purchasing goods themselves. This is not only time consuming, but it is extremely difficult to perform exhaustive searching on the Web (Vollrath et al., 1998). Current EC solutions do not provide a mutual mediation process to reach agreement among the buyers and sellers (Kang and Lee, 1998).

On-line marketplaces are both an opportunity and a threat to retail merchants. They are an opportunity because they offer a new channel to advertise and lower the transaction costs. They are also a threat because many on-line marketplaces are limited to price comparison—they do not consider added value services in their comparison. The retailers add value to manufacturers' products to distinguish themselves from their competitors (Guttman et al., 1998).

One of the problems in bid evaluation is the large number of seller's documents needed to win the tender. These documents are unstructured and vary from one seller to another. This limits the buyers' ability to choose the most qualified bidder.

A tender is a very complicated document. It has general terms, specific terms, optional terms, compulsory terms, items and specification for these items. Sellers like to add more specification and value-added services to win the tender. This make the comparison among bids a very complicated problem. Many EC applications are using the Internet as an underlying platform. Internet users need tools to search for information across heterogeneous systems and to match potential data sources with their needs. Consumers also need to search for information using terms from domains they are familiar with (ontologies) (Adam et al., 1998).

The integration among disparate information systems is needed to facilitate the automation of the tendering process. This will speed up the emergence of the new generation of business–to–business electronic commerce. The difficult problem here is how to combine disparate information sources to integrate them in an open environment like the Internet (Silberschatz et al., 1995).

The sheer volume of information available on the Web represents a very real problem (Jennings and Wooldridge, 1997). Everyday, we are presented with enormous amounts of information, only a tiny proportion of which is relevant or important. The volume of information available prevents us from finding information that meets our requirements.

Tendering process activities are dependent, i.e., simplifying one activity can simplify or complicate other activities. In the literature, the attempts to automate the tendering process were focused on one side of the problem, i.e., automating the interaction activities or the non-interaction activities. The challenge here is to link these disparate systems together and provide a new infrastructure that receives benefits from these systems.

The sealed auction *(tendering)* has different characteristics from the other types of auctions, in particular the outcry auction. The current auction protocols deal with the sealed auction without giving any attention to these characteristics. Sealed auction is not treated well in the on-line auction. Auctions deal with single-item, specific, well-known items, price mechanisms, simple terms, and are always centralized. On-line auctions provide a good background for the sealed auction, but for automating the tendering process there are many things still missing. The on-line auction automates an individual to business process while the tendering process is considered as a business–to–business process.

The seller side in the tendering process is well discussed in many disciplines. But very little attention was given to the buyer side. The role of the buyer is important in the tendering process and his activities (tender forming, bid evaluations, etc.) should be given more attention.

EDI and other standard protocols provide standards for content and transactions in the procurement process, but there are many things still missing. These standards need a super standard to be integrated. It is difficult to adopt a common domain-specific standard for content and transactions, particularly in cross-industry initiatives, where companies cooperate and compete with one another (Smith and Poulter, 1999). Moreover the open standards are not opened. Standards are inflexible, not scalable, expensive, and closed. Standards need a pre-agreement between the participants, and it takes time to be widely adopted.

PROPOSED SOLUTION

Tendering is well addressed in many disciplines and there are many commercial systems automated in the process or a part of the process. In summary, the tendering systems involve workflow, data analysis, security, EDI, DSS, searching, matching, monitoring, payments, and many other automated and non-automated activities. We are interested in automating the informational part of three activities: forming the tender, matchmaking, and bid evaluation. An agent-based system is needed for tender forming. A knowledge-based system is needed to store tender information and enable the mediator to perform matchmaking and bid filtration.

To deal with that huge number of participants, our solution will be agent-oriented. Agents are personalized, continuously running, and semiautonomous (Guttman et al., 1998). These features help us in resolving many problems. Software agents will help in filtering the huge number of tenders. This will help the buyer and the seller at the same time.

Our architecture is composed of three layers: the buyer (customer) layer, the mediator layer, and the seller (supplier) layer. Each layer communicates with other layers using direct or indirect messages. The buyer layer contains the coordinator management (CM) and the matching management (MM). The mediator layer has the trusted party (TP), ontology management (OM), and the advertising management (AM). The seller layer is composed of the coordinator management (CM), the matching management (MM), catalogs management (CAM), and the Web management WebM (Figure 1).

Our solution is mediator-based. The mediator performs two types of operations: service-oriented and system-oriented operation. Service-oriented covers the provision of services to customers. Service identification, service request, agreement, and past agreement are examples of service-oriented operations. The system-oriented operations cover the systems that provide the users with some Value-Added Operations. Search, browse, meta-data, profiles, and catalogs are examples of system services (Gallego et al., 1998).

A buyer can submit three types of request to the mediator. These are request for more information, request of invitation, or request of tendering advertising. On the seller side, sellers can submit two types of request: find relevant tenders or general request about any tender details.

The buyers' requests help them to advertise and form their tenders. For buyers we have two situations:

- Buyers know exactly their needs and are looking to advertise these needs in the mediator knowledge-based repositories in the terminology of the mediator.
- Buyers need more information about some of the items' specifications prior to performing step one.

The buyer creates an agent to collect information about some items or services. The agent asks the mediator (i.e., the AM agents). The mediator makes matching between the queries and the profile, and returns the address of the sellers' agents. The buyer agent asks the seller agent who may ask their catalog agent about this service. The buyer agent collects and summarizes the results for the buyer. CM coordinates the agent interactions and MM summarizes the answers with the help of OM agents.

We need the following components to implement our framework:

- Formal (logical) structures
- Formal ontologies
- Agent models
- Knowledge repositories and system tools

In the following subsections, we will discuss each component of the framework.

Formal (logical) Structures

Using natural language to model tendering makes any process associated with tendering automation extremely difficult. Since we are interested in storing the information in a knowledge base, we need a formal logical language to model our structures. In our system we use Conceptual Graphs (CGs). CGs are a method of knowledge representation developed by Sowa (1984) based on Charles Peirce's Existential Graphs and semantic networks in artificial in-

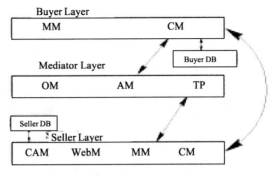

Figure 1. Tendering Framework Architecture

telligence (Sowa, 1995). According to Sowa (1984), CGs have a direct mapping to and from natural language and a graphic notation designed for human readability. Conceptual graphs have all the expressive power of logic but are more intuitive and readable. Many popular graphic notations and structures ranging from type hierarchies to entity-relationship or state transition diagrams can be viewed as special cases of CGs (Way, 1994). CGs are semantically equivalent graphic representation for first order logic (FOL) like Knowledge Interchange Format (KIF).

Using formal structures has advantages over the standardized approach (e.g., EDIFACT messages). The EDI approach needs a pre-agreement about everything, but here we just need to agree about the common ontology. The ontology contains abstract concepts that will form the primitives to construct a tender or a bid. This is more flexible and can be stored in a knowledge base. The ontology will make it easy to build tools to transfer from a friendly user interface (like the Web) to a logical structure (knowledge base). To build these structures, we modeled a real tender in conceptual graph. Then we extracted the primitive concepts from these models. These concepts were stored in the ontology. For specific situations, we built some tender templates using these formal structures. These concepts and templates were used to express the context, the rules and knowledge, and the agents (communication and queries). We will explain more about these structures in the following subsection.

Formal Ontologies

Since users tend to use their own tendering vocabulary, the mediator needs to maintain a common ontology to perform the service and the systems operations. Also the mediator uses the common ontology to define a context for similarity (Kashyap and Sheth, 1996).

In our project, we divided the ontology into three parts: collections of concepts, collections of conceptual structures, and collections of formal contexts. These all form our ontology (see Figure 2). The collections of concepts help us to build tools for translation and integration from one domain to another. The concept part

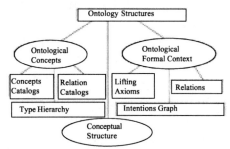

Figure 2. Ontology Structure

consists of three subparts. Those are: the catalog vocabularies, the relation vocabularies, and the hierarchical relation between concepts. The Conceptual Structures (CS) represents the basic element for the tendering system. Software agents use these CSs to communicate and interact. Buyers, sellers, and mediators use these structures to describe their needs, offers, responses, or queries. The formal context provides the mechanisms of defining the similarities between concepts. The formal contexts contain three parts: the intentions graph (the graph in which the graph will be asserted), the lifting axioms, and the relation (type-of, is-a, part-of, etc.). The lifting axioms help us in reusing the ontologies and knowledge.

Following our framework (Kayed and Colomb, 1999), we need four types of ontologies: meta-ontology, abstract domain ontology, domain ontology, and tendering ontology. In the following we will briefly describe each ontology.

The Meta-Ontology defines (describes) very general concepts for other ontologies. The meta-ontology helps to query the domain ontologies and to translate from and to the domain ontologies. This is a very abstract ontology and we built its components from other generic ontologies like Farquhar et al. (1997), Elkan and Greiner (1993), and Uschold et al. (1998). We reused the definition of time (Date, Days, Years, Hours) from the ontology server (Farquhar et al., 1997). We took the basic unit measures from Cyc ontology server (Elkan and Greiner, 1993). We also redefined some organizational concepts like entity, buyer, seller, agent, activity, process, etc. from the Enterprise Ontology (Uschold et al., 1998).

The Abstract Domain Ontology contains *Classes* which are abstract descriptions of objects in a domain. The class has Class-ID, Class-Properties, Class-Synonyms, Class-Type, Relation, Sub-Class, and Axioms. A relation is a link between classes, and axioms are rules that govern the behavior of the classes. The abstract domain ontology represents a container of abstract data types for sellers' catalogs. In this sense we should distinguish between the catalogs and the ontology. For example ontology may contain a PC as a concept, which has RAM and CPU as other concepts. Catalog may contain Pentium 3 with 32 MB RAM. In CGs sense, this can be translated to:

[PC:Dell]--->(Part-Of)--->[CPU-Type:Pentium3]--->(part-Of)--
>[Memory: RAM]<--(measure)<--[Memory-Unit: 32 MB]

The Domain Ontology is a collection of vocabularies mapped to concepts in the higher level ontology. Since the Abstract Domain Ontology (ADO) is a schema for the sellers catalogs, we should define mapping between these abstract concepts (in the ADO) and the catalog values. This is how we know that Dell computer is a PC concept.

The Tendering Ontology represents the core ontology in our system. The basic part of it is the Tendering Conceptual Structures (TCSs). We divide them into three models: buyer, seller, and mediator models. The buyer model is divided into advertising model, query model, and policy model. The advertising model again can be divided into tender invitation, terms, objects (services), specification, and returned forms. Two of the most important TCSs are the Tendering Invitation Structure (TIS) and the sellers' profile structure (SPS). It is beyond the scope of this chapter to describe everything in this ontology. Readers are encouraged to visit our ongoing works at Kayed (2000).

Agent Models

Buyers' agents contact the mediator through formal structures that are committed to the ontology which should be defined in the former stage. The mediator checks the profile repository, and depending on the buyers' strategies, determines the address of sellers' agents that match their needs. This stage is based on software agents. There are many methodologies to design an agent-oriented system. The common core of these methodologies is to define the internal agent model and external (environmental) agent model. The internal model focuses on modelling BDI (Belief, Desire, Intention). The external model focuses on how agents can interact and the role of each agent.

Since the agents work autonomously, the buyer provides the agent with strategies and policies to direct their behavior. These strategies are implemented in a matrix of desires (with default values) and some logical rules. A quality of service (QoS) is an example of these matrixes. QoS contains concepts from the ontology, and some fuzzy numbers measure seller's capability for that service. The TP is responsible for maintaining this matrix.

In our project we define three agent models. The role of agents is described in Agents Model. How the agents can interact is described in the

Interaction Agents Model. The internal behavior of each agent is defined in the BDI Model. In the following we will give a brief description for each model.

- Agents Model
  - Interface agents: Interface between user (buyers or sellers) and other agents (mediator agents)
  - Ontology agents: Maintain ontology, providing tools to browse ontologies, find the relation between two concepts, find equivalent concepts (terminology finder), etc.
  - Catalog agents: Maintain seller's catalog and answer other sellers' agents
  - Seller agents: Maintain seller's profile, answer buyer agent through the catalog's agents, look for new opportunities to inform the seller with relevant tenders
  - Matching agents: Determine how much two objects are similar. Object here may be a query, data source (seller profiles), tender, etc.
  - Summary agent: Summarize the returned answers in a table
- Interaction Agents Model
  - Agents Bulletin Board (ABB)
  - Agents messages
  - Global policies director
  - Ontological translator
  - Agent messages repository
- BDI model
  - Algorithms (Concepts matching, semantic correctness, similarity measures, etc.)
  - Local policies structures
  - Formal structures for messages, desire matrixes, strategies, quality of services, etc.
  - Translating tools

For more technical details, please visit Kayed (2000).

Knowledge Repository and System Tools

The mediator stores the tendering information in a knowledge-based repository and sends invitations to the relevant sellers. The mediator will be responsible for the following:

- Construct and maintain the knowledge base
- Construct and maintain the ontologies
- Maintain all the repositories (seller profiles, policies, agent profiles, etc.)

- Provide tools to use the above
- Tools provided by mediator are:
  - Repositories browsing tools
  - Matching tools and utilities
  - Tools to check the syntactic of profiles, tenders, queries, etc.
  - Translating tools + browsing the ontology
  - Tools to query ontology, profiles, tender, all the repositories
  - Bid filtration tools
- Repositories contains:
  - Logical messages
  - Rules of matching
  - Ontologies: tendering ontology, domain ontology, abstract domain ontology, and meta ontology
  - Profiles: buyers, sellers, and agent profiles
  - Policies
  - Advertising area
  - Bidding area

Discussion

Using ontological representation for tender modeling will facilitate bid evaluation. Following that, the procedure for bid selection will be simplified. Buyers submit their policies for bid selection, while the mediator checks the bids and tries to find the most bids that match the buyer policy.

As a business process, the mediator is not likely to decide which is the best bid. Mediator will perform a bid filtration by applying buyer desires and reduce the number of bids. Buyers are controlling the selection procedure through querying tools provided by mediator. Following these strategies, we will not violate any business rules.

One of the main operations of the mediator is matchmaking. In matchmaking the buyers/sellers advertise their needs/capabilities to the mediator (Sycara et al., 1999). The mediator uses the domain ontology to perform matchmaking. The needs/capabilities should be committed to the common ontology to perform this matchmaking.

Mediator receives users' structures (buyers or sellers) and checks their semantics. Mediator checks if the structures are canonically derived from the ontologies. Here we apply the algorithm of Mugnier and Chein (1993). This algorithm decides whether a conceptual graph is canonical relative to a given canonical basis (the repositories). The complexity of this algorithm is polynomial related to the complexity of computing a projection between two conceptual graphs. When the canonical basis is a set of trees, it is polynomial.

We defined two types of matching: soft-matching and concept matching. The soft-matching depends on the multi-attribute utility theory (MAUT) (Hatush, 1996). The tender is divided into classes, which may contain subclasses. The buyer provides a factor of importance (utility function) for each concept in each class in each level in the tender (the sum in each level should =100%). The mediator performs concept matching between the class concepts and the concepts in the seller profile. The concept matching returns a number which will be multiplied by the factor of importance up to a higher level which will determine the distance between the buyer request and sellers' offers.

Concept matching measures the distance between two concepts according to the common ontology. The distance between two concepts can be computed by the number of roles that subsume both concepts over the number of roles that subsume the buyer's concept. If the result is close to one, this means that the two concepts are similar.

CONCLUSION AND FUTURE WORK

Automating the tendering process is evolving and as it gets more advanced, the cost of automating this process will be reduced. Problems such as communication cost, legislation, security, and authentication will be reduced by that time. An open environment like the Internet and the huge number of participants will open new problems for both sellers and buyers. For the sellers, the problem is not just knowing about the tender; the problem will be whether this tender is relevant to the seller's domain. For the buyers, the problem is how to pick up only the relevant and qualified sellers that match their needs.

In this chapter we analyzed the tendering process, we surveyed the systems that automated fully or a part of the process. We pointed out the problem that should be resolved before putting the tendering on-line. We gave a general description of our framework.

We defined the role of ontology in automating the tendering process. We constructed our ontologies based on three components: the concepts, the structures, and the contexts. This decomposition facilitates the process of ontology building and reusing. We described our system of tendering automation focusing on the role of ontology. We clarified how the ontology would help in defining semantic matching. We have shown how the expressive power of CG helps in building ontologies and conceptual structures.

We introduced the concepts of layered ontologies. At the top level we used very abstract ontology which contains abstract data types for the domain ontology. Defining multiple levels of abstractions facilitates the transformation of catalog to ontology. One of the exciting areas here is to define the relation between the catalogs, standards, and ontologies. Catalogs are not interoperable. Standard catalogs are, but lack flexibility. The ontology is more flexible and provides interoperability between partners.

In future work, we will develop tools to translate from and to the common ontology. Besides soft matching and concepts matching, we will define data-mining facilities for bid evaluation. An expert agent will extract the concepts of a certain bid, using concept matching to find the items that best match the bid in similarity and cost. We intend to use the context to implement what we call soft-matching (Kayed and Colomb, 1999). This fuzziness will capture the buyers' policies that will direct the agent in finding buyers' needs.

ACKNOWLEDGMENT

The authors acknowledge the Department of CSEE at the University of Queensland for financial support for this project. Also we acknowledge anonymous referees who contributed to improving the ideas and readability of this chapter.

REFERENCES

Adam, N., Dogramaci, O., Gangopadhyay, A., and Yesha, Y. (August 1998). *Electronic Commerce: Technical, Business, and Legal Issues*. Prentice Hall (ISBN: 0-13-949082-5).

Ariba Technologies, Inc. (1999a). *Operating Resource Management System*. http://www.ariba.com/.

Bichler, M., Beam, C., and Segev, A. (1998). OFFER: A broker-centered object framework for electronic requisitioning. *Lecture Notes in Computer Science*, 1402, 154+.

BIDS (1999). *http://www.bids.ca/*.

Blomberg, P., and Lennartsson, S. (1997). *Technical Assistance in Electronic Tendering Development—FINAL REPORT*. Technical Assistance in Electronic Procurement to EDI—EEG 12 Subgroup 1. http://simaptest.infeurope.lu/EN/pub/src/main6.htm.

Business Gateway (1999). *www.businessgateway.com*.

Chavez, A., and Kasbah, P. M. (1996). Kasbah: An agent marketplace for buying and selling goods. In: *The First International Conference on the Practical Application of Intelligent Agent and Multi-Agent Technology*, UK, London.

Commerce Net Consortium (1999). *http://www.commercenet.org.uk.*

Collins, J., Jamison, S., Gini, M., and Mobasher, B. (1997). *Temporal Strategies in a Multi-Agent Contracting Protocol.* AAAI-97 Workshop on AI in Electronic Commerce.

Collins, J., Jamison, S., Mobasher, B., and Gini, M. (1998). A market architecture for multi-agent contracting. In: *Agent98, Proceedings of the Second International Conference on Autonomous Agents*, pages 285-292, ACM Press.

Commerce One, Inc.(1999b). *Real-Time Electronic Online System.* http://www.commerce-one.com/.

Compranet (1999). *Mexican On-line Trading.* http://crimson.compranet.gob.mx:8081/cnetii/plsql/principal.inicio.

Cutkosky, M., Fikes, R., Genesereth, M., Gruber, T., Mark, W., Tenenbaum, J., and Weber, J. (1993). *PACT: An Experiment in Integration Concurrent Engineering Systems.* http://www.eit.com/creations/papers/pact/.

Dawood, N. (1996). Strategy of knowledge elicitation for developing an integrated bidding/production management expert system for the precast industry. *Advances in Engineering Software [ADV ENG SOFTWARE]*, 25(2-3), 225-234.

Department of Defence (1994). *Costs of Tendering Industry Survey.* Australia Government Publishing Service, Canberra.

EIT, Inc. (1996). *http://www.eit.com/.*

Elkan, C., and Greiner, R. (1993). Book review of building large knowledge-based systems: Representation and inference in the CYC project (D.B. Lenat and R.V. Guha). *Artificial Intelligence*, 61(1), 41-52.

Farquhar, A., Fikes, R., and Rice, J. (1997). The ontolingua server: A tool for collaborative ontology construction. *International Journal of Human-Computer Studies*, 46(6), 707-727.

Franklin, M. K., and Reiter, M. K. (1996). The design and implementation of a secure auction service. *IEEE Transactions on Software Engineering*, 22(5), 302-312.

Gabb, A. P., and Henderson, D. E. (1996). Technical and operational tender evaluations for complex military systems. *Technical Report, Department of Defence–Defence Science and Technology Organisation (DSTO)-Australia*, Rep. No. DSTO-TR-0303.

Gallego, I., Delgado, J., and Acebron, J. (1998). Distributed models for brokerage on electronic commerce. *Lecture Notes in Computer Science*, 1402, 130-139.

GEIS Inc. (1999). *Trading Process Network.* http://tpn.geis.com/.

Glushko, R. J., Tenenbaum, J. M., and Meltzer, B. (1999). An XML framework for agent-based E-commerce. *Communications of the ACM*, 42(3), 106-109, 111-114.

Guttman, R. H., and Kasbah, P. M. (1998). Agent-mediated integrative negotiation for retail electronic commerce. *Knowledge Engineering Review*.

Guttman, R. H., Moukas, A. G., and Kasbah, P. M. (1998). Agent-mediated electronic commerce: A survey. *Knowledge Engineering Review*.

Hatush, Z. (1996). *PhD. Thesis: Contractor Selection Using Multi-Attribute Utility Theory*. School of Construction Management and Property, Queensland University of Technology-Australia.

Hatush, Z., and Skitmore, M. (1998). Contractor selection using multi-criteria utility theory: An additive model. *Building and Environment*, 33(2-3), 105-115.

Jennings, N. R., and Wooldridge, M. (1997). *Application of Intelligent Agents*. Queen Mary and Westfield College, University of London.

Kalakota, R., and Whinston, A. B. (1996). *Frontiers of Electronic Commerce*. Addison-Wesley Publishing Company, Inc.

Kang, J-Y., and Lee, E-S. (1998). *A Negotiation Model in Electronic Commerce to Reflect Multiple Transaction Factors and Learning*. Technical Report, School of Electrical and Computer Eng., SKKU, Seoul, Korea.

Kashyap, V., and Sheth, A. P. (1996). Semantic and schematic similarities between database objects: A context-based approach. *The VLDB Journal*, 5(4), 276-304.

Kayed, A. (2000). *Homepage*. http://www.csee.uq.edu.au/~kayed/.

Kayed, A., and Colomb, R. M. (1999). Infrastructure for electronic tendering interoperability. In *The Australian Workshop on AI in Electronic Commerce,* in conjunction with the *Australian Joint Conference on Artificial Intelligence (AI'99)* Sydney, Australia, ISBN 0643065520, pages 87-102.

Keller, A. M. (1995). Smart catalogs and virtual catalogs. In: *International Conference on Frontiers of Electronic Commerce*.

Kimbrough, S. O., and Moore, S. A. (1997). On automated message processing in electronic commerce and work support systems: Speech act theory and expressive felicity. *ACM-TOIS*, 15(4), 321-367.

King, M., and Mercer, A. (1988). Recurrent competitive bidding. *European Journal of Operations Research*, 33, 2-16.

King, M., and Phythian, G. J. (1992). Developing an expert support systems for tender enquiry evaluation: A case study. *European Journal of Operations Research*, 56, 15-29.

Lee, H. G. (1997). Electronic market intermediary: Transforming technical feasibility into institutional reality. In: *Thirtieth Annual Hawaii Interna-*

tional Conference on System Sciences, volume IV, pages 3-12.

Lee, R. M., and Dewitz, S. D. (1992). Facilitating international contracting: AI extensions to EDI. *International Information Systems,* January.

Lim, E-P., Ng, W-K., and Yan, G. (1998). Toolkits for a distributed, agent-based Web commerce system. In: *Proceedings of the International IFIP Working Conference on Trends in Distributed Systems for Electronic Commerce (TrEC'98)*, Hamburg, Germany.

Madden, J. and Shein, E. (1998). Web purchasing attracts some pioneers. *PC Week Online,* March 16.

McAfee, R. P., and McMillan, J. (1987). Auctions and bidding. *Journal of Economic Literature*, 25, 699-738.

MERX (1999). *http://www.merx.cebra.com/*.

Merz, M., Liberman, B., Muller-Jones, K., and Lamersdorf, W. (1996). Interorganisational workflow management with mobile agents in COSM. In: *Proceedings of PAAM96 Conference on the Practical Application of Agents and Multi-agent Systems*.

Michigan Internet AuctionBot (1998). *http://auction.eecs.mich.edu*.

Moukas, A., Guttman, R., and Maese, P. (1998). Agent-mediated electronic commerce: An mit media laboratory perspective. In: *The First International Conference on Electronic Commerce*, Seoul, Korea.

Mugnier, M. L., and Chein, M. (1993). Characterization and algorithmic recognition of canonical conceptual graphs. *Lecture Notes in Computer Science*, 699, 294+.

Mullen, T., and Wellman, M. P. (1998). The auction manager: Market middleware for large-scale electronic commerce. In: *Third USENIX Workshop on Electronic Commerce*, Boston, MA, USA.

New Brunswick Opportunities Network (1999). *http://inter.gov.nb.ca/index1.htm*.

Noriega, P. C. (1997). *PhD. Thesis: Agent Mediated Auctions: The Fishmarket Metaphor*. Universitat Autonoma de Barcelona–SPAIN.

O'Leary, D. E., Kuokka, D., and Plant, R. (1997). Artificial intelligence and virtual organizations. *Communications of the ACM*, 40(1), 52-59.

Ong, K-L. and Ng, W-K. (1998). A Survey of Multi-Agent Interaction Techniques and Protocols. *Technical Report, Centre of Advanced Information Systems*, CAIS-TR04-98, School of Applied Science, Nanyang Technological University, Singapore.

Onsale Auction (1998). *http://www.onsale.com*.

Robinson, W. N. (1997). Electronic brokering for assisted contracting of software applets. In: *Thirtieth Annual Hawaii International Conference on System Sciences*, volume IV, pages 449-458.

Rodríguez-Aguilar, J. A., Martín, F. J., Noriega, P., Garcia, P., and Sierra, C. (1998). Competitive scenarios for heterogeneous trading agents. In Sycara, K. P. and Wooldridge, M. (Eds.), *Proceedings of the 2nd International Conference on Autonomous Agents (AGENTS-98)*, pages 293-300, New York, ACM Press.

Sandholm, T. (1993). An implementation of the contract net protocol based on marginal cost calculations. In: *Eleventh National Conference on Artificial Intelligence (AAAI-93)*, pages 256-262, Washington DC.

Sandholm, T., and Lesser, V. (1995). Issues in automated negotiation and electronic commerce: Extending the contract net framework. In: *First International Conference on Multi-agent Systems*, San Francisco.

Sandholm, T. W. (1996). *PhD. Thesis: Negotiation Among Self-Interested Computationally Limited Agents*. Department of Computer Science, University of Massachusetts–Amherst.

Shein, E. (1998). Special Net delivery. *PC Week Online*, March 16.

Silberschatz, A., Stonebraker, M., and Ullman, J. (1995). Database research: Achievements and opportunities into the 21st century. *NSF Workshop on the Future of Database Systems Research*.

Simaptests Projects (1999). European Online Public Procurement. *http://simaptest.infeurope.lu/EN/pub/src/welcome.htm*.

Slone, A. (1992). Electronic data interchange and structured message usage. *Computer Standards and Interfaces*, 14(5-6), 411-414.

Smart Procurement (1996). *http://waltz.ncsl.nist.gov/ECIF/smart_procurement.html*.

Smith, H., and Poulter, K. (1999). Share the ontology in XML-based trading architectures. *Communications of the ACM*, 42(3), 110-111.

Smith, R. G. (1980). The contract net protocol: High level communication and control in a distributed problem solver. *IEEE Transaction on Computers*, C-29(12), 1104-1113.

Sowa, J. F. (1984). *Conceptual Structures: Information Processing in Minds and Machines*. Addison-Wesley, Reading, Mass.

Sowa, J. F. (1995). Syntax, semantics, and pragmatics of contexts. *Lecture Notes in Computer Science*, 954,1+

Stark, H., Stevenson, M., and Barling, B. (1997). *Online Commerce*. Ovum Ltd. UK London.

Stark, R. M., and Rothkope, M. H. (1979). Competitive bidding: A comprehensive bibliography. *Operations Research*, 27(1), 364-389.

Sun, Y., and Weld, D. S. (1995). *Automated Bargaining Agents (preliminary results)*. Technical Report TR-95-01-04, University of Washington, Department of Computer Science and Engineering.

Sycara, K., Lu, J., Klusch, M., and Widoff, S. (1999). Matchmaking among heterogeneous agents on the Internet. In: *Proceedings AAAI Spring Symposium on Intelligent Agents in Cyberspace,* Stanford, USA.

Tenders on the Web (1999).Homepage. http://www.tenders.co.uk/.

Tendersearch (1999). *http://www.tendersearch.com.au/info.html.*

Tenenbaum, J.M., Chowdhry, T. S., and Hughes, K. (1997). Eco system: An Internet commerce architecture. *Computer*, 30(5), 48-55.

Tsvetovatyy, M., Gini, M., Mobasher, B., and Wieckowski, Z. (1997). Magma: An agent-based virtual market for electronic commerce. *Journal of Applied Artificial Intelligence.*

Uschold, M., King, M., Moralee, S., and Zorgios, Y. (1998). The enterprise ontology. *The Knowledge Engineering Review*, 13(Special Issue on Putting Ontologies to Use).

Vanwelkenhuysen, J. (1998). The tender support system. *Knowledge-Based Systems*, 11, 363-372.

Vickrey, W. (1961). Counterspeculation, auctions, and competitive sealed tenders. *Journal of Finance*, 16, 8-37.

Vollrath, I., Wilke, W., and Bergmann, R. (1998). Case-based reasoning support for online catalog sales. *IEEE-Internet Computing*, pages 47-54.

Ward, S. C., and Chapman, C. B. (1988). Developing competitive bids: A framework for information processing. *Journal of Operations Research Society*, 39(2), 123-134.

Way, E. C. (1994). Conceptual graphs: Past, present, and future. In Tepfenhart, W. M., Dick, J. P., and Sowa, J. F. (Eds.), *Proceedings of the 2nd International Conference on Conceptual Structures : Current Practices*, volume 835 of *LNAI*, pages 11-30, Berlin, Springer.

Wing, H. (1998). *PhD. Thesis: Managing Complex, Open, Web-Deployable Trade Objects*. Department of Computer Science and Electrical Engineering, University of Queensland-Australia.

Workflow Management Coalition (1996). *Reference Model and API Specification*. http://www.aiai.ed.ac.uk/WfMC.

Wurman, P., Walsh, W., and Wellman, M. (1998a). Flexible double auctions for electronic commerce: Theory and implementation. *Decision Support Systems*, 24, 17-27.

Wurman, P. R., Wellman, M. P., and Walsh, W. E. (1998b). The Michigan Internet AuctionBot: A configurable auction server for human and software agents. In Sycara, K. P., and Wooldridge, M. (Eds.), *Proceedings of the 2nd International Conference on Autonomous Agents (AGENTS-98)*, pages 301-308, New York, ACM Press.

Section III

Value Chain Networks
and Research Issues

Chapter IX

Structuration Theory: Capturing the Complexity of Business-to-Business Intermediaries

Paul A. Pavlou and Ann Majchrzak
University of Southern California, USA

This chapter argues that the three most commonly used perspectives in conducting research on business-to-business (B2B) eCommerce-transaction cost economics, electronic market hypothesis, and network analysis-have inadequately explained the unfolding nature of how B2B intermediaries are being employed in industry today. We argue that these perspectives are insufficient because they assume that technology is deterministic and thus not worthy of critical analysis. This chapter proposes structuration theory as an alternative perspective, which differs from the traditional perspectives in several ways: a) structuration theory examines the impact of B2B intermediaries not just on economic indicators of business success but on such process outcomes as mutual trust, coordination, innovation, and utilization of shared knowledge; b) it examines not just technology, but the alignment between technology, the interorganizational structure, and the nature of the task (e.g., basic procurement vs. collaboration); and c) it recognizes that no technology is simply installed, but rather brought into an organization through a series of adaptations that affect both the technology and the organization over time. Examples of how structuration theory can apply to research on B2B intermediaries are presented. Moreover, we use this perspective to suggest new research questions and methodologies that eCommerce researchers could consider in the future.

This chapter is focused on business-to-business (B2B) intermediaries. B2B intermediaries can be viewed as extensions of interorganizational information systems (IOIS), which are defined as automated information systems shared by two or more organizations (Bakos, 1987; Cash and Konsynski, 1985; Johnston and Vitale, 1988). B2B intermediaries act as interorganizational intermediaries that match buyers and sellers, facilitate any-to-any online transactions, enable information sharing and collaboration, and provide the technological and institutional infrastructure to enable proper operation of these functions. With more than 1,000 currently established Internet-based B2B marketplaces (Bermudex et al., 2000), there is a substantial variation among B2B intermediaries (Choudhury, 1997). Being able to understand the impact of these variations on interorganizational relationships is essential for choosing among these intermediaries or predicting which intermediaries will be useful under different conditions. Attempts to address these issues solely based on the extant literature have been insufficient as explained in the next section.

LIMITATIONS IN THE EXTANT THEORIES FOR STUDYING B2B INTERMEDIARIES

According to the Electronic Market Hypothesis (EMH), electronic markets should be the mechanism of choice for exchanging low-specificity goods and services among organizations in the presence of electronic communication technologies (Malone, Yates, and Benjamin, 1987). This is because the technology of electronic communication is presumed to lead to better coordination and lower transaction and search costs (Bakos, 1987), following Williamson's (1975) Transaction Cost Economics (TCE) paradigm. Recent evidence suggests that the EMH might be wrong; according to Dai and Kauffman (2000), the adoption of private transacting mechanisms suggests that interorganizational coordination mechanisms are not moving towards the pure market that the EMH predicts in the presence of IT. These authors have found many private aggregating and matching networks, which involve only a few participants, contrary to the EMH predictions. For example, fasturn.com (www.fasturn.com), a B2B intermediary in the low-specificity apparel industry, has recently introduced private, buyer-driven marketplaces, despite the existence of its own global many-to-many electronic marketplace. This suggests that, simply because coordination costs go down with a B2B intermediary, organizations will not necessarily opt for an electronic market, even in the exchange of low specificity assets.

An alternative perspective that has been used to explain when and why B2B intermediaries would be useful is the theory of network externalities. B2B intermediaries provide open networks where a large number of organizations can participate without substantial time, space, and cost restrictions (Kaplan and Sawney, 2000). According to the theory of network externalities, the organizational adoption of electronic markets suggests that participants obtain a greater value when the number of organizations in the network increases (Riggins et al., 1994; Uzzi, 1996). Empirical evidence on B2B intermediaries does not appear to support Network Externality Theory (Dai and Kauffman, 2000). Despite the value that organizations obtain through network externalities, there is not much evidence to suggest that firms have embraced many-to-many B2B intermediaries. On the contrary, even if electronic market makers initially focused on the global market model (Latham, 2000), there is substantial evidence to suggest that firms move towards private B2B intermediaries where they have more control over their exchange relations (Sodhi, 2000). Therefore, the theory of network externalities has, similar to the EMH and TCE, not adequately explained the organizational adoption of B2B intermediaries.

AN ALTERNATIVE FRAMEWORK FOR STUDYING B2B INTERMEDIARIES: STRUCTURATION THEORY

Structuration theory (DeSanctis and Poole, 1994; Giddens, 1984; Leonard-Barton, 1988; Majchrzak et al., 2000; Orlikowski, 1992; Tyre and Orlikowski, 1994) explains how organizations adopt Internet intermediaries to collaborate with other organizations, execute transactions, and streamline their supply chain. An important focus of structuration theory is the process of the technology adoption rather than the mere outcome. Therefore, from a structuration perspective, measures of success of a technology adoption include both economic and process variables. Evidence from research on B2B intermediaries suggests that a focus on process outcomes is an important one. For example, research on B2B intermediaries has found profound changes in organizational structures and processes in order to realize interorganizational integration and Internet working (Brynjolfsson and Kahin, 2000; Sodhi, 2000; Zmud, 2000). Recent evidence on B2B intermediaries also suggests that companies engage in significant restructuring to effectively participate in eCommerce (Karpinski, 2000). Since B2B intermediaries are employed as interactive technologies that enable organizations to work together with other organizations, increase their reach to new partners, transform their supply chain, and increase the level of collaboration and organizational learning towards new product designs, process-related success measures might include elements of interfirm collaboration, such as trust, organizational learning, satisfaction, and confidence (Pavlou and Stewart, 2000).

Traditional measures of success in the extant literature on B2B intermediaries have not focused on these process-based outcomes, instead focusing on mostly economic measures of interorganizational success (North, 1990; Heide and Stump, 1995; Noordewier, George, and John, 1990). There are two reasons why this sole focus on economic performance limits our understanding of how B2B intermediaries are effectively utilized. First, when only economic measures of success are examined, the success of the technology deployment process, as opposed to the outcome, may be overlooked, such as the degree of mutual trust, participation, involvement, improvisation, comprehension, and satisfaction in the deployment process (Pavlou and Stewart, 2000). These process measures are important measures in their own right because they are related to successful economic outcomes (Hill, 1990), and because they are indicators of a high-performance organization (Van Tuijl and Van de Kraats, 2000). An additional aspect overlooked may be the long-term effects, such as time to deploy future technologies, improved supplier relationships, faster time to market for new products, or organizational learning (Cannon and Perrault, 1999; Ring and Van de Ven, 1992, 1994; Zaheer, McEvily and Perrone, 1998).

Second, when only economic measures of success are examined, the unplanned effects of technology are overlooked. Such unplanned effects of technology might include centralization of relevant information for strategic planning and scheduling, ease of accessibility for end-users, improved ability to handle increased amount of data for visibility and control, the development of better work strategies and policies, improvement in interorganizational collaboration and interaction, facilitation of coordination and learning among organizations, an increase in the utilization of shared knowledge, and an enhanced image of the organization both in the marketplace and by its employees (Orlikowski and Hofman, 1997). Other spontaneous outcomes of technology-enabled interorganizational relations may include generation of new ideas (innovation and improvisation); reduction in conflict; and better, faster and higher quality decision-making (DeSanctis and Poole, 1994).

Not only does structuration theory suggest a focus on process outcomes, but also it does not put technology as the central focus. Instead, the role of technology must be examined within the existing context to appreciate how the technology and context affect each other. As a result, the focus of research attention is not the technology but the alignment of technological characteristics, the existing organizational and interorganizational structures, and the nature of the work task (e.g., procurement, supply chain, and product development). When these three components are aligned, technology deployment will be successful (Leonard-Barton, 1988; Majchrzak et al., 2000; Orlikowski, 1992). This interrelationship is illustrated in Figure 1.

To understand how the three components can be aligned, let us first look at the alignment between task and technology in the B2B intermediary context. In the basic procurement task used for many B2B intermediaries, the specificity and complexity of the focal good will indicate which B2B intermediary is most appropriate (Malone et al., 1987, Williamson, 1975). Organizations purchasing products that are low in asset specificity and complexity of description are more likely to be successful using many-to-many electronic markets (Choudhury, 1997). This suggests that B2B technologies with high brokerage value (as one of the technology dimensions) will be more successful with procurement tasks, but only if the procurement task is limited to products of low asset specificity and complexity. In contrast, B2B intermediaries used for supply chain management tasks require different technology dimensions to explain the successful implementation of such intermediaries. In supply chain management, organizations need to make both transaction and relationship-specific investments to build an electronic supply chain (Heide and Stump, 1995). These investments are perceived as 'signals' of trustworthy intentions (Bakos and Brynjolfsson, 1993; Stump and Heide, 1996). This suggests that the degree to which the intermediary is compatible with existing trustworthy practices of relationship management (the compatibility dimension of technology) may be critical for successful use of supply chain management intermediaries.

Figure 1: Interdependence Among Technology, Structure and Task

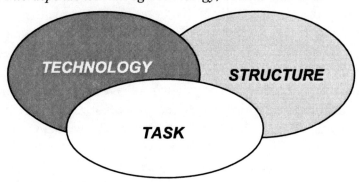

Aligning technology and task is insufficient; technology must also be aligned with the organizational and market structure. For B2B eCommerce, one source of market structure is the degree of reciprocity among organizations. For example, many-to-many B2B intermediaries promote low reciprocity among organizations since the large number of firms does not facilitate reciprocal relationships to develop (Beccera and Gupta, 1999). This is in contrast to private B2B intermediaries in which reciprocal relationships develop based on high levels of trust, joint action, and mutual understanding (Morgan and Hunt, 1994). This suggests that intermediaries that promote dyadic, long-term, trusting relationships (such as through electronic brokerage, compatibility, and electronic integration) may be more suitable for interorganizational structures based on reciprocity, while intermediaries that promote brief interactions among large numbers of organizations are better suited for other interorganizational structures.

Given structuration theory's focus on process (vs. economic) outcomes and alignment (not just deterministic technologies), it is perhaps not surprising that the final element of structuration theory we review for B2B intermediary research is structuration theory's focus on how technology structures and tasks are adapted (rather than assumed to be adopted as expected). Since new advanced technologies are almost never immediately adopted upon their initial introduction (Orlikowski, 1992), an adaptation process is necessary. Adaptations are actions intended to correct, extend, and modify the technology and the structural context (Tyre and Orlikowski, 1994). Adaptations occur when one group of organizations chooses to change or interpret a specific feature of the B2B intermediary differently than another group of organizations or differently from the vendor or intermediary host. Adaptations may involve modifications to particular organizational structures (centralization and formalization), or adaptations of existing legacy systems to integrate with the structural features of an advanced technology. In other words, adaptations are the actions that organizations take to modify the dimensions of the B2B technologies, tasks, and interorganizational structures to accomplish their interorganizational coordination needs.

Examining the adaptation process is critical to understanding what actions should be taken during the adaptation process to ensure that the B2B intermediary will be efficiently and effectively utilized. For example, compatibility issues usually arise when organizations have different existing technological infrastructures, which affect the degree of electronic integration. Hence, research from a structuration perspective can help organizations improve their interaction with B2B intermediaries by eliminating any friction between the emerging technology dimensions and the emerging structure and task.

A successful adaptation process usually passes through a series of misalignments and adaptations of existing structures until it achieves alignment of *all* pertinent structures. Many examples of misalignments and adaptation moves are present with B2B intermediaries. Public auctions were initially introduced as the method of choice for sellers to have many anonymous buyers compete for their products. However, despite the benefits of many buyers, sellers wanted to restrict their sales to known buyers; therefore, this misalignment has been adapted by private auctions where buyers can participate by invitation.

Various models have been proposed to describe the process by which these structures eventually become aligned (e.g., Leonard-Barton, 1998; Tyre and Orlikowski, 1994; DeSanctis and Poole, 1994). One model found in research by Majchrzak et al. (2000) may be particularly pertinent for B2B intermediaries. In the Majchrzak et al. model, misalignments were found to occur throughout the adaptation process, with some of them resulting from emerging, not just preexisting structures. Emerging new structures are likely to occur especially with B2B intermediaries. For example, the dimension of electronic brokerage can be adjusted to fit the organization's needs. Figure 2 (adapted by Majchrzak et al., 2000) graphically represents how the adaptation process may unfold: when structures are malleable, adaptation is likely to both resolve potential misalignments and create new ones.

IMPLICATIONS FOR RESEARCH

Applying a structuration theory perspective to B2B eCommerce research offers a very important advantage over the existing frameworks: it enables the complex interrelationship among multiple factors that influence B2B success to be simultaneously addressed and examined over time, while allowing room for a wide spectrum of organizational outcomes. In the context of B2B intermediaries, a large number of variables concurrently affect interorganizational relations. Previous attempts to examine multiple interactions (e.g., three-way interactions) among various constructs using existing frameworks have not produced a meaningful theory. For example, Buvik and John (2000), using TCE, hypothesized the effect of a three-way interaction among the degree of vertical coordination, uncertainty, and supplier asset specificity on transaction costs. Despite the partial support for this hypothesis, the authors expressed concern that a static view of the interaction was insufficient for explaining transaction costs: "The deleterious effect of vertical coordination would have remained uncovered if we had studied a single exchange problem in isolation" (p. 61). As another example, Rindfleisch

Figure 2: The Adaptation Process (Adapted by Majchrzak et al., 2000 with permission)

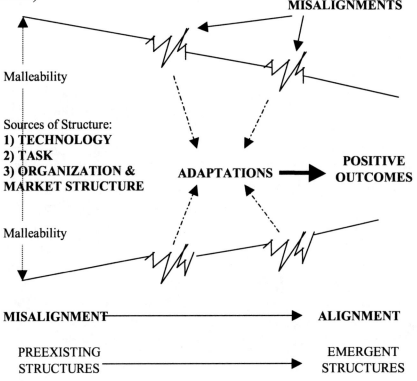

and Heide (1997) proposed that individual governance may serve multiple purposes, and research should understand how to align governance mechanisms with multiple problems simultaneously. Therefore, given the increasing complexity of online B2B relationships, the importance of alignment of multiple structures, the salience of alignment, and the deleterious effect of misalignments should all be considered.

In this section, we offer several research questions that would be suggested by a structuration theory framework for studying B2B intermediaries:

- What are the characteristics of B2B intermediaries (possibly using the technology dimensions identified in this chapter) that are likely to be most aligned with different types of interorganizational structures, given different types of tasks? How can B2B intermediaries positively influence the interorganizational relationship between structure and task?
- What kind of tasks will B2B intermediaries encourage? On which task-procurement, supply chain management, or coordination-would the most benefits from technology arise?
- How can asymmetrically dependent organizational relations

(misalignments) be made to work for either or both partners following an adaptation process? How can B2B intermediaries help this process?

- How important is the malleability of certain interorganizational structures (e.g., markets, hierarchies, joint ventures) and how do important social structures such as trust and relationship commitment affect the adaptation process towards high levels of interfirm collaboration and joint action?

- What factors prevent favorable adaptations from occurring, such as governance mechanisms for managing opportunism that discourage trust, commitment, and joint action? How can B2B intermediaries promote favorable adaptations and avoid rigid structures that prevent alignment?

- Are the dimensions of technology identified the right ones for capturing the types of adaptations required to be promoted by B2B technologies to promote interorganizational collaboration? Which other dimensions can be identified to explain better the alignment required between technology, organizational structure, and task?

- Is it possible to make inferences about the future of B2B eCommerce over time, based on the existing and emerging structures, the nature of the adaptation process, the malleability of structures, and the nature of organizational relationships?

- Are there ideal adaptation profiles for different configurations of B2B intermediary technologies, interorganizational structures, and tasks that describe how the adaptation process should ideally unfold over time?

These important questions that are likely to puzzle researchers in B2B eCommerce are likely to be better answered if analyzed under the lens of structuration theory. Thus, we offer a set of guidelines on how to conduct research under this perspective.

Measure Process-Not Solely Economic-Outcomes As Dependent Variables

Since organizations usually form ongoing, formal business relationships to achieve common goals, it is imperative that research departs from the basic economic efficiency of the focal transaction to encompass outcomes arising from innovation, risk sharing, and new resources (Bleeke and Ernst, 1993). To assess success of an interorganizational relationship using a B2B intermediary, such dependent variables as enhanced coordination, satisfaction with the intermediary, efficiency improvements in the work process, and the ability to perform tasks in more creative ways should be considered. In addition, dependent variables that explicitly examine whether unintended negative consequences accrued as a result of the intermediary technology should be considered. For example, the lack of work-arounds, where organizations must identify alternative ways to do certain tasks because the technology prevents them from doing it in a straightforward manner, should be examined.

Measure Adaptations-Not Static Structures-As Independent Variables

Examining structures (such as dimensions of technology, organization, work task, or interorganizational relationships) as if they were static, or as if a measure at one point in time was indicative of a state at a later point in time, is misleading. Thus, research must recognize the dynamic nature of these structures and examine changes to those structures, such as a change in the state from pre-intermediary to mid-use of intermediary. Moreover, the adaptation process itself should be examined, such as what decisions were made to make changes to these structures and why these decisions were made.

Many studies take a single point in time using cross-sectional data and ultimately admit that no causal relationships can be empirically inferred using this method. Despite the ease of conducting this type of research, there are many instances where different studies find conflicting results. Perhaps the most controversial examples are the empirical validations of the predictions of the TCE where some researchers find support (e.g., Houston and Johnson, 2000) and others do not (e.g., Brown et al., 2000). Measuring the adaptations where organizations move from one governance structure to another might help resolve this controversial issue.

Obtain Data Using Ethnography Observations, Monitoring, and Multiple Methods

To learn about adaptations, surveys are insufficient. Instead, the adaptation processes must be observed as they occur. This can be done through in-person observations, through electronic monitoring, or through virtual monitoring, such as by attending teleconference meetings. Observation protocols must be established. In addition, the ideal study is one that does not rely on a single source of data to draw inferences about what transpired, but instead collects data from a variety of different sources, using many different methods. Despite the inherent difficulties from collecting data from multiple organizations, companies can benefit from learning about their adaptation processes, as opposed to providing one-time data. Therefore, researchers can establish long-term relationships with organizations by following the adaptation process, and jointly attempt to solve misalignments and reach an alignment.

Follow Interorganizational Relationships Over Time

To study adaptation processes over time requires that the interorganizational relationship be examined over time. Thus, longitudinal research designs must be utilized. Ideally, the research begins prior to the selection of a B2B intermediary and continues throughout the adaptation process. Obviously, the involvement in an intermediary never ends, so at some point the researcher will need to determine when continued observation is no longer providing additional evidence for conclusions.

Conduct Experiments to Examine Impacts of Alternative Structures

While the above methods will help researchers to describe structuration processes as they occur, they do not help to answer the question of the differential impacts of different dimensions of structures under different conditions. One way to assess these different impacts is by observing different B2B intermediaries varying along particular dimensions, and controlled in other dimensions. Alternatively, intermediary hosts must be convinced to systematically experiment with different dimensions and the results closely observed. Experimentation is not as infeasible as it might initially sound. Intermediary hosts are always rolling out new versions of software; influencing how those versions are rolled out, and which features are highlighted in a particular version, needs to become part of the researcher's role.

CONCLUDING REMARKS

In sum, then, a structuration perspective allows not only a new focus on research, but also a new way that research should be conducted in the B2B arena. The theoretical implications of this perspective are pronounced. Research would be conducted in a longitudinal fashion that would allow causal relationships to be derived. Moreover, the adaptation process is more likely to allow better predictions on how future adaptations need to take place to solve potential emerging misalignments. Moreover, the inclusion of a broader context of dependent variables would allow research to explore new, unexplored measures of success.

The purpose of this chapter is not to denounce research on B2B eCommerce with alternative methods. Research from a structuration perspective does not preclude research using other more traditional perspectives. Given that structuration theory might be more time-consuming that current research methods, structuration theory might be used where the complex set of interrelationships among various constructs cannot be otherwise adequately resolved. Moreover, research from a structuration theory can attack problems where the time component might be particularly important. For example, when rapid changes occur in B2B eCommerce, structuration theory methods would be especially beneficial.

This chapter conveys the challenges of B2B eCommerce, the paradoxical results from the extant literature, the limitations of traditional research methods, and, most important a novel paradigm to guide research in this area– to tempt researchers to look for answers.

REFERENCES

Bakos, J. Y. (1987). Inter-organizational information systems: Strategic implications for competition and cooperation. *Doctoral Thesis*, MIT Sloan School of Management, Cambridge, MA.

Bakos, J. Y. and Brynjolfsson, E. (1993). Information technology, incentives and the optimal number of suppliers. *Journal of Information Systems*, 10(2), 37-51.

Bermudex, J., Kraus, B., O'Brien, D., Parker, B. and Lapide, L. (2000). B2B commerce forecast: $5.7T by 2004. Available on the World Wide Web at: http://www.amrresearch.com. Accessed on November 9, 2000.

Bleeke, J. and Ernst, D. (1993). Collaborating to compete: Using strategic alliances and acquisitions in the global marketplace. New York: John Wiley & Sons.

Brown, J. R., Dev, C. S. and Lee, D. J. (2000). Managing marketing channel opportunism: The efficacy of alternative governance mechanisms. *Journal of Marketing*, April (64), 51-65.

Brynjolfsson, E. and Kahin, B. (2000). *Understanding the Digital Economy: Data, Tools, and Research*, Cambridge, MA: MIT Press.

Buvik, A. and John, G. (2000). When does vertical coordination improve industrial purchasing relationships. *Journal of Marketing*, October (64), 52-64.

Cash, Jr. J. I. and Konsynski, B. R. (1985). IS redraws competitive boundaries. *Harvard Business Review*, March-April, 134-142.

Choudhury, V. (1997). Strategic choices in the development of interorganizational information systems. *Information Systems Research*, 8(1), 1-24.

Dai, Q. and Kauffman, R. J. (2000). Business models for Internet-based eprocurement systems and B2B electronic markets: An exploratory assessment. *Proceedings of the 34th Hawaii International Conference on Systems Science*, Maui, Hawaii (forthcoming).

DeSanctis, G. and Poole, M. S. (1994). Capturing the complexity in advanced technology use: Adaptive structuration theory. *Organization Science*, 5(2), 121-147.

Gates, S. (1993). *Strategic Alliances: Guidelines for Successful Management*. New York: The Conference Board, Inc.

Giddens, A. (1984). *The Constitution of Society: Outline of the Theory of Structure*. Berkley, CA: University of California Press.

Heide, J. B. and Stump, R. L. (1995). Performance implications of buyer-supplier relationships in industrial exchanges: A transaction cost explanation. *Journal of Business Research*, 32, 57-66.

Hill, C. W. L. (1990). Cooperation, opportunism and the invisible hand: Implications for transaction cost theory. *Academy of Management Review*, 15, 500-513.

Houston, M. B. and Johnson, S. A. (2000). Buyer-supplier contracts versus joint ventures: Determinants and consequences of transaction structure. *Journal of Marketing Research*, 37, 1-15.

Johnston, H. R. and Vitale, M. R. (1988). Creating competitive advantage with inter-organizational information systems. *MIS Quarterly*, June, 153-166.

Kaplan S. and Sawhney, M. (2000). E-hubs: The new B2B marketplaces. *Harvard Business Review*, May-June, 97-103.

Karpinski, R. (2000). Behind the B2B scenes. Available on the World Wide Web at: http://www.btobonline.com/cgi-bin/article.pl?id=4296. Accessed on November 9, 2000.

Latham, S. (2000). Evaluating the independent trading exchanges. Available on the World Wide Web at: http://www.amrresearch.com. Accessed on November 9, 2000.

Leonard-Barton, D. (1988). Implementation as mutual adaptation of technology and organization. *Research Policy*, 17, 251-267.

Majchrzak, A., Rice, R. E., Malhotra, A., King, N. and Ba, S. (2000). Technology adaptation: The case of a computer-supported interorganizational virtual team. *MIS Quarterly*, December.

Morgan, R. M. and Hunt, S. D. (1994). The commitment-trust theory of relationship marketing. *Journal of Marketing*, July (58), 20-38.

Noordewier, T. G., George, J. and John, R. N. (1990). Performance outcomes of purchasing arrangements in industrial buyer-vendor relationships. *Journal of Marketing*, 54, 80-94.

North, D. (1990). *Institutions, Institutional Change, and Economic Performance*, New York: Cambridge University Press.

Orlikowski, W. J. (1992). The duality of technology: Rethinking the concept of technology in organizations. *Organization Science*, 3(3), 398-427.

Orlikowski, W. J. and Hofman, J. D. (1997). An improvisational model of change management: The case of Groupware Technologies. *Sloan Management Review*, 38(2), 11-21.

Pavlou, P. A. and Stewart, D. W. (2000). Measuring the effects and effectiveness of interactive advertising: A research agenda. *Journal of Interactive Advertising*, 1(1). Available on the World Wide Web at: http://jiad.org/vol1/no1/pavlou/index.html.

Rindfleisch, A. and Heide, J. B. (1997). Transaction cost analysis: Past, present and future analysis. *Journal of Marketing*, October (61), 30-55.

Ring, P. S. and Van de Ven, A. H. (1992). Structuring cooperative relationships between organizations. *Strategic Management Journal*, 13, 483-498.

Sodhi, M. S. (2000). Supply chain planners are on Mars, B2B marketplaces are on Venus. *OR/MS TODAY*, October, 10.

Stump, R. L. and Heide, J. B. (1996). Controlling supplier opportunism in industrial relationships. *Journal of Marketing Research*, 33, 431-441.

Tyre, M. J. and Orlikowski. W. J. (1994). Windows of opportunity: Temporal patterns of technological adaptation in organizations. *Organization Science*, 5(1), 98-116.

Uzzi, B. (1996). The sources and consequences of embeddedness for the economic performance of organizations: The network effect. *American Sociological Review*, 61, 674-698.

Van Tuijl, H. and Van de Kraats. A. (2000). Value people, the missing link in creating high performance organizations. *International Journal of Technology Management*, 19(6), 559-570.

Williamson, O. E. (1975). *Markets and Hierarchies*. New York: The Free Press.

Zaheer, A., McEvily, B. and Perrone, V. (1998). Does trust matter? Exploring the effects of interorganizational and interpersonal trust on performance. *Organization Science*, 9(2), 141-159.

Zmud, R. W. (2000). *Framing the Domains of IT Management*. Cincinnati, OH: Pinnaflex Educational Resources, Inc.

Chapter X

Agent Technologies and Business Models for Electronic Commerce[1]

Paul Timmers and Jorge Gasós
European Commission, Directorate-General Information Society,
Belgium

Agent technologies have proved to provide adequate solutions to some of the challenges posed by the new business models that are arising in the field of electronic commerce. In this chapter, we present some of the key challenges in turning agents' research into commercial applications, provide an overview of the electronic commerce business models, and discuss how they can benefit from the new developments in agent technologies. We illustrate the discussion with examples of the work that is being developed by projects from the IST research program of the European Union.

INTRODUCTION

In line with the rapid expansion of electronic commerce in the recent years, there has been a parallel evolution in the associated business models in order to address the new market needs and opportunities. Initial models, like e-shop and e-procurement, showed relatively little innovation when compared to traditional ways of doing business: in many cases they consist of a Web site displaying electronic product catalogues, marketing material or procurement specifications. More innovative models, like third-party marketplaces or value chain integration, bring together multiple suppliers or multiple steps of the value chain, and add value by their potential to provide broader services while minimizing costs and by their potential to exploit the information flows. Current trends in business models focus on dynamic markets/networks, where consumers and businesses can seamlessly and dynamically come together, even for short-term relationships, in response to or in anticipation of new market opportunities.

These new business models require the development of a wide range of supporting technologies to allow the efficient implementation of the required processes and services. These technologies range from customer relationship management and marketing support to collaborative working tools and negotiation schemes, from security issues to automatic contractual arrangements and conflict mediation. In this context, agent technologies have contributed with appropriate solutions to some of these technological challenges (Maes et al., 1999).

Electronic commerce has proved to be a domain where the full potential of intelligent agents can be demonstrated. It requires managing enormous amounts of information, which in many cases is heterogeneous, not structured, and distributed in space, and needs to be dealt with in a personalized way with decision making that may need to be validated in a negotiation process. This combination of complex information from multiple sources that requires a personalized treatment and negotiation between different actors, calls for automatic solutions that show a certain degree of autonomy, intelligence, and ability to adapt/react to the particular environment/circumstances. Agent technologies fit these requirements since they provide an architecture for the implementation of autonomous, intelligent, and reactive behaviors. Furthermore, it is an enabling technology that is not restricted to specific reasoning or knowledge representation paradigms, and hence, it can be applied to the solution of many different problems from different perspectives and approaches (Maes, 1994; Bailey & Bakos, 1997; Ephrati & Rosenschein, 1994; Moukas, 1997).

The first agent systems that were developed for electronic commerce can be typified as *individual agents*: they have specific objectives and act on behalf of the user without interacting with other agents. This lack of interaction with other agents significantly simplifies the development of individual agents. Each agent can be programmed in an ad hoc fashion without concerns about protocols, semantics, or standards. Individual agents are already emerging in the market being incorporated into products and services. Examples include information agents, such as share price tracking or personalized newspapers, that retrieve, analyze, and integrate information available from multiple distributed sources. Examples of individual agents implemented for e-shops include user profiling and personalized marketing.

The next level in terms of complexity is *collaborative agents*: communities of agents that cooperate to achieve a goal, and that have been implemented following a detailed design and with a global view of the problem. The key point here is that, even if many agents have to interact, there is a certain control of the system and there exists previous agreement on the tasks to be performed by each agent and on the proprietary protocols and semantics for the exchange of information. Examples include agents cooperating to resolve network faults, decentralized management of limited common resources, and applications for static electronic marketplaces or value chain integration such as 'traditional' supply chain management. For the integration of collaborative agent systems into commercial applications it is still required to significantly improve in the area of agent engineering. These include rigorous methodologies for requirement analysis and system specifications, as well as tools for the verification, validation, and testing of the system functionality. In the case of large-scale collaborative agent systems, a better understanding is also needed of how individual agent's behaviors combine dynamically to generate the system behavior, since it will be different from a 'sum' of the individual behaviors in static environments. Issues such as social dynamics, self-organization, self-regulation, and adaptive behaviors become critical to avoid undesirable effects.

The most complex model is the *society of agents*: agents developed by different users or providers, implementing different objectives and strategies, and that have to inter-operate in a complex and dynamic environment. Global standards are the key issue to make possible these open agent platforms, including protocols for communication and common semantics for information exchange. Furthermore, legal and security issues, e.g. liability of contracts made by autonomous software and protection from malicious agents, need also to be addressed.

In this chapter we analyze the relation between agents' applications and electronic commerce business models. The context of advanced work in these subjects is the Information Society Technologies (IST) Research Program of the European Union.[2] This program supports collaboration between industry, research institutes, and public bodies for R&D and pilot projects with a European added value and on a co-financed basis. The program is structured around four key actions (see Figure 1). Most of the applications discussed

Figure 1. The European Union IST Programme

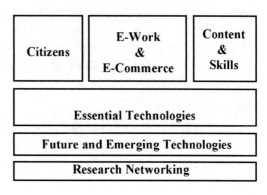

Information Society Technologies Programme

Citizens	E-Work & E-Commerce	Content & Skills

Essential Technologies

Future and Emerging Technologies

Research Networking

in this paper have been developed in projects that fall in the 'eCommerce and e-work' key action.[3] The rest of the applications come from projects in the other key actions that address: services for the citizens and ICT (Information and Communication Technologies) supported public services; digital content and ICT support for education and training; and the underpinning information and communication technologies, including hardware, software, and services for next-generation networks. The IST program is completed with specific actions for long-term research and collaboration in research networks.

This chapter brings together several separate pieces of work by the IST projects, and connects them to provide a global overview of the different approaches to integrate agent technologies in electronic commerce business models. All the individual approaches have been reported in greater detail in the technical literature and in public documents of the projects. The goal of this paper is not to explain the technicalities of any of these approaches, but rather to provide a glimpse of the ways in which research on agent technologies is being applied to face the challenges posed by the new business models that are arising in the field of electronic commerce.

AGENT TECHNOLOGIES AND BUSINESS MODELS

'Business models' is certainly one of the most discussed topics in electronic commerce. Virtually every electronic commerce provider uses 'business models' in its advertising. Investors are asking 'What is your business model,' meaning, where are you going to make the money, why are people paying and continuing to pay for your service? Surveys of SMEs have shown that one of the most frequently mentioned barriers to electronic commerce, next to cost concerns, is 'the lack of a business model.'

In the literature several taxonomies of business models can be found. Some provide a broad overview such as Merz (1999) or Rappa (2000); others focus on specific business models such as virtual communities (Hagel & Armstrong, 1997). Often Internet technology companies provide their own taxonomies, for an example see Intershop.[4] An overview of references to business models and an additional taxonomy can be found in Rappa (2000). Rayport (1999) provides an historic perspective on the quest for successful business models.

Beyond business models it is also useful to consider larger-scale economic structures, that is, business networks like supply chains and e-markets or 'e-business communities' as defined and analyzed by Kalakota and

Robinson (1999) and Tapscott et al. (1999). Timmers (1999) provided such an analysis of 'e-economy' structures in terms of value networks and dynamic markets, as will be discussed below.

For the business models classification, we will make use of the approach published in the *International Journal of Electronic Markets* (Timmers, 1998). This paper is one of the few to provide a formal definition of a business model, namely that it consists of the architecture of business processes or value chain steps, together with a description of the product or service, information, and money flows. The business model should also list the business actors involved, their roles, and the benefits they get. This approach also provides a methodology to construct new business models.

A business model in itself does not yet provide understanding of how it will contribute to realizing the business mission and objectives of any of the companies who is an actor within the model. We also need to know about the companies' marketing strategies in order to assess the commercial viability of the business model and to answer questions like: how is competitive advantage being built, what is the positioning, what is the marketing mix, which product-market strategy is being followed? Therefore it is also useful to define beyond a business model the 'marketing model' of a company, which consists of a business model in combination with the marketing strategy of the company (for a more profound analysis see Timmers, 1999).

In principle many new business models can be conceived by deconstructing the value chain into its constituent steps or by decomposing the business into its set of business processes, followed by reconstructing the value chain or set of business processes, again using electronic commerce technologies to build up the business operation. In practice only a limited number of business models are being realized in Internet electronic commerce. Figure 2 shows these most common eCommerce business models. The dimensions in this mapping are the degree of innovation relative to the nonelectronic way of doing business, and the degree of integration of business functions. In the discussion below these business models are briefly explained and put in the context of agent technologies.

E-Shop, E-Procurement

In their basic form e-shops (and e-procurement) are about bringing selling (responsible for buying) on-line by offering an electronic interface to the sales (responsibility for procurement) function. Initial models showed relatively little innovation and consisted of a Web site displaying electronic catalogues or marketing material. Extensions to this basic model integrated ordering and payment, as well as existing information systems, logistics, and distribution. Agent technologies have been successfully implemented to improve the front-office aspects of e-shops: mainly to build customer loyalty and to provide marketing support (Terpsidis et al., 1997).

Figure 2. Electronic Commerce Business Models

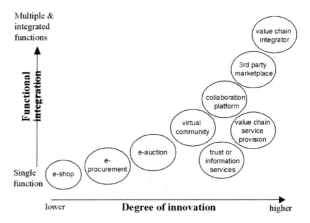

Customer support can be implemented at different levels: providing the basic information that allows the selection of a product, providing additional technical advice, and personalizing the advice and information using extensive knowledge of the customer. In this line, COGITO[5] is a recently started EU project aiming at developing personalized assistants using intelligent agents. Starting from a chatbox enhanced by 2D and 3D animations, it will use agents to support customers through proactive advice and through intelligent and personalized dialogues, product search and offers. User profiles generated during the dialogues will allow users to learn their preferences and attitudes, and to improve the naturalness of the new dialogues. User profiles and domain knowledge will be used to assist the customer with situation-specific advice in the selection process.

The EU NECTAR[6] project is an example of the use of individual agents in the retail sector. The project aims at building and enhancing customer loyalty by means of actions that satisfy customer expectations and satisfaction, while improving the perceived benefits. The system automatically creates user profiles based on the transactions and product or brand preferences. They are used to generate personalized offers by the automatic monitoring of catalogues and products, seeking out items that match the personalized shopping profiles. Agents are also used for the dynamic presentation of affinity products, once the customer shows interest in a particular item. Furthermore, they have developed one-to-one marketing tools for targeted advertising and special promotional messages fitting the user interests. This strategy tries to generate impulse shopping, increases transaction rates, and provides real-time feedback on the effectiveness of the messages. Full tracking, data analysis, and reporting capabilities allow the marketing departments to improve their strategies and get a deeper knowledge of their customers and their campaigns.

Additional examples of EU projects in this area are: MIMIC,[7] that provides tools for tracking and analysis of pre-sales customer behavior with a view to optimizing the content of a Web site by identifying critical decision points; ACTIVE, that focuses on home shopping with filtering and recommendation capabilities, targeted promotion techniques, and provision of cost fluctuation and flexible advertising schemes; and AIMEDIA, that uses agents for personalized advertising in interactive media.

E-Auctions

Auctions are used to decide the price of a good, mainly when the seller cannot easily determine the market price or when there are fluctuations of demand and/or supply. Examples range from areas as diverse as secondhand products to electricity production to surplus electronic components and to advertising space. Real-world auctions often have an element of excitement and entertainment, and virtual world auctions are trying to reproduce this (see e.g., the auction clock in the EU project INFOMAR, now marketed as Multi-trade by SCS,[8], or the simulated real-time counter in Wehkamp's on-line auction[9]).

In the case of agent-automated auctions, the excitement of a real-world auction is replaced by the carefully studied bidding strategy implemented in the agent. One area particularly suited for agent implementation is commodities, e.g., similar, interchangeable goods that can be easily defined by a common ontology (Vetter & Pitsch, 1999a). An effect of the unprecedented degree of information available through electronic commerce is that many products that before required specialized advice are now starting to be sold as commodities. The power of information and the possibility of comparing competing products are further moving industry towards an auction market-place where commodity products are sold based on cost, reliability, and speed of delivery.

Price-based auctions are the simplest type of auctions, where most efforts are focusing on their automation by means of agents. Multivariable auctions, based on price plus other factors such as delivery times, service contracts, or negotiable bundles of products and services, are starting to attract the interest of the research community. An example of a multivariable auction is the outsourcing of work or services (e.g., outsourcing software development). An additional issue to consider is the legal liability of the result of the auction that, being of concern in virtual auctions, is more critical in the case of bids made by autonomous software.

CASBA[10] is an example of integration of agent-driven auctions in the electronic marketplace. All participants in the automated auctions are agents that can take one of four roles (Vetter & Pitsch, 1999a). The *sell agent* initiates the process by sending an order to the *administrator agent*, including the descriptions of the good and the rules for the auction. The administrator agent informs of the auction terms to all *buy agents* that may be interested according to the available information in the buy agents' database. It also creates an *auctioneer agent*, in charge of handling the auction according to the agreed rules. The interested buy agents have to subscribe to the auction and, once the auction starts, can make bids executing the strategies of their users. A prototype is being developed for (last-minute) airline tickets, a good that has a clear ontology and therefore is well suited for automated auctions.

Third–Party Marketplaces

In a third-party marketplace (TPM) or 'distributive network,' the provider puts the catalogues of suppliers on-line, and offers catalogue search, ordering, and payment facilities in a secure environment to purchasers. The TPM provider might also add branding, one-to-one marketing support, and logistics to this, as well as more advanced functions such as risk management and insurance, tax/customs handling, and product bundling. In short, the TPM provider relieves suppliers and buyers of much of the burden to go on-line. This approach is particularly important since it is well suited for volume trading of routine supplies between businesses. These MRO goods (which are routine industrial goods that are needed to keep operations going but that are not of strategic importance to the production and are also called Maintenance, Repair, and Operations goods) constitute 50% of all eCommerce.

Agent technologies have an important role in the automation of some of the key processes involved in TPM: information brokerage and mediation, as well as negotiation of offers. TPM requires the development of multi-agent systems (*collaborative agents* as explained in the introduction) that match the demand and supply processes in a commercial mediation environment (Laasri et al., 1992; Rosenschein & Zlotkin, 1994).

The EU project ABROSE[11] is an example of an electronic commerce application that builds an agent technology architecture for brokerage and mediation. The main challenges faced by the project in the automation of information brokerage are:

- knowledge representation, processing, and retrieval to enable the matching of demand and supply; and
- managing the distributed access, flows, and update of information in time.

ABROSE has built a virtual marketplace, populated by agents from providers and users, which negotiate offers, supply, and demand. Transaction agents represent users and providers in the brokerage domain, encapsulating knowledge about them and learnings about other transaction agents. Each time a request is issued, the communication agent in charge of it contacts the transaction agent of the user. Based on specific mediation knowledge, relevant providers' agents are identified and contacted. Providers' agents analyze and adapt the request to issue a proposal that is transmitted to the user domain. Here decision support is provided by specialized agents that own specific domain knowledge, and that is updated based on the evaluation of the obtained results. A symmetric scenario is used for offer propagation (advertising).

The EU project CASBA implements advanced marketplaces providing services that improve customer focus and flexibility. It allows dynamic pricing according to the real demand and customer-specific offers; as a result, the customer and the vendor can negotiate the details of a deal. CASBA has developed a framework for electronic marketplaces using multi-agent technology: a set of tools for setting up and administrating electronic markets, and a tool for the creation of specialized agents to access these markets. An overview of the main features of the system includes (Vetter & Pitsch, 1999b):

- it allows the buyer set specific priorities on the attributes of the desired product;
- this enables the selling agents to answer with related products and/or alternatives according to the buyer preferences;
- using filtering rules the buyer can pre-select the sellers he wants to negotiate with; and
- the agents negotiate with each other using sophisticated strategies based on rule systems and a utility function defined by the individual user. CASBA also includes a secure electronic payment system.

Value Chain Integration

Value chain integrators focus on bringing together multiple steps of the value chain, with the potential to exploit the information flow between those steps for further added value. Improved information exchange that allows tight integration of all partners in the value chain is one of the main benefits of this model. However, it also allows the provision of new services where intelligent agents can play an important role: as personalized advice to buyers of complex products, customized configuration of the products, and after sales support. All these services require the integration of information to come from all actors in the value chain.

The new IST project LIAISE[12] will use intelligent agents to bring together sellers and suppliers with long-term relationships in order to let the user to do his personal configuration of high complexity products. Agents on the seller side will interact with agents on the user and suppliers' sides. They will provide advice to the user and assure that the requested product configuration is well formed and fulfills all restrictions. They will interact with the suppliers to confirm the availability of the parts and to negotiate their optimal supply. Each user request requires constructing a new solution by assembling a compatible collection of parts chosen from the different suppliers in the value chain. Furthermore, the system will be integrated with the back-office functions of the organizations in the value chain. As test bed, the system will be applied to the selling process of industrial automation systems, where complexity and modularity of the configuration and allowed architectures are strongly increasing.

Other Business Models

The business models classification can be further extended with more business models that have emerged over the past few years. New business models include Application Service Provision (ASP), where the service consists of hosting business applications for a service fee. Access to the applications is over the Internet. ASP as a business model needs reliable and high-performance networking. Witnessing the recent huge investments in ASP there seems to be considerable confidence in this new business model. New forms of value chain service provision are also coming up, such as call centre support and order taking. An example of this is the announcement at the end of 1999 of USA Network[13] to form such an eCommerce services unit. Amongst specialized value chain services, also bill hosting has caught the spotlights for B-to-C transactions.

There are in principle many more business models that can be imagined. A systematic approach to this has been outlined in Timmers (1999). Agent technologies will be critical to enable some of these new models, especially those that focus on added value by targeting higher levels of semantics rather than only automating existing business processes.

AGENT TECHNOLOGIES AND THE
ORGANIZATION OF THE ECONOMY

In the quest for efficiency, agility, and competitive advantage, companies constantly need to reassess what is core to their activities, which relationships are strategic, and in which markets they need to be active. For example, companies need to consider rearranging their cost structure, trading off production, which is organized in-house against sourcing from the market or partners. While the make-or-buy question has always existed for companies, it is the opportunities in particular from the Internet, as well as from enabling agent technologies, that have put this question very much into the spotlight again.

Such assessment and consideration lead to rethinking how business processes should be organized, that is, both inside the company as well as in relationship to other companies and to the market. All processes that add to value creation should be analyzed to assess their added value and the appropriate position inside the organization or external to it. In other words, the company is (re-)defining its business model.

However, business models are in fact a single-company-focused view of the organization of the digital economy at large. If we take a helicopter view, we see that business models are critically dependent upon some form of ICT-based networking between business partners and are therefore reflecting the local implementation of the general organization of the economy. Two of the particularly interesting patterns that are emerging in the organization of the information economy at large are *value networks* and *dynamic markets*. These are defined as follows:

A value network is a multi-enterprise set of relationships focused on integration of information flows to exploit information and knowledge in the business network for strategic business objectives.

A dynamic market configuration is a market-mediated set of relationships focused on increasing flexibility and opportunity for strategic business objectives.

A comparison of value network and dynamic market on some key characteristics is given in Table 1.

Value networks generally consist of relationships between a limited number of companies. The focus is on deepening these internal relationships, that is, in between the companies and inside each of the companies. The set of partners may change gradually over time as new competitive suppliers or

Table 1. Characteristics of Value Networks and Dynamic Markets

	Focus	*Time scales*	*Mutual commitment*	*Investment per relation*	*Relations*
Value Network	Increasing value through internal relations	Medium-long	High	High	Few
Dynamic Market	Increasing value through external relations	Short-medium	Low	Low	Many

buyers are added and others are being dropped. The actual value chain at any given moment in time may involve a subset of partners from the value network, and this may change over time too.

Dynamic networks would typically involve a larger or very large number of parties, with a focus on seeking to maximize value from those external relationships. In a dynamic network the approach is to maximize price or delivery opportunity or flexibility or agility by selecting the most appropriate business partner (buyer, component supplier, service provider, etc.) at any moment in time.

Figure 3 shows how value networks and digital markets relate to each other by reorganizing value creation processes. It suggests that a company can evolve to become a member of a value network by setting up ICT-supported relationships with other companies who provide goods and services that are no longer produced in-house. It also suggests that these relationships can become more dynamic by being contracted from digital markets for goods and services. In other words, the value network can evolve into a dynamic market configuration. Certainly an evolution in this direction, from single company to value network to dynamic market configuration, is not the only path a company can take. It may also make sense to strengthen the ties with some of the ad-hoc partners in a dynamic market setup and thus go into the direction of a value network. It may even be appropriate to merge with other companies in the value network and thus internalize the business relations (vertical or horizontal integration). Furthermore, new Internet businesses can start in any configuration. By the very nature of the Internet, many of them in fact will start

Figure 3. From Value Chain to Value Network and Dynamic Markets

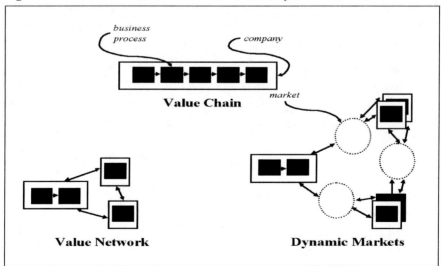

with a dynamic partnership with market parties, rather than as a traditional, tightly integrated company.

These definitions show that there can be overlap between the two forms, namely where market-mediated relationships are combined with tight integration of information systems. Also hybrid forms are conceivable, where a company is at the same time a partner in a value network for some of its business processes, as well as operating in a dynamic market setting for other processes. This can happen when collaboration with suppliers is tightly integrated and relatively static or of long duration, while collaboration with distributors is loosely integrated and more dynamic and of shorter duration. Another example is when critical components are sourced from a limited number of pre-selected suppliers, while the less critical parts are obtained from one out of many suppliers, which is dynamically selected on the basis of best price or fastest delivery.

A qualitative mapping of business models into the value network/ dynamic market space is given in Figure 4, where investment specificity corresponds to the amount of sunk investment per business relationship. For a more detailed discussion of electronic commerce scenarios, such as value networks and dynamic markets, see Timmers (1999).

Value Networks

Most current implementations of the value chain integrator and third-party marketplace provider business models are examples of value network

Figure 4. Business Models and Value Networks / Dynamic Markets

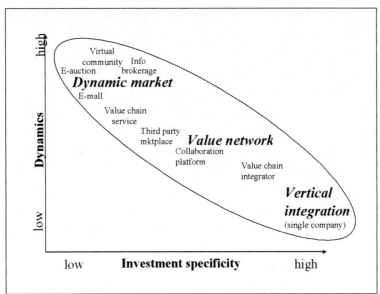

configurations. The agent technologies that have been mentioned above for these business models are relevant for value networks in general. Further complexity may come in as in the near future the depth of the value network increases. For example, some companies seek to tightly integrate *all* partners along the whole value chain, in order to implement customer-driven production, also called value chain reversal. Collaborative agents that can rely upon a shared semantics along the value chain clearly find application in such cases. While the alignment of business processes and business semantics across enterprises is a significant challenge, it is in principle possible. An example is the RosettaNet pilot in the PC supply chain, which has delivered such common ontology.[14] The ontology should not only address the 'what' of the value network (the product) but also the 'how,' that is the processes and roles and conditions, including business contracts. The variable parts in a value network are demand and supply (production) but not so much business partners or processes, let alone semantics. Value network agents have to negotiate production schedules and distribution schemes, matching demand and supply. Value network agents would also detect demand patterns and, if a business strategy such as customer-driven production is pursued, trigger the upstream part of the network.

Dynamic Value Networks

In the case of dynamic value chains, the main difference is the possibility of having short-term business relationships: companies or individuals may access the system on an ad-hoc basis and just for a specific kind of transaction. This flexibility brings complexity to the technological development. Collaborative agents developed centrally and deployed on the newcomer server may limit the type of activities performed or require an effort that is not worthy of a single transaction. The solution of a society of agents, developed by different users or providers and negotiating in a complex and dynamic environment, is the appropriate solution but still requires significant developments in agent interoperability, business semantics, and more generally ontologies. A particular challenge will be in detecting common semantics or the lack thereof 'on the fly.' Furthermore, these large-scale open platforms require a better understanding of issues as scalability and stability (including self-organization, self-regulation, and adaptive behaviors), as well as clear solutions for the legal and security aspects.

Dynamic value networks are a challenging research area for agent technologies since they require addressing all the key problems of open agent platforms, and they also provide a test bed where the full potentiality of agents can be demonstrated. Dynamic value networks are the subject of the Year 2000 calls for project proposals of the eCommerce key action of the IST program.

STANDARDS AND RESEARCH NETWORKS

Standardization is a key issue to advance towards the development of open agent platforms. Today, two major standards addressing interoperability of agents are available, namely the Object Management Group (OMG) Mobile Agent System Interoperability Facility (OMG-MASIF) and the Foundation of Physical Intelligent Agents (FIPA) specifications. OMG-MASIF[15] aims at enabling mobile agents to migrate between agent systems of the same profile via standardized CORBA IDL interfaces. FIPA[16] works on enabling the intelligent agents' interoperability via standardized agent communication and content languages. Beside the generic communication framework, FIPA is also specifying ontology and negotiation protocols to support interoperability in specific application areas. However, these standards are far from being complete; they require validation, further enhancements, and most importantly integration.

FACTS[17] is a EU project that aims at validating the work of FIPA, OMG-MASIF, and other standards groups by constructing a number of demonstrator systems based on proposed standards. By building real demonstrator systems, it proves the overall technical approach adopted by the standardization bodies, identifies their strengths and weaknesses, and generates proven suggestions for changes and enhancements. Application areas include audio-visual entertainment and broadcasting, service reservation, and electronic trading.

The cluster CLIMATE[18] represents a pool of agent technology-related projects within the EU collaborative research and development program. Its mission is to optimize the information exchange and to promote cooperation between these projects in order to enable the harmonization of work, which ideally will result in a flexible common agent middle ware, which could be used for different application domains. CLIMATE promotes the agent project activities and results towards the outside world, and takes an active part in contributing to relevant agent standards and telecommunication standards.

The AGENTLINK[19] network of excellence brings together industry, users, universities, and research centres with a common interest in agent-based computing. It provides a communication and cooperation framework, and supports a range of activities aimed at raising the profile, quality, and industrial relevance of agent systems in Europe. Activities are organized through Special Interest Groups that cover the main research issues discussed in this chapter, and include: intelligent information agents, methodologies/ software engineering, agent-based social simulation, agent-mediated electronic commerce, multi-agent coordination and control, telecommunication applications, and telematics services.

CONCLUSIONS

New business models for electronic commerce have been emerging over the past few years, which require a parallel evolution in the supporting technologies to allow the efficient implementation of the required processes and services. Throughout this paper it has been analyzed how agent technologies provide an appropriate framework for the solution of some of the emerging problems. However, there is still a long way to go until it becomes a common practice to incorporate agent-based systems into products and services, in particular, when we consider the most innovative business models. This will require addressing the key challenges of agent technologies, which are mainly related to the problems generated by large-scale open and highly dynamic systems. These include among others: agent software engineering, scalability and stability of agent systems, standards, and legal and security issues. The new IST program of the EU offers opportunities for collaboration between industry, research institutes, and public bodies by supporting research and development projects that can meet these challenges.

REFERENCES

Bailey, J., & Bakos, Y. (1997). An exploratory study of the emerging role of electronic intermediaries. *International Journal of Electronic Commerce,* 1(3).

Ephrati, E., & Rosenschein, J. (1994). Multi-agent planning as search for a consensus that maximizes social welfare. *Lecture Notes in Artificial Intelligence* 830, pages 207-226, Springer-Verlag.

Hagel, J., & Armstrong. A. (1997). *Net Gain: Expanding Markets Through Virtual Communities.* Harvard Business School Press.

Kalakota, R., & Robinson, M. (1999). *e-Business, Roadmap for Success.* Addison-Wesley.

Laasri, B., Laasri, H., Lander, S., & Lesser, V. (1992). A generic model for intelligent negotiating agents. *International Journal of Intelligent and Cooperative Information Systems,* Vol. 1.

Maes, P. (1994). Agents that reduce work and information overload. *Communications of the ACM,* 37(7).

Maes, P., Guttman, R., & Moukas, A. (1999). Agents that buy and sell. *Communications of the ACM*, 42(3).

Merz, M. (1999). *Electronic Commerce: Marktmodelle, Anwendungen, und Technologien.* dpunkt.verlag, Heidelberg.

Moukas, A. (1997). Amalthaea: Information filtering and discovery using a multiagent evolving system. *Journal of Applied AI*, 11(5).

Rappa, M. (2000). *Business Models on the Web.* http://ecommerce.ncsu.edu/business_models.html (May 25).

Rayport, J.R. (1999), The Truth about Internet Business Models. *Strategy + Business*, 3rd Quarter 1999, http://www.strategy-business.com/ (May 25).

Rosenschein, J., & Zlotkin, G. (1994). *Rules of encounter: Designing conventions for automated negotiations among computers.* MIT Press.

Tapscott, D., Lowy, A., & Ticoll, D.(1999). *Blueprint to the Digital Economy.* McGraw-Hill.

Terpsidis, I., Moukas, A., Pergioudakis, B., Doukidis, G., & Maes, P. (1997). The potential of electronic commerce in re-engineering consumer-retail relationships through intelligent agents. In: *Advances in information technologies: the business challenge,* J-Y. Roger et al. (Eds.), IOS Press.

Timmers, P. (1998). Business Models for Electronic Markets. *International Journal of Electronic Markets*, 98(2), Available: http://www.electronicmarkets.org (2000, May 25)

Timmers, P. (1999). *Electronic Commerce: Strategies and Models for Business-to-Business Trading.* Wiley & Sons Ltd.

Vetter, M., & Pitsch, S. (1999a). An Agent-based Market Supporting Multiple Auction Protocols, Agents 99. in: *WS 4: Agent-Based Decision-Support for Managing the Internet-Enabled Supply-Chain*, Goodwin, R. (ed.)

Vetter, M., & Pitsch, S. (1999b). Using autonomous agents to expand business models in electronic commerce. in: *Business and Work in The Information Society, EMMSEC'99*, Roger, Y., Stanford-Smith, B., Kidd, P.T. (Eds.), IOS Press.

ENDNOTES

1   Views expressed in this paper are the authors and do not necessarily reflect the opinions of the European Commission.

2   For information on the IST program, the current workprogram, and calls for project proposals, see http://www.cordis.lu/ist (2000, May 25)

3   For an overview of electronic commerce projects of the European Commission, see the publication, *Accelerating Electronic Commerce in Europe*, which lists about 300 EU eCommerce-related projects. The book is also available on-line at http://www.ispo.cec.be/ecommerce/books/aecebook.html,

(2000, May 25).

4 Intershop makes a distinction between business models for direct and indirect sales (i.e., marketplaces, affiliate schemes, and distributor channels). See http://www.intershop.com (2000, May 25).

5 More detailed information about the project is available at http://www.darmstadt.gmd.de/~cogito/ (2000, May 25).

6 More detailed information about the project is available at http://www.etnoteam.it/nectar/ (2000, May 25).

7 More detailed information about the project is available at http://www.atinternet.fr/mimic/ (2000, May 25).

8 See http://www.schelfhout.com (2000, May 25). As a case study this is analyzed in-depth in Timmers (1999).

9 http://www.wehkamp.nl (2000, May 25) which also has a 'publiekstribune.'

10 More detailed information about the project is available at http://www.casba-market.org (2000, May 25).

11 More detailed information about the project is available at http://b5www.berkom.de/ABROSE.

12 More detailed information about the project is available at http://www.orsiweb.com/rtd/liaise.htm (2000, May 25).

13 http://www.thestandard.net/articles/display/0,1449,6956,00.html?1447 (2000, May 25).

14 RosettaNet: http://www.rosettanet.org (2000, May 25) is a project supported by a wide industry consortium and managed by CommerceNet since 1998.

15 Detailed information about OMG-MASIF is available at http://www.fokus.gmd.de/research/cc/ecco/masif (2000, May 25).

16 Detailed information about FIPA is available at http://drogo.cselt.stet.it/fipa (2000, May 25).

17 More detailed information about the project is available at http://www.labs.bt.com/profsoc/facts (2000, May 25).

18 More detailed information is available at http://www.fokus.gmd.de/research/cc/ecco/climate (2000, May 25).

19 More detailed information is available at http://www.agentlink.org (2000, May 25).

Chapter XI

The Role of eServices and Transactions for Integrated Value Chains

Michael P. Papazoglou and Jian Yang
INFOLAB, Tilburg University, The Netherlands

Aphrodite Tsalgatidou
University of Athens, Greece

eCommerce has been well established for several years, particularly using Electronic Data Interchange (EDI) over private or value-added networks. The advent of the Internet and the World Wide Web has given a further push to eCommerce and has been dramatically changing the way business is conducted. Enterprises, in order to be competitive, form powerful business alliances that offer services and products by utilizing the autonomous and heterogeneous infrastructure provided by the independent partners. Such extended corporations reach out not only with business relationships. They also integrate their business processes and information systems with company value chains being transformed to integrated value chains for efficiently supporting this new model of extended enterprises. This chapter gives an overview of the technological challenges for B2B eCommerce and integrated value chains. It explains how adaptive business objects and controlled interoperability on one hand, and e-services on the other, are the key enabling technologies to the challenge of integrated value chains and then discusses how business transactions can be combined with eServices to provide flexible electronic business solutions.

INTRODUCTION

eBusiness is a fast growing area in the new Internet economy. The rapid adoption of eBusiness models is shaping the future of global businesses. The enterprise is no longer limited to the internal systems of a company, but spans the entire value chain, incorporating trading and distribution partners as well as customers. As a consequence, businesses increasingly integrate their value chains by redesigning their structures to move from hierarchical-with a focus on management control-to horizontal organizations-built around business processes, teamwork and empowerment. Thus, by coordinating, collaborating and integrating with other partners, enterprises create an extended virtual enterprise. Company value chains are transformed to integrated value chains in order to support the requirements of the new extended enterprises.

Value system integration can be defined as the process by which multiple enterprises within a shared market segment collaboratively plan, implement and manage the flow of goods, services and information along the value system in a way that increases customer-perceived value and optimizes the efficiency of the chain (Dobbs, 1998). Company value chains are transformed into integrated value systems if they are designed to act as an "extended enterprise," creating and enhancing customer-perceived value by means of cross enterprise collaboration. The concept of integrated value system is expected to have major impact, allowing companies, and ultimately customers, to benefit from reduced inventories, cost savings, improved value added goods and services to customers, and tighter links with business partners. In these settings, business systems can no longer be confined to internal processes, applications and data repositories; rather they span networks of enterprises, incorporating systems of trading-and distribution-partners as well as customers.

Connectivity to the Internet, and the effective exploitation of available Internet service technologies is both the cause and the effect of new ways to conduct business electronically. A number of business and technology-driven requirements are key driving forces that enable successful development and deployment of integrated value system applications. Success in this environment requires adoption of methods and technologies that support this expanded model of the networked enterprise. These include:

1. efficient business process management technology for modeling and automation of business processes that span business entities;
2. efficient business-to-business communication for secure and reliable exchange of information and transactions with trading partners over public networks such as the Internet;

3. efficient enterprise application integration technology for combining mission-critical legacy systems-throughout the networked enterprise-with new business components.

These technologies make it possible to support cross-enterprise collaboration at various levels of granularity:

·   Supporting discrete, and possibly short-term, activities between small teams working across enterprise boundaries, e.g., participating in isolated business processes.
·   Enabling a tactical response, for example at a business unit level, to capture a market opportunity or to react to a competitive threat.
·   Sustaining long-term, strategic eBusiness arrangements that integrate an enterprise's core processes with its supply and value chain, and affinity groups, resulting thus in complex multifaceted virtual businesses.

This chapter gives an overview of the information infrastructure to support eBusiness and integrated value chains and, in particular, discusses the role of eServices and transactions. Firstly, it describes some essential requirements for integrated value chains, namely new business models that offer a new way to deliver value to customers, cross-enterprise interoperability that is essential for the operation of the entire value chain and aspects related with leveraging legacy systems. Subsequently, it discusses the role of legacy systems for integrated value chains. It then concentrates on two main approaches to creating integrated value chains: the homogeneous vs. the heterogeneous approach and the corresponding enabling technologies. Business objects and frameworks are considered as enabling technologies for homogeneous approaches while eServices is the enabling technology for developing networked applications within a heterogeneous framework of business processes and infrastructure. Finally, the transition from eServices to transactions is described.

ESSENTIAL REQUIREMENTS FOR INTEGRATED VALUE CHAINS

Success in today's global marketplace will depend on creating networks of cross-industry partners to provide products and services related to the customer's basic needs. In order for companies to be successful, they need to evaluate innovative new strategies that capitalize on both the power of the Internet and the changes in market demands. Once the movement of information extends beyond the confines of a single organization, it requires the introduction of changes to the modeling of business activities manifested in the introduction of new improved business models. Moreover, it requires interoperable technology that allows business process to cross-organizational, computing and geographic boundaries.

eBusiness-Enabled Models

Enterprises can only become an effective link in a leading value chain by re-conceptualizing the company as a collection of business operations and processes, by reshaping corporate structures around modern business processes and by making their internal processes align with and support the integrated value-chain. This requires that new business models are created to offer a new way to deliver value to customers. Business modeling is the practice of abstracting and representing a business in a way that illuminates particular aspects for better understanding and communication. Models can represent enterprise or business area, markets, resource supplies, demographics and so on. Models also represent business processes or data, such as business process reengineering (BPR) process models.

Over the past two decades, businesses had to adapt and transform their organizations. A number of changed models have been introduced and tried during that time, but at best, they produced incremental improvements on the "fringes" with marginal bottom line results. Many involved change strategies that launched several change initiatives within the organization simultaneously, each narrowly focused on specific aspects of the organization with little or no pre-planning and coordination. Such an approach tries to change the organization's parts, but ultimately results in sub-optimizing the whole system for marginal bottom line performance. Any initiative to transform or change an enterprise must consider how that particular enterprise operates as an integrated whole, and its relationships with its suppliers, business partners and customers.

Most traditional seller- or product-driven businesses create value primarily at the product or line-of-business level. In contrast to this, the integrated value chain business model is customer-centric, where value is created at the relationship level across products and channels rather than at the individual product level. One important area of focus in the customer-centric model is on bundling different products and services within the same industry to create solutions. Many companies are adopting a customer-centric business model, becoming more responsive to and developing deeper relationships with customers. Relationships with suppliers, partners and customers need to be mediated almost exclusively using Internet technology, and the integration possible is becoming deeper, broader and more seamless than was ever deemed possible.

Value-chain integration is necessary if vendors are to coordinate between "upstream" suppliers, internal operations (e.g., manufacturing processes), and "downstream" shippers and customers effectively. With this model, processes once perceived as internal to the company, now span the entire value chain. Effective service providers integrate their operations directly into the processes of their customers. With this model every company in the chain performs a set or sequence of activities to produce its products. The links between those activities provide a prime opportunity for competitive advantage, whether due to exceptional efficiency or some form of product differentiation. This chain of partners that work in sequence to create, market and move goods and services grows ever more complex. For example, take SouthWest Airlines value chains which have as strategic partners not only the Boeing Co., with all of their aircraft, but also General Electric Co., which makes the engines that Boeing uses. In addition, the airline has partners including jet fuel makers, travel agents, long-distance vendors and computer hardware and software markets in its value chain.

Cross-Enterprise Interoperability

Another important requirement is that integrated value chains take advantage of existing and emerging technologies and systems that can be used to link and enable the entire value chain. The foundation of this barrier-free environment is interoperability: the ability of one system to process information from and to another at a syntactic and semantic level without requiring either system to make changes to accommodate the other (Yang, 2000). Interoperability provides a solution for integrating technology incompatible and fragmented business processes and for managing end-to-end business processes in integrated value chains. Information systems play a major part in this drive for competitive edge as their interoperation allows business allied partners to use information much more effectively in the rapid delivery of goods and services to customers.

Value-chain integration means that an enterprise's business systems can no longer be confined to internal processes, programs and data repositories, rather they must interoperate with other such systems that support links in the supply chain. Unfortunately, present eBusiness implementations automate only a small portion of the electronic transaction process. For example, although ordering and distribution of goods can be fast, the supporting accounting and inventory information, payment and actual funds transfer-which require communication of business processes with business application systems-tends to lag by a substantial amount of time. A classic example of a business application system, which typically relies on database support, is an accounts receivable system that keeps track of invoices sent and payments received. This time-lag, and the decoupling of accounting and payment information systems from the ordering and delivery of goods and service (business) processes, increases the transactions credit risks. Moreover, it may often introduce discrepancies between various information sources requiring expensive and time-consuming reconciliations. Ideally, an eBusiness application should eliminate the gaps between ordering, distribution and payment, enabling the development of interoperable links to record-keeping and accounting information systems. This requires that system incompatibilities be overcome and that business processes and information systems not only harmonize, but they are also combined with legacy assets to accommodate a broader range of business process variability and evolution. This important issue is covered in some length in the following section.

LEVERAGING LEGACY ASSETS

In an enterprise framework there is a pressing demand to integrate "new generation" business processes with legacy perspectives, processes and applications. Legacy systems are systems that are critical for the day-to-day functioning of an organization; they normally comprise monolithic applications that consist of millions of lines of code in older programming languages (e.g., COBOL), are technically obsolete with a poor performance and hard to adapt and maintain (Umar, 1997; Brodie, 1995). Few businesses can afford to completely abandon their existing information systems to implement new ones. Beyond the volumes of data collected in those systems, there are key features and functions that need to be continuously used even when new systems are introduced. Thus in addition to improved business modeling and interoperability, it is important to make sure that critical applications are not obstacles to new ways of conducting business.

The break-up of monolithic business units and processes from a business perspective requires structuring of the applications that support them and, at a minimum, finding a way to integrate them. Additionally, the nature of many of these new processes means that they must be integrated at the transaction level, not just via replication and batch transfers of data.

We can identify various types of legacy systems, ranging from highly decomposable legacy systems to monolithic (non-decomposable) systems (Brodie, 1995; Umar, 1997). The highly decomposable systems can be decomposed in user interface components, application components and database components. However, it is not likely that most of the legacy systems will meet these requirements. Needs for legacy componentization could be met depending upon the business objectives. These may include:

1. *Discarding*. This strategy should be followed in case the legacy system has a low business value and a low technical condition, for example if the legacy system is non-decomposable.

2. *Replacement*. This strategy allows the implementation of the whole or parts of the legacy application to be upgraded or replaced at the component level, without having impact on other components.

3. *Enhancement*. The function of the legacy applications must be changed to meet new requirements.

4. *Separation of concerns*. This strategy separate a service a component provides and determines how to invoke it via its interface.

5. *Selective integration*. This strategy makes it easier to integrate parts of the legacy application into new systems. Reusing the services locked inside the legacy may not require reworking the existing application, just the ability to access it and integrate it into new systems. This option can be used if one wants to use (part of) the legacy system in current and future implementations.

The tactics used to leverage existing investments in legacy systems by including them in a new computing environment can be summarized in the following:

· Identify the logical content of the existing system in terms of its data content and functionality.

· Restructure the source of the legacy into separate component interfaces and express them as abstract interfaces that exclude implementation details.

· Publicize the interfaces and direct new applications to access this interface rather than the legacy system.

Object wrappers are a successful technology for combining business objects with legacy systems. Object wrapping is the practice of implementing a software architecture given pre-existing heterogeneous components. It allows mixing legacy systems with newly developed applications by providing access to the legacy systems. This is achieved by creating a wrapped interface to post an entry to a desired (legacy) business process such as Accounts Receivable (see Figure 1). The wrapped legacy system can then communicate with new generation business components such as Invoice and Receivable. The wrapper specifies services that can be invoked on legacy systems by completely hiding implementation details. It provides external applications a clean legacy Application Programming Interface (API) that

Figure 1: Connecting Legacy Systems with New Generation Applications

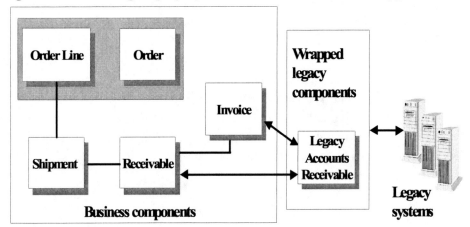

supports a host of abstract services irrespective of the complexity of internal representations of the legacy systems. This legacy API is the software access path to the legacy implementations' supported functions. Wrapping provides an opportunity to include a system's semantic contents and patterns of usage in the public definition of the system. The advantage of this approach is that it promotes conceptual simplicity and language transparency. Further examples on wrappers may be found in Umar (1997).

This technological advancement can be achieved by harnessing the emerging distributed object management technology and by appropriately compartmentalizing existing software and applications. For example, a simple layer of software mapping the legacy APIs to, for example, CORBA IDL, provides for broader system interoperation and distribution of legacy system services through CORBA. Encapsulation is used to partition and componentize legacy systems. Each component can be objectified separately, and then the system can be re-integrated using object-based messaging. The benefits of this approach are that each component can be reused, and system upgrades can happen incrementally. A detailed study of how legacy relational databases can be transformed to semantically equivalent representations accessible via object-oriented interfaces can be found in Papazoglou (1999).

TECHNOLOGY CHALLENGES FOR EBUSINESS AND INTEGRATED VALUE CHAINS

An important consequence of business modeling is that key competitive advantages can be gained by rethinking business processes both internally as well as externally. External rethinking examines the business partner's or customer's view of the enterprise, its product and services. Its goal is to make the enterprise more responsive and effective. Internal rethinking analyzes the flow of work that produces these products and services. This may include the usual intra-enterprise activities such as sales, marketing, manufacturing, distribution, accounting (fiscal). To accomplish the objective of business modeling, business processes must be (re)engineered in a manner which is both natural and leads to interoperable solutions in that they manage end-to-end business processes that span value chains. From a technology standpoint we distinguish between two possible interoperable frameworks within which diverse eBusiness processes and applications can be represented and performed. These include frameworks for the development of eBusiness applications based on homogeneous and heterogeneous infrastructure.

Homogeneous Approach: Business Components and Frameworks

The eBusiness objectives demand a fully integrated information framework and infrastructure. From a technology perspective, the challenge of integrated enterprise computing is to support the new management structures and the work procedures evolving in global markets. Business objects provide a powerful mechanism for dynamic business modeling and re-engineering. Business objects can be used for packaging shared business policy, process and data definitions, and provide pre-assembled business functionality that can be used to wire together and customize business applications. They provide a natural way for describing application-independent concepts such as customers, products, orders, trades, bills, financial instruments and so on. Business-objects add value to a business by providing a way of managing complexity and giving a higher level perspective that is understandable by the business (Manola, 1998). Moreover, business objects help to manage the architectural complexity of distributed objects and three-tier client/server computing. The whole concept of distributed computing can be viewed as simply a global network of cooperating business objects. Furthermore, mission-critical legacy systems can be "wrapped" (see next section) to participate in this distributed object environment.

Business objects package together essential business characteristics such as business procedures, policies and controls around business data. This creates a semantic construct that holds together in a coherent unit the right business policy with the right data, and ensures that the data is used in a manner consistent with the business intent. In contrast to a business object, a business process is characterized by a set of interrelated activities that collectively accomplish a specific business objective, possibly, according to a set of pre-specified policies. A business object is data with behavior, while a business process operates on business objects, i.e., it changes their states and coordinates their interactions. Business processes interact in a predictable, repeatable manner to produce a recognized business activity of generic nature in a specific business domain, e.g., procurement management, general ledger, etc. Business processes are initiated by events that trigger activities in the organization (Curran, 1998). These events can be internal (e.g., rules) or external (e.g., customer requests). The business processes are initiated on the basis of an incoming event (e.g., a customer request), and result in an outgoing event (e.g., the notification that a product is ordered). We collectively refer to business objects and processes as business components.

Business processes that operate within, across or between organizations in order to implement value chains that deliver eBusiness transactions may be implemented using a set of workflow definitions that are created to support discrete segments of the overall process. Workflow management systems support the definition, execution and controlling of the business processes. Workflow applications rely on an extensive foundation of reusable business components, i.e., the core business processes, that form the basis for building new applications. Workflow support for integrated value chains provide the infrastructure to allow business processes to interact, cooperate and execute in a distributed manner across enterprise boundaries. This leads to reuse and sharing of business components across several eBusiness applications.

Figure 2 illustrates a stratified integrated value chain framework for modeling business applications and for developing and delivering enterprise solutions. This enterprise framework provides business (and system) services that are necessary for functional organization and lifecycle of business components, and its (vertical components) are the building blocks of applications targeted for business process or function-specific industries. This enterprise framework consists of business components, processes and workflow applications defined within a specific "vertical" industry, or across such industries. The integrated enterprise framework in Figure 2 provides a base for the effective encapsulation of business practices, policies and tactics in modular high-level components. In other words it includes the basic (generic) business logic for a particular domain. Specialized applications can then be built by enhancing and extending this type of framework instead of having to build entire applications from scratch. This framework supports multiple eBusiness initiatives, integrates with legacy and ERP systems, and assists in quick development and deployment of eBusiness-enabled applications. The infrastructure provides separation of programming and administrative roles so that areas such as object location and security can be administered separately from program flow. Finally, it masks any specific platform, which increases the portability of applications and business components.

The component assembly approach of eBusiness applications is one in which each layer in the enterprise framework uses services (functionality) from one layer and offers services to another layer while hiding the details of the implementation. Interfaces (APIs) offer and receive this functionality. The interfaces define the services that the business component relies on and provides, as well as the semantics of the services offered. The highest two layers in the enterprise framework provide the core business functionality and facilities to develop eBusiness-enabled (workflow) applications that can be easily combined and extended to offer a complete cross-organizational business solution. The enterprise framework comprises the following layers:

1. **Workflow-Enabled eCommerce Applications Layer:** Traditional workflow environments concentrate on the internal business process-routing work from one user to the next. However, when we consider the needs of the modern enterprise, with its outsourced processes and complex partnerships, traditional models of internal control delivered via workflow are no longer relevant. The business processes evolve too quickly, and when it comes to linking those evolving applications across organizational boundaries, all of the established approaches are inadequate. What the workflow layer in Figure 2 delivers is the ability to easily thread together distributed applications, supporting the integration of diverse users and other applications and systems.

    The workflow layer provides the means for developing inter-business applications which interconnect and manage communication among disparate workflow-based business applications and put the business processes in motion. Distributed workflows use functionality provided by business process and objects, and are normally built on a distributed object network infrastructure (Paul, 1998; Schmidt, 1998), such as that provided by the middleware infrastructure layer. The purpose of distributed workflow technology for integrated value chains is to manage long-running, process-oriented applications that automate business processes over enterprise-wide networks. For example, an order activity in a production planning process may start an appropriate order entry process at a closely aligned parts supplier. This type of cooperation can only be achieved if the workflow systems of the cooperating companies are loosely coupled. This results in the elimination of supply chain discontinuities that produce delays and waste. Workflow-enabled business processes can track transactions across department, company and enterprise boundaries, looking at the status of business activities, coordination of the flow of information of (inter and intra-) organizational activities and the possibility to decide among alternative execution paths (Papazoglou, 1997).

One of the key aspects of multilateral electronic business is to effectively and seamlessly provide real-time integration of databases across multiple organizations. Thus workflow activities may invoke components from existing applications, for instance legacy (wrapped) objects, and combine them with newly developed applications comprising business objects and processes.

2.   **Business Process Layer:** The core business process layer provides business objects and default business logic for selected vertical domains. This layer comprises two sublayers: the specialized business services and the generic business process sublayer. The specialized business process sublayer provides business processes, business objects and default business logic for a particular vertical domain, e.g., financial, manufacturing or health-care applications. These are used to develop customized workflow-enabled applications in a specific vertical domain by extending or overriding the default business behavior. The generic business process sub-layer represents generic business services common to multiple vertical industries, e.g.,

Figure 2: Layers of the Business Object Framework

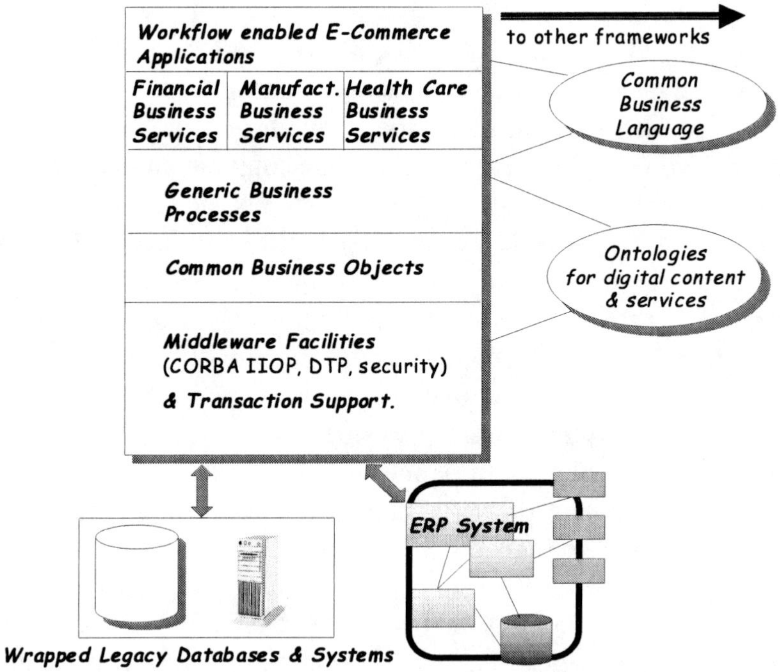

retail (shopping order fulfillment and shipping) and business-to-business functions (procurement, order management, financials, inventory, supply chain management, etc).

The approach taken here is to develop fragments of business processes with the relevant application functionality attached. These fragments are then combined as required to suit the needs of each workflow-enabled application. Rather than having to compose ever more complex end-to-end offerings, the enterprise can leave it to the knowledge worker to choose those elements that are most appropriate, combining the process fragments into a cohesive whole.

If business objects and processes are well defined and modelled using some kind of meta-model (e.g., UML), the building of integrated workflow-enabled eCommerce applications on top of them can be facilitated with the help of the Meta-Object Facility (MOF) (www.omg.org/technology/documents/formal/meta.htm). MOF is a standardized repository for meta-data that contains the descriptions and definitions of the fundamental concepts that applications work with. As a meta-data modelling tool from OMG, the MOF goal is to allow interoperability across the application development cycle by supporting the definition of multiple meta models. To achieve this goal, the MOF specification defines a set of CORBA IDL interfaces that can be used to define and manipulate a set of interoperable meta-models and their corresponding models. It specifies precise mapping rules that enable the CORBA interfaces for meta-models to be automatically generated, thus encouraging consistency in manipulating meta-data in all phases of the distributed application development cycle.

However, there are two constraints when using MOF: (1) the generation of a concrete IDL for a meta-model is feasible only if the meta-model at hand is MOF compliant; (2) interoperability support is limited to CORBA-based application design (as the provided mapping rules generate automatically only CORBA interfaces for the meta-models) and thus interoperation is not facilitated if other middleware or no middleware facility is used.

3. **Common Business Object Layer:** The common business objects (CBOs) are of three types: business objects commonly used in multiple application domains, business object interfaces that provide interoperability between applications and objects that implement frequently useful design patterns for business applications (Abinavam, 1998). The first type of function is found in business-objects which provide pre-assembled business functionality that can be used to bring together and customize applications. These provide a natural way for describing application-independent (common) concepts such as customers, products, orders, bills, financial instruments and temporal information, such as a quarterly earnings period or annual tax cycle. The

second type of CBOs provides functions of commonly used business objects that can be used as the foundation for interoperability between applications by providing interfaces to core business processes. These CBOs allow independently developed applications to work together and enterprise framework applications to interoperate with legacy and ERP applications. The last type of CBOs supports design patterns that are useful in many different application domains. Typical examples of these include: classification types–used to represent user-defined types that modify business policies; and keyables–used to support balances across different composite keys (Abinavam, 1998).

4. **Middleware Services Layer:** This layer provides the run-time environment and the distribution, reliability and security services required to support the common business objects and the core business processes. It caters for initiating, executing, sequencing and controlling instances of a process definition in conjunction with multi-cast protocols, delivery receipts, authenticated packages and smart firewalls (McConnel, 1997). Many of the services of this layer are based on object service definitions from the Object Management Group (OMG). For example, this layer provides object transaction services, collection handling, communication between distributed objects and persistence management. These functions may be provided by a CORBA-compliant Object Request Broker (ORB), or they may be merged and combined with functions provided with Java as these provided by the San Fransisco framework (Abinavam, 1998). San Fransisco uses Java and Java's remote method invocation (RMI) as a basis for the object communication infrastructure. ORB functionality can be extended with functionality offered by Distributed Transaction Processing (DTP) monitors, such as for example Encina and Tuxedo, to provide the transactional properties required for supporting business-like transactions.

Since document exchange is an important step in automated business transaction for integrated value chains, there has been some work done in the area of providing framework for (meta)data description and processing so that (Web) documents can be machine-understandable and therefore processed. Resource Description Framework (RDF) (www.w3.org/RDF) is one of the representative works in this area. RDF has been endorsed as a W3C Recommendation for the model to represent meta-data, as well as the syntax to encode and transport this meta-data in a manner that maximizes the interoperability of independently developed Web servers and clients. RDF emphasizes providing facilities with the ability to automated processing of

Web resources, which can be used in a variety of application areas, e.g., in resource discovery to provide better search engine capabilities, in cataloguing for describing the content and content relationships available at a particular Web site by intelligent software agents to facilitate knowledge sharing and exchange, etc.

Although RDF can be used to automate some business processes, its main purpose is for (Web) document exchange. Therefore it does not facilitate the need to describe transaction scenarios and processes capabilities which are core in the integrated value chain. On the other hand, the BizTalk is an XML framework designed specifically for application integration and eCommerce. It includes a design framework for implementing an XML schema and a set of XML tags used in messages sent between applications. The design emphasis is to leverage the existing data models, solutions and application infrastructure, and adapt them for eCommerce through the use of XML. The information about publishing XML, XSL and information models and business processes supported by applications that support the BizTalk Framework can be found at www.biztalk.org.

Interoperation in integrated value chains is achieved mainly at the workflow and business process level, where cross-enterprise applications may invoke business services or script together business objects from different organizations. However, as eBusiness focuses increasingly on transenterprise communications and as the number of trading partners and sophistication of commerce applications increases, the need to harmonize business models, processes, terminology and representation formats rises rapidly. Many companies have already begun to organize and standardize their digital services in order to create and maintain sustainable network relationships with their trading partners. Common ontologies www.ontology.org are being developed in several industry sectors so that trading companies can interact by sharing a common terminology to avoid misunderstandings. For example, many industries such as electronics, automotive and aerospace have already established standard XML DTDs to create a standard shared terminology for their respective vertical industry.

The generic enterprise framework shown in Figure 3 was influenced by projects like the eCo architecture (McConnel, 1997) and business frameworks such as San Francisco (Abinavam, 1998). The objective of the eCo framework is to define an architecture through which information on eCommerce systems can be communicated and within which the diverse world of eCommerce can be represented. eCo offers a suite of services providing business components interconnected using a distributed object management protocol (like CORBA). San Francisco is a multi-layered

Figure 3: Conducting eBusiness Using ebXML (Copyright © ebXML, 2000).

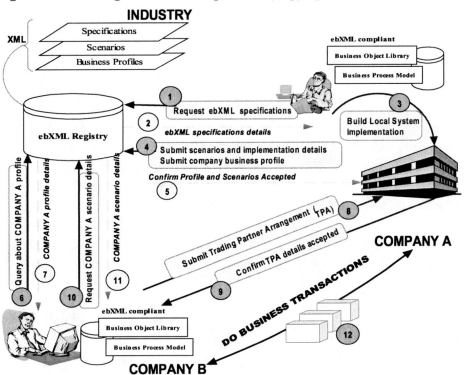

architecture using distributed object and framework technologies to provide an infrastructure that can be used to build eBusiness applications. It also provides object models for specific domain business processes and default business logic that can be used to start building applications in these domains. San Francisco is implemented using the Java language this makes San Francisco and applications developed using it portable across many platforms. The current product contains implementations for the following business activities: General Ledger, Accounts Receivable/Payable, Order Management and Warehouse Management.

In many situations it is desirable to facilitate spontaneous commerce between trading partners without custom integration or prior agreement on specific industry-wide standards. In such cases business documents represent a more intuitive and flexible way to access business services than programming business process APIs. In such situations it is much easier to interconnect companies in terms of the documents they exchange, on which they largely agree, rather than in terms of their business system interfaces (Glushko, 1999). The coupling in such situations is looser and interoperation is achieved by means of a Common Business Language such as the electronic business XML (ebXML) (www.ebxml.org). ebXML consists of a set of XML document type definitions that are common for business-to-business (ANSI X12 EDI) transactions across most industries. Its purpose is to preserve and extend the EDI infrastructure, by leveraging semantics and structure of EDI standards such as X12 and EDIFACT. Some concepts and constructs needed in these "vertical" specifications apply to all business domains and are expressed in a common way across vendors to enable ebXML-based eBusiness. These constructs include descriptions of businesses, products and individuals, measurements, date, time, location, currencies, business classification codes and so on. Translation services can be developed to handle the mapping from one company's XML documents onto document formats used by its trading partner and into data formats required by its own legacy systems. A complete business integration solution along the lines of ebXML requires: standardized tags (meta-data) for each industry sector; a means for mapping between different meta-data descriptions; and means for processing XML documents and invoking business applications and services provided by business processes and workflows.

Figure 3 shows a conceptual model for two trading partners, engaging in a simple business transaction interchange. This model is provided as an illustration of the processes and steps that may typically be required using ebXML Applications and related Components and is adapted from ebXML (2000). In Figure 3, Company A requests an ebXML specification from an ebXML Registry that contains a set of ebXML specifications in order to determine if it wants to become an ebXML-compliant participant (Figure 3, step 1). Company A, after reviewing the specification that it receives, decides to build and deploy its own ebXML-compliant application (Figure 3, steps 2 and 3). Company A then submits its own implementation details, reference links and Trading Partner Profile (TPP) as a request to the ebXML Registry (Figure 3, step 4). The TPP submitted describes the company's ebXML capabilities and constraints, as well as its supported business scenarios (XML versions of the business processes). The TPP is verified and acknowledged by the ebXML Registry (Figure 3, step 5). Company B is then informed by Company A that they would like to engage in a business transaction using ebXML. Subsequently, Company B queries the ebXML Registry about Company A and Company A's profile is retrieved (Figure 3, steps 6 and 7). Based on the TPP, the application determines that it is able to execute a specific scenario that Company A supports. Before engaging in that scenario, Company B submits a proposed Trading Partner Agreement (TPA) directly to Company A's ebXML-compliant software interface. The TPA outlines the eBusiness scenario and specific arrangement(s) it wants to use with Company A, as well as certain messaging, contingency and security-related requirements (Figure 3, step 8). Company A accepts the TPA and acknowledgement is sent directly to Company B (Figure 3, step 9). Since the scenario from Company A was not available in the software package that Company B is using, the application requests it and receives it from the ebXML Registry (Figure 3, step 10 and 11). Based on the business processes (contained in the process models) and business messages exchanged, Companies A and B are now engaging in eBusiness utilizing ebXML specifications via their respective software applications (Figure 3, step 12).

Interoperability in ebXML is achieved by applying business objects across business models that enable representation of business relationships between interacting companies in a shared business process. Business objects and business processes are contained in a business library which is used in conjunction with a lexicon that contains data and process definitions as expressed in business terminology and organized per industry sector. The fact that component technology is also used to support ebXML business activities makes it easy to integrate ebXML-based applications with business object frameworks such as those depicted in Figure 2.

Heterogeneous Approaches: eServices

Traditionally, integrated value chain applications have been viewed as a collection of cooperating business components that run over multiple organizations in a relatively closed network. As a result, these environments are geared toward a homogeneous infrastructure and tightly coupled applications where a client process expects a particular server interaction syntax and semantics. However, these environments do not facilitate spontaneous or dynamic commerce between trading partners without prior custom integration. There is a need for computing infrastructure that enables the building of complex applications by combining (heterogeneous) data and processes offered in the form of services available across the network. Applications in an open Internet environment are better characterized as a collection of independent eServices from different vendors, or enterprise applications, interacting with (or using) other eServices owned by different vendors or even different divisions within a company. These eServices normally have very diverse data structures, processing capabilities and qualities and are offered by different providers.

Businesses in an integrated value chain may offer a set of eBusiness "services" to each other. Broadly speaking we may characterize an eService as a software component that performs business-related activities and may conduct transactions over the Internet. Examples of such services include catalogue browsing, ordering products, making payment, checking order status, product lifecycle, new product introduction and so on. Each business describes the types of business services offered, their interfaces and other information needed to use a particular service offering. The types of services and their interfaces can vary among business providers, although a group of businesses or marketplace may adopt some common conventions. For example, in a specific vertical industry, businesses participating in that industry could agree on a common catalog update service, a product data exchange service, a failure analysis service and so on.

Each provided eService contains a service interface and a service description and may be composed of sub-services. eServices can continue to recur until an atomic service is reached. In addition to sub-services, a service may invoke other services in order to complete that service. For example, a service might "wrap" a traditional EDI system defined in accordance with a human readable specification. By examining the service interface, potential partners can be made aware of each others' offerings or get the specification. Regardless of the method used, a potential trading partner must be able to fully determine the protocols required for using a service by examining the information available through the service description environment.

Each eService represents an interface to a business process. At the highest level, businesses interact by using the services of each other within the context of some business process. At the most abstract level, eServices refer to the resources accessible via the Web which provide structured data sources (e.g., databases), semi-structured (e.g., HTML documents) or unstructured information sources (e.g., text files, images), and computational software (e.g., business processes/applications, workflows or agents). The availability of diverse electronic services on the Web has raised high expectations for flexible and efficient sharing of services, which has been witnessed in the areas such as electronic catalogs, digital libraries, Web-based value chain networks, Web-based healthcare systems, just to mention a few. Integrated value chains have significant competitive advantages over traditional enterprises. They can provide new services and products without the investment and delays a traditional enterprise requires, and may utilize the best-in-their-class component services without having to develop them.

The development of cooperative applications which share Web-accessible services is still an ad hoc very demanding and time-consuming task. It typically requires an enormous effort of low-level programming. The problem is further aggravated by the fact that the service space in the Web is dynamic, diverse and very large. The main goal of this section is to enhance the fundamental understanding of how to describe the Web-accessible services so that they can be efficiently and effectively created, searched, shared and combined in order to develop integrated value systems applications. This involves providing high-level modeling constructs to describe services (by means of their interfaces and semantics), to query services and to compose new services from available services. In the following sections we discuss the stages in eService development and the issues in describing services. We also describe our approach as well as the state-of-the-art enabling technology in service development.

Steps in eService-Based Integrated Value Chain Application Development
    In order to develop integrated value chain applications based on eServices through the Web, an organization needs to go through the following steps:
- **Service Presentation:** Firstly, business application functionality has to be offered in the form of eServices for online access. Typical technologies that can be used at this step are XML, Java applets and servlets, CGI and homegrown software for the communication with the back-end databases. During this step, legacy applications of the organization can be integrated with the Web front-end, allowing customers to effectively use eServices that map to legacy components. Typical examples are enterprise portals and Web interfaces for accessing various services.
- **Service Registration and Publication:** The second step involves the publication of the service interfaces in a form that can be understood and queried by other organizations when developing a networked application. Therefore an expressive and declarative service description language needs to be developed so that services can be searched, selected and combined.
- **Service Selection:** Tools and facilities should be offered for querying the service descriptions with the aim of understanding their functionality and appropriateness for an application. The ultimate goal is to be able to select advertised services from various organizations in an integrated value system setting.
- **Service Composition:** The final step is the availability of facilities that enable the construction of an integrated value system application by means of combining existing services and composing new services on the basis of a service library. This step involves issues such as service composability, compatibility, conformance and substitutability.

    Once the service is properly described and advertised, it is ready to be retrieved and used in building integrated value system applications (eServices). Services that belong to different enterprises can then be fused together and become part of an integrated value system application. Existing integrated value system applications can be stored in an application library and can be also re-used and specialized, just like services, to develop newer applications. In essence, existing applications are another form of high-level service. In this way eServices may transparently invoke legacy (wrapped) applications and combine them with newer generation business processes.

We assume that (1) individual business service designers require no direct knowledge or access of the models and implementations used by other enterprises; (2) services that belong to different enterprises are integrated and interact only via their inter-enterprise interface specifications. Inter-enterprise services are functional abstractions of a collection of (business) services provided by individual enterprises.

Issues in Service Modeling and Description

The current advances in Web technology represent an important development in information processing. However, there is no model or methodology available for describing (advertising), querying and composing eServices in a systematic manner which make them easy to adapt, to verify and to deploy. This is poorly supported by existing process models for the following reasons:

- **Service Heterogeneity:** Different enterprises typically model their processes using different conceptual, process and/or execution models. Even if workflow and data exchange standards are followed, each process requires different handling and there doesn't seem to be a general solution for dealing with heterogeneity in any model. A solution to this problem is provided by (Georgakopoulos et al, 1999) who suggest that process models that capture application semantics and provide effective abstractions via sub-classing can deal better with heterogeneity than other process models that bury integration semantics in the code of some integration programs and, based on this rationale, they propose the Collaboration Management Model (CMM).

- **Service Autonomy**: The integration of the individual (business) services can be captured by the use of generic invocation and feedback activities. We also note that using such existing process technology to integrate services can only be accomplished by a tight integration of services and this leads to specification explosion. An orthogonal problem is that service integration using low-level activities may not be possible at all since it requires that the designer or an integrator has detailed knowledge and access of the services that are used by the other enterprises. This assumption and approach of modeling is not possible with usual enterprise policies. Enterprises often protect their processes and their related implementation, since they can be observed, measured and analyzed to reveal important details about the efficiency of an enterprise in delivering a service of a product (e.g., required cost, time, etc.). Preliminary research contribution in this area is the Service-Oriented Process (SOP) model (Georgakopoulos et al, 2000) that models supply chains as multi-enterprise processes that integrate, dynamically select and invoke services offered by external businesses. SOP decouples service interfaces from service implementation and thus enables multi-enterprise processes to include activities specified only as an abstract interface, i.e., to include activity place holders.

- **Multiple Service Providers**: There may be multiple service providers that offer the same or similar services, i.e., their services can be used to achieve the same or similar objectives. Normally a customer may use the services that offer the most favorable terms in achieving its business objectives. To select the best collection of services, a service integrator may perform dynamic service selection and integration to dynamically construct a new service. This task is heavily dependent on the way the services are modeled and described. There are preliminary research contributions in the area of service quality and automatic service selection via service brokering in the literature (Geppert, 1998; Bichler, 1998).

Representation of eServices

Most existing work in representing services is done by interface specification, e.g., CORBA IDL. However a service interface is only a declarative specification of service syntax and is therefore not sufficient on its own to develop integrated value chain applications. It normally includes application-specific activities, operations and application-specific states. These capture the complex interactions between clients and service providers. In addition, service interfaces specify input and output parameters. Additional means to advertise and discover services in an integrated value chain environment (such as the semantics) are required that support the service lifecycle that covers the time even before a service is captured and wrapped by a basic service activity and service wrapper processes.

In this section we propose to use a declarative service description language (SDL) for service describing, advertising and service assembling. In contrast to traditional database and programming languages, SDL will not focus on providing query and computation constructs. Instead, it will offer constructs for describing existing services; facilitating, creating and composing new services; capturing their interaction; and invoking their operations. Note that CORBA's IDL and scripting languages such as Perl are too low level to provide for efficient sharing for the available eServices. More importantly, these languages interleave the code for service access and integration which makes the reuse and evolution of the service very complex. The language we propose accepts as input information from the business model and is expressive enough to supplement the business modeling constructs with the following:

- Provide a comprehensive description of the service semantics. This includes the description of:
  - o *Service properties*, i.e., service general information (e.g., identification, owner), service access information (e.g., service location-URL, the maximum time for a conversation between the service and a service requester, public key certificate).
  - o *Service ontology*, i.e., what is the service about and the terminology that is needed to discover the service.
  - o *Service cost*, i.e., the estimated cost for using the service or the information provided by the service.
  - o *Payment*, i.e., the way the service receives the payment from the customers.
  - o *Actors*, i.e., the people or organizations who are using the service.
  - o *Authorization/security/visibility*, i.e., who can see/use what (service contents and functions).
  - o *Service contents*, which specifies the content and the structure of the underling service, e.g., the attributes, objects, the constraints on use of attributes/objects, etc.
  - o *Service capability*, which specifies the access patterns that the service supports. For example at the system level, one can look at the service interface, conditions for combining services and deriving consistent results; while at the data level, one may look at such services as selection of objects on the basis of values of attributes, a join across objects and delivery of data as an XML file. The access pattern declared for a service provides the way of describing applications supported by the service or the functionalities supported by the service wrapper.

In other words, this is a set of meta-information that is needed for the service to be selected, retrieved and reused. Figure 4 gives a description for a hypothetical Bidding service offered by some enterprise in SDL.

- *Support service extensibility*. The language will provide a set of generic classes and composition operators. The generic classes provide a minimal set of features required for accessing, monitoring and controlling services. The composition operators can be used to reuse, extend and customize existing services in order to develop quickly and deploy new value-added services.

- Cater for the creation of both dynamic and transient relationships as well as long-term relationships among services to enable flexible integration and re-use of existing services. More precisely, since scalability and flexibility are of great importance in Web-based environments, we anticipate that the proposed language will provide operators for:

  o The creation of a value-added service from integration of a small number of known and loosely coupled services. In this case, the integrator (i.e., the developer of the value- added service) defines value chains as the desired service by examining all the services to be integrated. A typical example is the creation of an integrated value system that provides, e.g., product manufacturing value chain. A participant service focuses on one activity in the value-added service and partners with multiple other services in other value chains.

  o The creation of a value-added service from a potential large number of (unknown) loosely coupled services. In this case, the integrator defines value chains as a description of desired activities in the service (e.g., searching books, buying books, etc.). This creates a container of a desired actual service that can offer (fully or partially) the desired activities. At any time during the lifespan of a service, an actual service provider can locate containers of interest and register the service in them. By doing so, the proposed language provides appropriate abstractions for creating virtual services. A typical example is the creation of a virtual enterprise where service providers dynamically form temporary alliances, joining their services in order to share their costs, skills and resources in offering the value-added service. The service can then be dispensed with when it is no longer profitable or actual.

Figure 5, illustrates the process of service composition and creating value-added services. In this figure we assume that this enterprise is offering an Auctioning service created by combining hypothetical Bidding and Billing services.

Figure 4: SDL for Bidding Service

service Bidding
begin
    Owner: eService company
    Location: www.eservice.com

    Ontology: auction, bidding

    Cost: …

Payment: credit cards

Actors: bidders

Contents

    User_details

 attributes

    (user, company_name,

    company_address,

    email_address)

 visibility: public

Item_details

 attributes

    (item_name, item_amount,

    item_quality, item_pickup_date,

    item_no, current_price,

    minimum_increment, no_of_bids,

    auction_started, auction_ends,

    seller, description)

    visibility: public

Functions

 Browse

    input: none

    output: item_details

    visibility: public

 Search

    input: item_no **or** item_name

    output: item_details

    visibility: public

Bid

    input: item_no, amount, price_increment

    output: purchase_details

    visibility: subscribers

end;

Figure 5: Service Composition

service Auctioning

begin

 Owner: eService company;

Location: www.eservice.com;
Ontology: auction, biding, billing;
Cost: …
Payment: credit cards;
Actors: bidders;
Use: service Bidding, service Billing;
    Visibility: private;
Contents: …// which is the combination from Bidding and Billing services;
  Functions: …// which is the combination from Bidding and Billing services;
end;

Enabling Technologies

One of the most recent and relevant initiatives in eService development is E-speak (www.e-speak.net) from Hewlett Packard (www.hp.com) which is an open software platform designed specifically for the development, deployment and intelligent interaction of eServices. Once services become e-speak enabled, they can dynamically discover and negotiate with each other, can mediate on behalf of their users and can compose themselves into more complex services with strategies, development environments or device capabilities.

The E-speak platform consists of the following two components:

• The *E-speak Service Framework Specification (SFS)* that defines integrated value chains as standard business interactions and conventions, such as XML documents. It provides a detailed framework in which Internet B2B eServices can discover each other; negotiate according to user-defined criteria, reach agreement on product, pricing and delivery terms; and combine other eServices to provide value-added services.

• The *E-speak Service Engine*, a high-performance software implementation of the SFS, which implements business collaboration conventions expressed as both Java and XML APIs. It supports (1) dynamic discovery of other eServices that meet specific attributes; (2) negotiation between requester and service provider; (3) monitoring transactions in real-time; (4) composition of independent eServices into a complex end-to-end solution.

In summary, E-speak allows the clients/service to interact with each other in a more abstract way. Once an E-service is E-speak-enabled, the provider has to register the service with a host system by creating a description of the service that consists of its specific attributes. Users looking for eServices then describe the type of service they want and E-speak will automatically discover registered services that have the desired attributes.

Compared with other middleware such as CORBA, E-speak supports higher level concepts, i.e., services, rather then interfaces between applications distributed over the Internet. In contrast with the middleware, E-speak doesn't require applications to have fixed locations or interactions, so it allows broader, dynamic access to data. Currently, E-speak has the following limitations:

- It does not provide query facilities that allow users to ask sophisticated questions about the information of services besides the contents and the structure, e.g., the status, interaction mode, etc., to have a feel of what the service is about, how it looks, and how to access it:

- It doesn't address the critical factors for service registration, i.e., what should be described from the services so that accurate service searching can be performed.

Nevertheless, E-speak can be used as a platform to implement our framework for service description discussed in this section. It is worth mentioning here that some reflective operations, e.g., *refMetaObject, refItself, reflsInstanceOf,* provided by the CORBA reflective module (defined in the reflective interfaces), can be used for retrieving object meta-data, if MOF is used. However, these operations are rather primitive, non-declarative and therefore not suitable for the end-user.

The most recent industry initiative in service registration, discovering and integration is the Universal Description, Discovery and Integration (UDDI) standard (www.uddi.org). UDDI is a specification for distributed Web-based information registries of eServices that can be used in conjunction with E-speak to remedy some of the problems stated above. It takes advantage of standards such as XML (eXtensible Markup Language) and TCP/IP, HTTP, DNS (Domain Name System) and SOAP (Simple Object Access Protocol) protocols to create a uniform service description format and service discovery protocol. More specifically, the UDDI specifications consist of an XML schema for SOAP messages and a description of the UDDI API specification. These together form a base information model and interaction framework that provides the ability to publish information about a wide range of Web services.

The core component of UDDI is the UDDI business registration, an XML file used to describe a business entity and its eServices. The UDDI business registry is a logically centralized, physically distributed service with multiple root nodes that replicate data with each other on a regular basis. Once a business registers with a single instance of the business registry service, the data is automatically shared with other UDDI root nodes and becomes freely available to anyone who needs to discover what services are exposed by a given business. In this way, the UDDI business registry provides "registered once, published everywhere" access to information about Web services.

Conceptually, a UDDI business registration contains three components: 'white pages' including address, contact and known identifiers; 'yellow pages' including industrial categorizations based on standard taxonomies; and 'green pages' that contain the technical information about the services exposed by the business. Green pages include references to specifications for eServices as well as support for pointers to various file and URL-based discovery mechanisms if required.

UDDI is designed to complement existing online marketplaces and search engines by providing them with standardized formats for programmatic business and service discovery. The ability to locate parties that can provide a specific product or service at a given price or within a specific geographic boundary in a given timeframe is not directly covered by UDDI specifications. These kinds of advanced discovery features require further collaboration and design work between buyers and sellers. Instead, UDDI forms the basis for defining theses services at a higher level.

The UDDI founding companies (Ariba, IBM and Microsoft) are launching a jointly operated UDDI business registry on the Web. Registration of businesses and services is not available at the time this chapter is being written, but it is planned to be available soon.

FROM ESERVICES TO BUSINESS TRANSACTIONS

Transactions in the eBusiness arena are usually long-lived propositions involving negotiations, commitments, contracts, floating exchange rates, shipping and logistics, tracking, varied payment instruments, exception handling and customer satisfaction. Performance of these tasks requires involving collaborative computing technologies to support the eService paradigm. In this section we present our vision regarding business transactions.

eService technology can serve to manage long-running, process-oriented applications that automate business processes over enterprise-wide networks and deliver the semantics of database-like transactions for eBusiness. A *business transaction (BT)* can be perceived as a script prescribing the combination—and subsequent interoperation—of business processes and objects to reach a joint business goal. A BT-service can be viewed as comprising two types of eServices: atomic eServices and non-atomic eServices. A BT-service identifies which eServices should be executed in an atomic (all or nothing) fashion. Atomicity guarantees that if for some reason the transaction fails, e.g., is aborted, all of its changes are undone, and it will be as though the transaction never ran. *Atomic eServices* as activity implementations frequently appear when the business model represents one of the core business processes (order entry, etc.) of an enterprise. *Non-atomic eService* activity implementations are frequently found within support processes (travel expense accounts, etc.). If for some reason the atomic eService identified by the BT-service cannot be successfully completed, then all running eServices should be aborted, and completed ones are compensated by having their effects revoked.

Rather than having to compose ever more complex end-to-end offerings as in the case of the homogeneous approach, the enterprise can leave it to the application developer to choose those elements that are most appropriate, combining the eService fragments into a cohesive BT-service whole. At run-time the BT-service management system will manage the flow of control and data between the business processes and will establish transaction boundaries around them as defined in the transaction script. A BT-service may utilize workflow technology to bundle eServices together and provide the sequence of business activities, arrangement for the delivery of work to the appropriate organizational resources; tracking of the status of business activities; coordination of the flow of information of (inter and intra-) organizational activities and the possibility to decide among alternative execution paths (Papazoglou, 1997).

Business transactions have several distinguishing characteristics when compared with traditional database transactions. Firstly, they extend the scope of traditional transaction processing as they may encompass classical transactions which they combine with non-transactional processes. Secondly, they group both classical atomic as well as non-atomic computations together into a unit of work that reflects the semantics and behavior of their underlying business task. Thirdly, they are governed by unconventional types of atomicity. We may distinguish between four broad types of atomicity (Yang, 2000):

- *Payment atomicity*: Payment-atomic protocols affect the transfer of funds from one party to another. Payment atomicity is the basic level of atomicity that each electronic commerce protocol should satisfy.
- *Goods atomicity*: Goods atomicity protocols are payment-atomic, and also affect an exact transfer of goods for money.
- *Delivery atomicity*: Delivery-atomic protocols are payment- and goods-

atomic protocols that allow both transacting parties to prove exactly which goods were delivered.

- *Contract atomicity*: In addition to these basic atomicity protocols, business transactions are generally governed by contracts and update accounts. These are normally based on electronic commerce protocols which include the exchange of financial information services and the exchange of bills and invoices. Thus payment-atomic protocols must also be contract-atomic.

In the world of eBusiness, traditional database transactions are replaced with long lived, multi-level collaborations. It is therefore not surprising that they require support for a variety of unconventional behavioral features which can be summarized in the following:

1. *Generic characteristics*:
   (a) who is involved in the transaction;
   (b) what is being transacted;
   (c) the destination of payment and delivery;
   (d) the transaction timeframe;
   (e) permissible operations.
2. *Special purpose characteristics*:
   (a) links to other transactions;
   (b) receipts and acknowledgments;
   (c) identification of money transferred outside national boundaries.
3. *Advanced characteristics*:
   (a) the ability to support reversible (compensatible) and repaired (contin gency) transactions;
   (b) the ability to reconcile and link transactions with other transactions;
   (c) the ability to specify contractual agreements, liabilities and dispute resolution policies;
   (d) the ability to support secure EDI, e.g., SET (www.setco.org), transactions that guarantee integrity of information, confidentiality and non-repudiation;
   (e) the ability for transactions to be monitored, logged and recovered.

A key activity in integrated value chains is the collection, management, analysis and interpretation of the various commercial data to make more intelligent and effective transaction-related decisions. Examples include collecting business references, coordinating and managing marketing strategies, determining new product offerings, granting/extending credit and managing market risk. Business transactions usually operate on document-based information objects such as documents and forms. A document is traditionally associated with items such as manuals, letters, bids and proposals. A form is traditionally associated with items such as invoices, purchase orders and travel requests. Both these media are arranged according to some predefined structure. Forms-based objects are closely aligned with business transactions which have numerical nature, while document-based objects are associated with contracts or bids. This allows business transactions to interchange everything from product information and pricing proposals to financial and legal statements. By using XML as the common format for exchanging document and forms-based information associated with business transactions, organizations can simplify and streamline the exchange of commercial data. In a recent development IBM has submitted a specification for defining and implementing eContracts called Trading Partner Agreement Markup Language (tapML) (Sachs, 2000). The foundation of tpaML is the Trading Partner Agreement (TPA). A TPA is an eContract that uses XML to stipulate the general terms and conditions, participant roles, e.g., buyers and sellers, communication and security protocols, and a business protocol (such as valid actions and sequencing rules). A TPA thus defines how trading partners will interact at the transport, document exchange and business protocol levels. XML-based TPA documents capture the essential information upon which the trading partner must agree in order for their applications and business processes to communicate.

The combination of eService technology with XML-based development can lead to a flexible BT environment. Consider the following business transaction scenario involving two companies. A company (buyer) is placing an order with a supplier company. This could be an XML document which can be routed to the appropriate manger for approval. The invocation parameters together with the eService name (purchase order) is then dispatched to the supplier together with an ensuing contract specifying the terms and conditions

Figure 6: Business Transaction in Terms of eService and XML

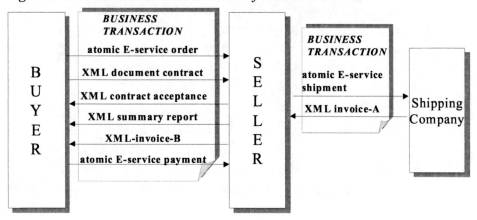

of the purchase in a similar manner to that outlined above. The supplier then accepts the contract and a summary is returned to the buyer. The supplier then issues the appropriate shipping instructions to a shipping company (in the form of an eService). An invoice is then sent to the buyer in XML. Appropriate changes are made to the invoice systems to reflect the order, inventory and accounting changes from this particular business transaction (see Figure 6).

For eBusiness transactions to become a more viable vehicle for integrated value chains, there are a number of security issues that must be resolved. Among the technical efforts to address these concerns is the development of a *secure electronic transaction (SET)* specification for payment over the Web.

The *Secure Electronic Transaction (SET)* protocol (www.setco.org) was developed jointly by payment card companies, specifically Visa and MasterCard, and software manufacturers. SET offers advancements in the Internet and is the first end-to-end solution. SET makes use of Netscape's Secure Sockets Layer (SSL), Microsoft's Secure Transaction Technology (STT) and Terisa System's Secure Hypertext Transfer Protocol, and uses aspects of a public key infrastructure. The SET specification is designed to enable payment security for all involved, authenticate card-holders and merchants, provide confidentiality of payment data, and define protocols for potential electronic security service providers. Currently, IBM and Verisign are extending SET to achieve product interoperability (www.setco.org/interoperability.html). The three basic types of payment interoperability pursued are: consumer/merchant interoperability where any consumer may purchase from any merchant; merchant/gateway interoperability which indicates the ability for any gateway to acquire transactions from any merchant; and SET component/certificate authority interoperability which indicates the ability for any SET component (such as cardholder wallet or merchant) to obtain SET certificates from any SET certificate authority.

Such activities address several of the security requirements of integrated value chains and can provide the basic infrastructure necessary for the development of a secure transaction framework that will guarantee interoperability at the level of secure business transactions.

SUMMARY

The broadening of an enterprise's view beyond its direct suppliers and customers, the optimisation of business practices for an entire value chain and the drive towards strategic partnerships and integrated value chains is among the most important factors for remaining competitive in the digital era. However, the incompatibility and heterogeneity of business models and systems across different enterprises is still a major obstacle. Efficient business process management technology and business-to-business communication, as well as efficient enterprise application integration technology for combining mission-critical legacy systems with new business components, are necessary prerequisites for success in this environment.

In this chapter we have given a detailed account of the business and technology considerations, as well as infrastructural support, that are required to enable the transition of organizations from relative independence and functionally oriented business thinking to integrated value chains. More specifically, we have examined new business models and cross-enterprise interoperability which, along with leveraging legacy systems, constitute essential requirements for integrated value chains, and then we demonstrated how business processes and information systems can be combined with legacy assets in order to accommodate a broader range of business process variability and evolution. Subsequently, we distinguished between two possible interoperable frameworks (from technology point of view) for implementing integrated value chains: the homogeneous vs. the heterogeneous framework for eBusiness applications development. We considered business components and frameworks as enabling technologies within a homogeneous framework and demonstrated how they can be used for developing networked applications within such an environment. eServices were then considered as enabling technology for developing integrated value chain applications within a heterogeneous framework. Along these lines, we described issues related to eService-based application development as well as enabling technologies, and we analyzed our approach for eService application development. We finally illustrated how business transactions can be combined with eServices to provide flexible electronic business solutions.

REFERENCES

Abinavam, S., et al. (1998). *San Francisco Concepts & Facilities*. International Technical Support Organization, IBM, February, SG24-2157-00.

Benson, R. J. (1996). Infrastructures, architectures and utilities. In Oonincx, J. A. M., Ribbers, P. M. and Th. Takkenberg, C. A. (Eds). *Organisatie, Besturing en Informatie*. Samsom.

Bichler, M., Segev, A. and Bean, C. (1998). A electronic broker for business-to-business electronic commerce in the Internet. *International Journal of Cooperative Information Systems*, 7(4), 315-330.

Brodie, M.L. and Stonebraker, M. (1995). *Migrating Legacy Systems: Gateways, Interfaces and the Incremental Approach*. Morgan Kaufman Publishing Company.

Curran, T., Keller, G. and Ladd, A. (1998). *SAP R/3 Business Blueprint: Understanding the Business Process Reference Model*. NJ: Prentice-Hall.

Data Access Technologies. (1997). *Business Object Architecture (BOA) Proposal*. BOM/97-11-09, OMG Business Object Domain Task Force.

Dobbs, J. H. (1998). *Competition's New Battleground: The Integrated Value Chain"*. Cambridge Technology Partners. Available on the World Wide Web at: http://www.ctp.com/.

EbXML. (2000). ebXML technical architecture specification. *OASIS*, October.

Georgakopoulos, D., et. al. (1999). Managing process and service fusion in virtual enterprises. *Information Systems, Special Issue on Information Systems Support for Electronic Commerce*, 24(6), 429-456.

Georgakopoulos, D., Cichocki, A., Schuster, H. and Baker, D. (2000). Process-based eService integration. In *Proceedings of 1st Workshop on Technologies for E-Services*, in cooperation with VLDB 2000, Cairo, Egypt, September 14-15.

Geppert, A., Kradolfer, M. and Tombros, D. (1998). Market-based workflow management. *International Journal of Cooperative Information Systems*, 7(4), 297-314.

Glushko, R. J, Tenenbaum, J. M. and Meltzer, B. (1999). An XML framework for agent-based eCommerce. *Communications of the ACM*, 42(3), 106-109.

Manola, F., et al. (1998). Supporting cooperation in enterprise scale distributed object systems. In Papazoglou, M. P. and Schlageter, G. (Eds.), *Cooperative Information Systems: Trends and Directions*. London: Academic Press.

McConnel, S. (1997). *The OMG/CommerceNet Joint Electronic Commerce White-Paper*, July, EC/97-06-09, Object Management Group.

Papazoglou, M. P., Delis, A., Bouguettaya, A. and Haghjoo, M. (1997). Class library support for workflow environments and applications. *IEEE Transactions on Computer Systems*, 46(6), 673-686.

Papazoglou, M. P. and van den Heuvel, W. J. (1999). Leveraging legacy assets. In Papazoglou, M., Spaccapietra, S. and Tari, Z. (Eds.), *Advances in Object-Oriented Modeling*. MIT Press.

Paul, S., et. al. (1997). Essential requirements for a workflow standard. *OOPSLA '97 Business Object Workshop III*. Available on the World Wide Web at: http://www.jeffsutherland.org/oopsla97/. Atlanta.

Sachs, M., et. al. (2000). Executable trading-partner agreements in electronic commerce. *T. J. Watson Research Center*, IBM.

Schmidt, M. T. (1998) Building workflow business objects, object-oriented programming systems languages applications. *OOPSLA '98 Business Object Workshop IV*,

OOPSLA '98. (1998). Available on the World Wide Web at: http://www.jeffsutherland.org/oopsla98/, Vancouver, California, October.

Umar, A. (1997). Application (Re)*Engineering: Building Web-based Applications and Dealing with Legacies*. NJ: Prentice Hall.

Yang, J. and Papazoglou, M. (2000). Interoperation support for electronic business. *Communications of the ACM*, 43(6), 39-47.

Chapter XII

Creating Virtual Alliances Through Value Chain Management: An Innovative Approach to eBusiness Strategy

Janice M. Burn
Edith Cowan University, Australia

Ray Hackney
Manchester Metropolitan University, UK

This chapter proposes a new approach to strategic planning for eBusiness systems which incorporates a three-stage investigation using value, supply and demand chain models. The resulting analysis can define the strategy and structure for an eBusiness enterprise as a value alliance network with a robust approach to evolutionary eBusiness development and the management of change. Initially an overview of the characteristics of virtual markets are presented and the opportunities for IT-enabled intermediation are examined. The chapter reviews the concepts of supply chain management (SCM), demand chains and value chains in the context of electronically networked organizations and then relates these to the evolution of a virtual value chain. The virtual value chain is used as a basis for the development of an effective organizational structure and the value alliance model in a virtual networked environment. Finally, this is reviewed in the context of the retail market and interactive home shopping systems (IAHS) and illustrated by a case study within the e-grocery business.

INTRODUCTION

Driven by such phenomena as the World Wide Web, mass customization, compressed product lifecycles, new distribution channels and new forms of integrated organizations, the most fundamental elements of doing business are changing and a totally new business environment is emerging (Turban et al., 1999). This environment variously described as the Electronic Business Community (EBC) (Ticoll et al., 1998), electronic economy (El Sawy et al., 1999), electronic market (Wigand and Benjamin, 1995), electronic marketplace or space (Jansen et al., 1999; Rayport and Sviokola, 1995) and virtual market (Burn and Barnett, 2000) is characterized by rapid exchange of information within a virtual network of customers and suppliers working together to create value-added processes.

This virtual market brings with it new forms of IT-enabled intermediation, virtual supply chains, increasing knowledge intensity and information-based business architecture strategies. Core business processes may need to be rethought and redesigned, new organizational forms and inter-organizational forms may need to be developed and the emphasis will be on collaboration rather than competition within the virtual market. Eisenhardt and Galunic (2000) point out, however, that the new roles of collaboration in eBusiness are actually counter-intuitive and that collaboration does not naturally lead to synergy. Where synergies are achieved, the managers have mastered the corporate strategic process of coevolving. These managers routinely change the Web of collaborative links-everything from information exchanges to shared assets to multi-business strategies-among businesses.

Figure 1: Traditional Collaboration Versus Coevolution (Eisenhardt and Galunic, 2000)

	Traditional Collaboration	Coevolution
Form of collaboration	Frozen links among static businesses	Shifting webs among evolving businesses
Objectives	Efficiency and economies of scale	Growth, agility, and economies of scope
Internal dynamics	Collaborate	Collaborate and compete
Focus	Content of collaboration	Content and number of collaborative links
Corporate role	Drive Collaboration	Set Collaborative Content
Business role	Execute collaboration	Drive/execute collaboration
Incentive	Varied	Self-interest, based on individual business unit performance
Business metrics	Performance against budget, preceding year, or sister-business performance	Performance against competitors in growth, share and profits

The result is a shifting Web of relationships that exploits fresh opportunities for synergies and drops deteriorating ones, as shown in Figure 1.

One such business model can be identified as a value network alliance where organizations define their roles in the context of a complex virtual market interaction. This can provide the organization with an effective strategy and supporting business structure which can be leveraged to improve business performance (Hackney et al., 1999).

SUPPLY CHAIN MANAGEMENT

Supply chain management (SCM) is a well-accepted concept in logistics and operations management theory, and aims to improve coordination and competitiveness beyond the enterprise level to include interorganizational relationships (Strader et al., 1999). Supply chains exist in virtually every industry and generally involve the procurement processes, transformation of raw materials into finished products and delivery of the product to customers through a distribution system. The supply chain of a packaged consumer goods manufacturer, for instance, comprises manufacturing, packaging, distribution, warehousing and retailing. Managing this involves the coordination of the materials inventory and production capacity availability across several organizations to produce products that can satisfy forecasted demand in an environment with a high level of uncertainty. While often regarded as a manufacturing concept (IT systems for Bill of Materials Processing [BOMP] have been around in the manufacturing sector since the late '60s), it can equally well apply in a University or any other service industry, and may specifically relate to the management of information rather than materials.

Consequently, however, SCM has become a "hot" topic for a number of different reasons. These include the trend towards multi-site operations with several independent entities involved in the production and delivery process, new and increasingly cut-throat marketing channels and the electronic marketplace. Traditional supply chains and trading partner relationships are exploding into intricate and dynamic virtual networks of trading partners and service providers. The emphasis in these relationships is to derive significant value through increased revenues and decreased costs as shown in Figure 2.

Companies have redefined their supply chain management by focusing on their core competence. This means that instead of covering all the operations of manufacturing, distribution and sales in-house, they are outsourcing areas to other partner companies. This has led to the build-up of supply chain communities where in the most extreme example, a company may outsource all elements from production to selling and retain only the brand image, as in the case of Nike. Achieving this in any organization directly depends on the performance of all the others in the network and their willingness and ability to coordinate (Swaminathan et al., 1998). One mistake in manufacturing could reduce the perceived quality of the brand. These communities have taken the supply chain one step higher by sharing information throughout the supply chain, with each specialising in its own core competence. The customer is now placed at the center of the supply chain rather than at the end, and the organization will now concentrate on finding out exactly what the customer needs and manufacturing this to customer specifications. This means significant changes to business processes and much faster product lifecycles, and companies have had to utilize IT in new and innovative ways to enable them to fulfil orders on demand and guide the changes needed to make new supply chain communities work.

However, eCommerce and Web-based transactions have not proved to be the success that was expected (Elliot, 2000). Many online retailing companies have suffered losses over the last two years with takeovers and mergers becoming the norm in the electronic grocery markets. A UK-based supermarket, Sainsbury, lost millions in its first year of online shopping and even online e-tailers such as Greengrocer.com and Homegrocer.com have had turbulent histories. One of the reasons for this poor performance has been the inability of companies to change from a traditional mindset with regard to the supply chain operation. Frequently customers can buy online but the fulfilment of the order will then take place through a normal supply chain mode via a retail outlet. Costs increase and service is diminished. Companies need to rethink their approach to supply chain management, and this means returning to the basics of the value chain, extending this to supply and demand chain analysis, and evaluating virtual value chains within the context of their industry.

THE VALUE ANALYSIS PROCESS

Value Chains

Porter (1980) considered these concepts when he derived his classic internal value chain showing primary activities which a business must do to exist, and the secondary activities required to control and develop the business and which are common across the primary activities. An organization today must consider the effect of Internet-enabled commerce on their distribution

Figure 2: Value from Networked Processes Along the Supply Chain (adapted from Benchmarking Partners, Inc., 1999)

Networked Processes	Value
Design and product management	• Competitive advantage through faster time-to-market • Reduced R and D expenses • Lower unit costs
Order management, planning, forecasting and replenishment	• Competitive advantage and higher revenues from reduced stock outs • Lower costs through reduced inventory • Lower costs through reduced return rates
Distribution	• Lower costs through optimised shipping and fulfillment
Sourcing	• Competitive advantage and increased revenue through faster product introductions • Decreased costs through and increased revenue from higher quality
Customer relationship management	• Increased revenue through improved customer segmenting and targeting • Increased revenue through improved customer service • Decreased costs from efficient salesforce automation
Merchandising/ Category management	• Competitive advantage and increased revenue through the proper product assortment, pricing and promotional strategies, and shelf placement

channels and the value chain, as illustrated in Figure 3.

Which parts of the chain will be Internet enabled? Which activities will the company retain in-house and which should be outsourced to others in the supply chain alliance? How will the intranet be used to improve internal coordination and communication? Which primary activities are most suitable for eCommerce delivery?

Demand Chains

Traditionally, suppliers reengineered only their end of the supply chain by reducing obsolete inventory and cutting down cost and time of goods to market. However, a much more powerful concept lies in the Demand Chain where, for example, a retailer's demand chain would consist of assortment planning (deciding what to sell), inventory management (deciding the quantity of supplies needed) and the actual purchase. Together with SCM we have the Demand-Supply Chain and these are linked and managed in two places-the order penetration point (OPP) and the value offering point (VOP), as shown in Figures 4 and 5.

The OPP is the place in the supply chain where the supplier allocates the goods ordered by the customer. Goods might be produced after orders come in (make to order) or allocated from a warehouse once the orders have been received (package to order) or from distribution (ship to order). Each order penetration point has different costs and benefits for the supplier and its customer-for example rapid delivery (a benefit for the customer) depends on holding a large inventory (a cost for the supplier).

The further back in the supply chain the supplier moves the OPP, the more steps there are to complete without disruption and the more difficult it becomes to fulfill orders promptly. The advantage to the supplier of this approach depends on the amount of cost savings it can achieve from lower inventory, on the one hand, compared with the reduction in sales that may be brought about by longer delivery times and higher total costs for customers, on the other. Customers and suppliers never benefit equally.

VOP—the second place where the demand and supply chains meet—is where the supplier fulfills demand in the customer's demand chain. Moving the VOP back in the demand chain largely benefits the customer, requiring more work from the supplier. There are three principal VOPs. In the conventional buyer-seller relationship, the VOP is the purchasing department, which

Figure 3: Internet-Enabled Commerce and the Value Chain (Porter, 1980)

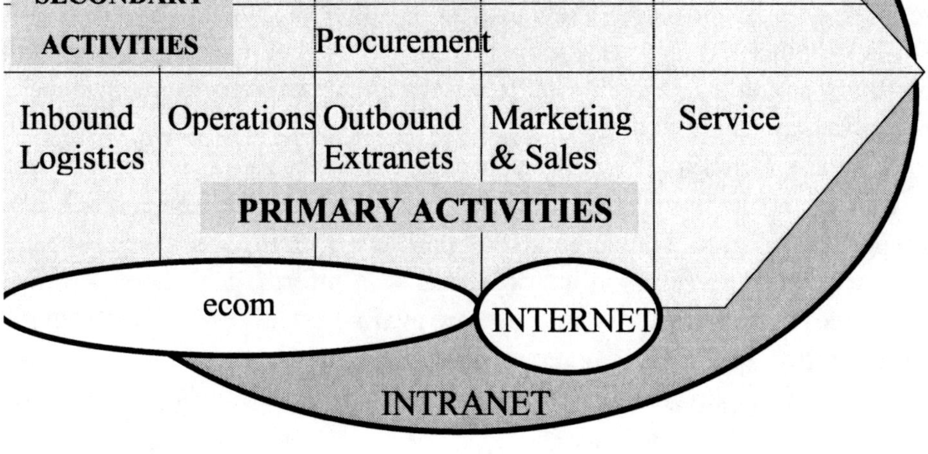

Figure 4: The OOPs (adapted from Holstrom et al., 2000)

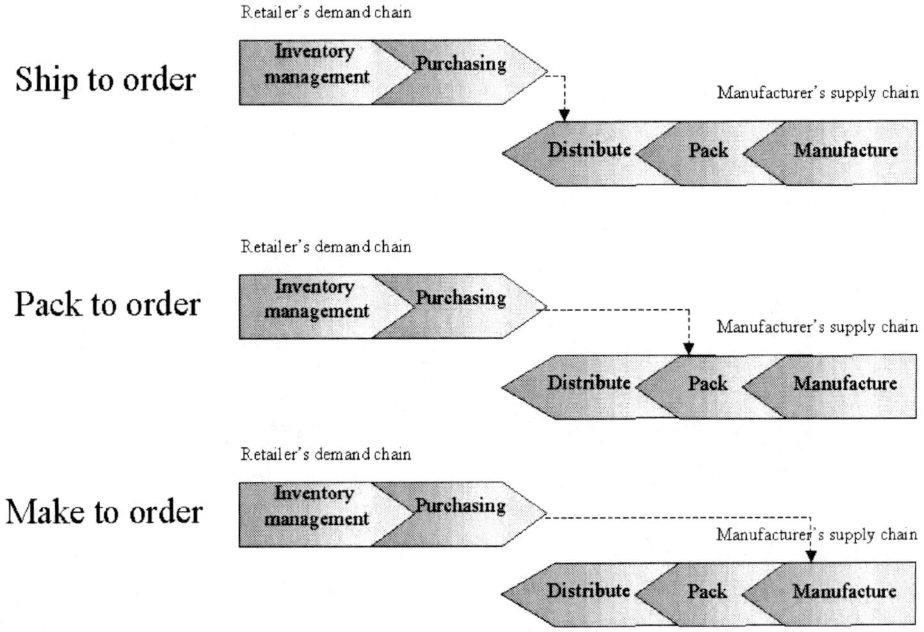

accepts an "offer to purchasing" by choosing the supplier and deciding when goods are needed. An "offer to inventory management" moves the VOP further back in the demand chain: by carefully monitoring the customer's inventory levels, a supplier can cut down on stock that is unlikely to sell and ensure that the customer never runs out of fast-moving goods. An "offer to planning" moves the VOP back to merchandising or production. As the VOP is moved back, this means more work for suppliers and greater benefits for retailers or even end users. The fourth VOP is the "offer to end user," such as Dell Computer's direct-sales model for business clients. Rather than fulfill orders from wholesalers (an offer to purchasing), Dell went all the way back in the demand chain to the end consumer by fulfilling orders for customized PCs—complete with software and network configuration. As we have noted, however, an inherent disadvantage of this model is the longer lead time needed for delivery. To overcome this problem, Dell provides the estimated delivery time as well as online order tracking information for each order. When the product inventory and parts are available, Dell can deliver a simple configuration in 2-3 days, average in 5 days, and complex in 7-10 days. However, if the parts are not readily available, the lead time is estimated and

Figure 5: The VOPs (adapted from Holstrom et al., 2000)

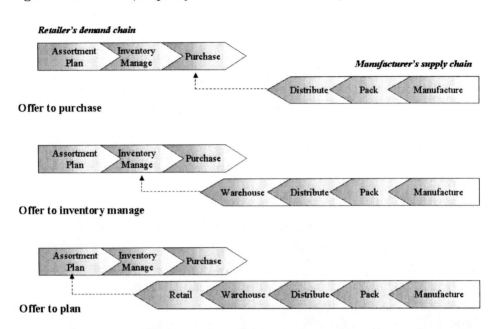

the customers informed.

In this way, by coordinating changes in both the supply and demand chains, a supplier can raise its customers' efficiency, as well as its own, i.e. simultaneous movements of the OPP and VOP will be of mutual benefit to customer and supplier. Effectively, this can result in the development of a virtual value chain.

Virtual Value Chains

Mougayar (1998) suggests an eBusiness must then consider the following two questions:

· Can you increase the number of electronic connections, simplify interorganizational processes and at the same time discover ways to shrink, speed up or virtualize the value chain?

· What is likely to happen with your wholesalers, distributors or retailers? Are they going to be disintermediated or are they likely to survive by transforming their businesses into new types of intermediaries operating in a neutral market (Berryman et al., 1998)?

One obvious scenario is that the old value chain gets smaller, so more efficient as you bypass some of the steps in the supply chain (for example online delivery of soft products). In some cases as you disintermediate previous links in your supply chain, new intermediaries will arise (for example you may change to selling through a portal or vortal to reach a larger market). This dynamic reconstruction of intermediaries can also lead to dynamic allocation of intermediaries where the channels become invisible or even non-existent, so creating the virtual value chain (Rayport and and Sviokola, 1995), as shown in Figure 6.

The value chain of the firm does not exist in isolation but exists as part of an industry value system, and the whole value system will consist of the value chains of suppliers, customers and competitors. This can become the model for the virtual organization as it links electronically into value networks.

THE VALUE NETWORK ALLIANCE

Once an organization has performed a full value chain analysis, it is then in a position to form viable value alliances through an electronic network. This may form the basis for a virtual organization where the alliance combines a range of products, services and facilities in one package, forming one single supply chain. Participants may come together on a project-by-project basis, but generally the general contractor provides coordination. Where longer

Figure 6: The Evolving Virtual Value Chain

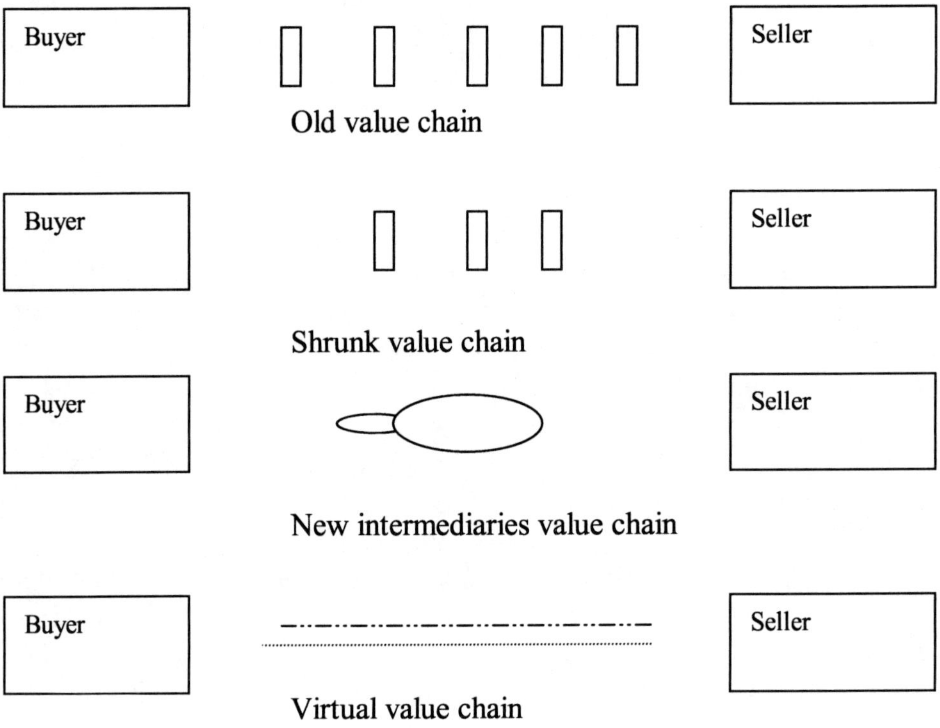

Old value chain

Shrunk value chain

New intermediaries value chain

Virtual value chain

term relationships have developed, the value alliance often adopts the form of value constellations where firms supply each of the companies in the value chain, and a complex and enduring communications structure is embedded within the alliance (Burn and Barnett, 2000), as shown in Figure 7. Substitutability has traditionally been a function of efficiency and transaction costs: searching for, evaluating and commencing operations with potential partners has been a costly and slow business procedure, relying as it does on information transfer, the establishment of trust and business rules across time zones, culture, currency and legal frameworks. These have determined the relative positioning of partners on the chain and the reciprocity of the relationship.

This model is particularly suited to taking advantage of communications efficiencies not previously available and therefore changing components extremely rapidly in response to evanescent market forces and opportunities. Different models present themselves to retailers and manufacturers and this has particular significance in the developing electronic grocery market where market alliances are in a continual process of evelution.

RETAILING AND E-GROCERY MARKETS

The retail grocery trade in developed countries accounts for between 30–50% of all retail spending on physical products, depending on income levels and definitions (Wileman and Jary, 1997). As each person in a cash-based economy buys food, this puts retail grocers in a market class of their own. This has given rise to sophisticated networks of supermarket chains expanding by virtue of their advantages of economy of scale, buying power, brand marketing and cross-marketing with loyalty and group promotion packages. Food retailers are by far the largest retailing group in the UK accounting for almost 38% of UK retail sales, while the large grocery retailers alone account for 30% of all UK retail sales. There are a relatively small number of large grocery retailers, each of which operates a large number of stores (on average the large

Figure 7: Value Alliance

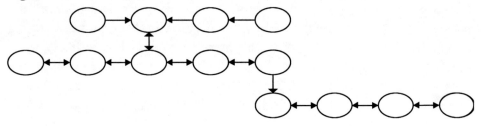

grocers operate 113 stores each, compared to an average of 1.3 stores per retailer for the food sector as a whole), generating a large per-store turnover. The top five large grocery retailers account for 48% of all sales (London Economics, 1997).

In comparison, clothing retailers represent 7% of total UK retail turnover. There are some multiples in this sector, although nowhere near as many as in food retailing, with an average of 1.9 stores are operated by each retailer. Electrical and music goods retailers make over 5% of all UK retail sales. The emergence of larger retail operators has enabled the use of more efficient methods of distribution. Over time, wholesalers have more or less disappeared from many of the retail markets, with large retailers dealing directly with manufacturers. This trend has probably been greatest in the grocery retail market; between 1982 and 1992, retail turnover increased by 125% while turnover from delivered wholesale trade increased by only 59%. At the same time the method of delivery has changed enormously as retailers have become more efficient. Before the emergence of multiple retailers, most deliveries to retailers were made by manufacturers or wholesalers. Such deliveries were of an assortment of products to individual retail outlets. Nowadays, manufacturers tend to deliver large amounts of a particular product in each delivery to a retailer's own centralised warehouse. The retailer has, in effect, internalised the wholesaling and transportation function into its own activities. The advantages of centralised warehousing include: reduced stock levels, reduced delivery visits per store, reduction of necessary storage space in stores themselves, fewer incidents of running out of stocks and empty shelves in the outlet; and lower shrinkage.

The increasing quantity of data that can now be collected and collated by retailers has improved their ability to judge how consumer preferences change over time. As a method of exploiting this new information advantage, many grocery and other retailers have developed stronger relationships with suppliers and have become involved in product development (Hogarth-Scott and Parkinson, 1994). Advances in technology also have consequences for the nature of retailing itself. The traditional, and still by far the most popular, form of shopping is one where consumers travel to the retailer to purchase products. However, other forms of retailing, such as mail order, teleshopping and interactive television are all viable alternatives. Moreover, home shopping, especially through teleshopping and interactive television, is likely to increase as technology progresses. It is difficult to know how directly these new forms of retailing compete with more traditional retailers, not least because data on home shopping is currently not collected very rigorously. Clearly, though, any significant growth in these new forms of retailing will be detrimental to traditional retailers and will have considerable effects on the structure of the retail market. The question, of course, is whether there will be a significant growth in these new forms of shopping and whether traditional retailers will adapt to provide these new channels to market, or whether new entrants will occupy the market niche first.

It has been suggested that Interactive Home Shopping (IAHS) might threaten the established supermarket presence by disintermediating the bricks and mortar real estate and associated management capital. Supermarkets are currently testing the potential for IAHS to alter their methods of dealing with customer requests. Trials are under way on at least 70 Web sites in more than 17 countries at present (Bos, 1999), but what is not clear is the management strategies behind the deployment of resources in this way. It is likely that virtual forms of organization will arise to extend or replace existing business models in the grocery trade. To understand therefore the stages of growth and management of organizational change, it is helpful to identify useful models for this industry.

Figure 8 summarises the current and potential supply chain structures for electronic channels in retailing. Models 1 and 2 represent the current structures for e-tailers and Models 3 and 4 represent potential structures for IAHS.

Figure 9 summarises how manufacturers of fast-moving consumer goods (FMCG) in models three and four have applied the supply-demand chain to cut out retailers and sell direct to the consumer. The savings for consumers are

Figure 8: Supply Chain Structures for Retailers (adapted from Younger, 1999)

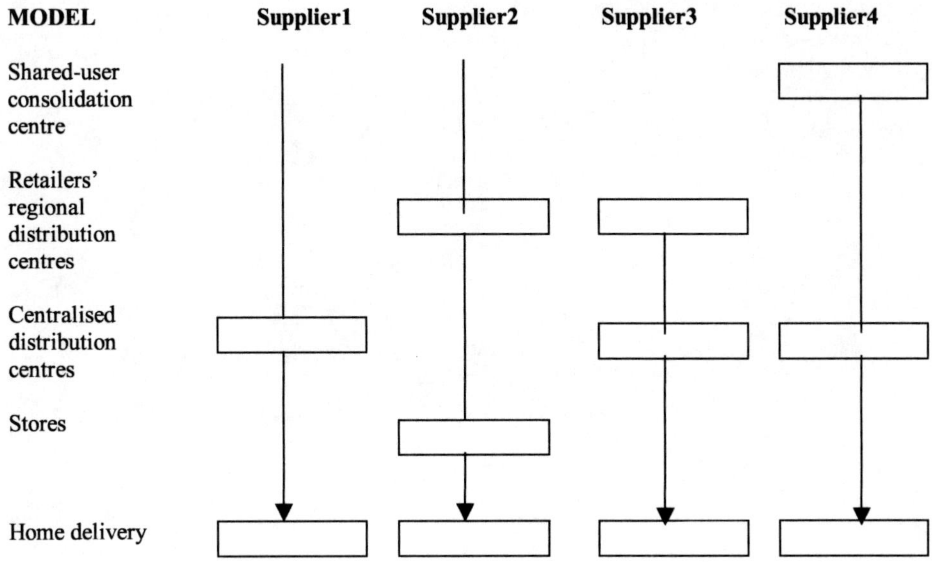

Figure 9: Supply Chain Structures for Non FMCG (Younger, 1999)

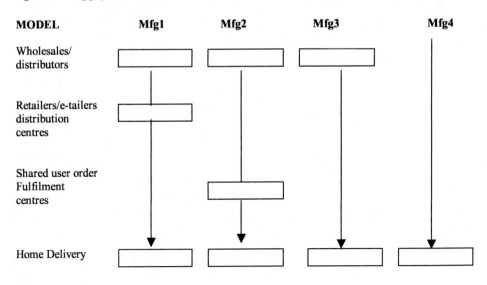

Figure 10: Value Network Alliance

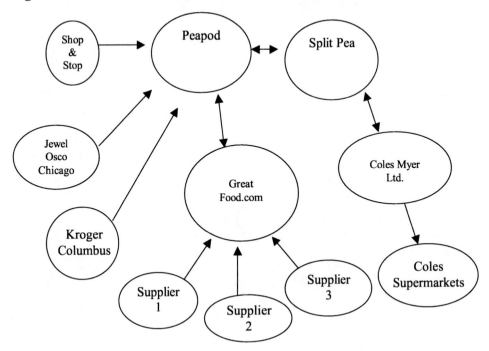

clearly significant, and from a manufacturing perspective the increased profit margins will undoubtedly accelerate the process. This model is particularly suited to taking advantage of communications efficiencies not previously available and therefore changing components extremely rapidly in response to evanescent market forces and opportunities.

An example of a value network alliance is Peapod.com (Figure 10) within the context of its virtual market.

Peapod.com operates in eight major U.S. conurbations (at the end of 1999) supplying grocery and pharmacy items using interactive home shopping through Web ordering, credit card processing and home/office delivery. They offer a range of items selected from partner stores in each area. (Only three are displayed for clarity.) The company solicits active Web recruitment partners by offering a reward program to owners of Web sites who accept links on their sites–rewards are provided in the form of set payments for each referred customer's first and third purchase. The company developed proprietary software and logistics to support its operations and then spun these away from the core grocery delivery business.

Split Pea Software was formed in December 1998 to act as an independent licensing arm for the IAHS shopping and delivery systems and technology. These systems include the server-based shopping application together with business applications such as fulfilment management, product database administration, customer support and Peapod's one-to-one targeting engine. Peapod is only a minority interest in Split Pea, which is majority owned by senior management.

Split Pea was formed upon the successful conclusion of negotiations leading to a licensing agreement with the large Australian Retail chain operator, Coles Myer Ltd. Coles Myer has exclusive use of the Split Pea technology within Australia and New Zealand, but Split Pea is seeking to license its software and delivery services elsewhere. Coles Myer is currently testing the system for Coles Online, the virtual face of its Coles retail grocery chain, with an introduction in Sydney.

Coles Online is the virtual face of a large retail grocery chain operating across much of Australia under the name of Coles. This company has no links to other companies or services on its site as yet, and operates by selecting goods from existing Coles grocery stores and operating a home delivery service, despite the fact that Coles Myer owns and operates other large chains with non-competing interests, such as the Target clothing stores and the Officeworks office supply and stationery chain. One of the most interesting aspects of these networks is the speed at which companies are focusing on core competencies and outsourcing non-core functions to other service providers in the value network. With virtual relationships, companies can more easily outsource but still integrate these outsourced functions into their virtual organization. A manufacturing company with superior strengths in branding and selling could transform their organization to focus on these and outsource the manufacturing into its virtual value chain. Many organizations have moved towards this model (particularly the new dot.com companies) and are becoming virtually integrated rather than vertically integrated. These companies can now focus specifically on their customer communities who act as information gathering and information dissemination conduits (Venkatraman and Henderson, 1998). This will involve increased personalisation and customisation of product offerings, and the aggregation and disaggregation of information-based product components to match customer needs and to support new pricing strategies (Bakos, 1998). This requires the organization to identify the framework for market mediation and the management implications involved in such value-network alliances.

FRAMEWORK FOR MARKET MEDIATION

As organizations form and reform, these value-network alliances also have to develop capabilities to cope with strategic, technical, cultural and operational change. Logistics, manufacturing and customer interfacing functions will become prime areas for outsourcing or incorporation into the virtual value chain, and the ability to form and manage these is of critical importance. As the virtual value chain is formed, facilitating direct exchange between the producer and consumer, we see the role of intermediaries being threatened (Wigand and Benjamin, 1995), but at the same time opportunities for new intermediaries arise.

Intermediaries

In traditional consumer markets, intermediaries (such as a traditional retail store) provide a variety of explicit and implicit services for their customers. These include assistance in searching and evaluation, needs assessment and product matching, risk reduction and product distribution and delivery (Sarkar et al., 1995). They also benefit producers by creating and disseminating product information and creating product awareness, influencing customer purchasing, providing customer information, reducing exposure to risk and reducing costs of distribution through economies of scale. A large supermarket chain can provide market opportunities that a small producer would find impossible to generate on its own. The mediation role for customers and producers are normally juxtaposed, and so part of the role of intermediaries is to balance this situation. While the truly virtual organization with a virtual value chain may be able to fully disintermediate, the fact remains that most organizations will still rely on an intermediary to integrate producer and consumer services and present the consumer market with a large-scale community front-end and one that can take advantages of economy of scale (Gallaugher, 1999). Interestingly, some of the biggest Internet businesses act as major intermediaries between other players. Amazon, CD-Now, Egghead.com and E*Trade can all be thought of as middlemen. Portals and vortals are both some form of electronic intermediary. This suggests that rather than disintermediation becoming the norm, a new form of intermediary, cybermediaries, may evolve.

Cybermediaries

Sarkar et al (1995) suggest the following list of cybermediaries: Gateways, Directories, Search Services, Malls, Publishers, Virtual Resellers, Web Site Evaluators, Auditors, Forums, Fan Clubs and User Groups, Financial Intermediaries, Spot Market Makers and Barter Networks, Intelligent Agents.

These intermediaries will continue to be necessary where customers demand choice, require quality assurance and want additional social and entertainment value. Producers may be unable to impose producer-centric structures on the market and may also be threatened by the power of retaliation from the existing intermediaries. They may also choose to operate along known trust relationships in certain cultures and, indeed, using this system may be actually reducing the costs implied by legal contractual arrangements in place between producer and consumer. In many cases, electronic sites will continue to complement existing physical infrastructures, but certainly restructuring of the processes is likely and the networked organization needs to be fully aware of the impact of such changing relationships.

STRATEGIES FOR VIRTUAL ALLIANCES

Virtual alliances involve collaborations among multiple organizations with several complex economic, strategic, social and conflict management issues as well as major organizational and technological factors. Planning and managing such systems requires an integrated multidimensional approach across the eBusiness (Kumar and Crook, 1999).

As a first step the following questions need answering:

- What do consumers ideally want to buy?
- What business should I be in?
- What are my current core competencies?

- What are the opportunities for new products or service lines?
- What are the opportunities for new business channels?
- What is the most effective value proposition in the short, medium and long run?
- What roles should I play—make, sell or service—and who are my customers?
- Who are my competitors, and how do I need to be positioned?
- What is my operating model?
- With whom should I partner/network?

The answers, if they are guided by a deep understanding of the economic implications and opportunity of the eEconomy, will produce a very different picture of the company. For many companies, achieving this vision will require building greater expertise in the strategic and operational application of technology which is driving the rapid evolution of eCommerce. Consequently it will be necessary to temper the technology focus by applying cross-disciplinary, cross-functional and cross-industry perspectives and expertise; this is because industry boundaries will be shaped by customer needs rather than by core competencies.

CONCLUSION

This chapter has argued that value, supply and demand chain analysis are methodologies which have been applied to IT strategies for the last two decades but they tend to imply linear relationships. Using them in a comprehensive framework, they can effectively model the value network of a complex eBusiness environment. As organizations form and reform these value-network alliances, they also have to develop capabilities to cope with strategic, technical, cultural and operational change. Logistics, manufacturing and customer interfacing functions will become prime areas for outsourcing or incorporation into the virtual value chain, and the ability to form and manage these is of critical importance. Continual re-evaluation of the value chains will become an essential tool for developing strategies for eBusiness and managing ongoing global change processes.

REFERENCES

Bakos, Y. (1998). The emerging role of electronic marketplaces on the Internet. *Communications of the ACM*, 41(8), 35-42.

Benchmarking Partners Inc. (1999). *Driving Business Value Through E-Collaboration*. Available on the World Wide Web at: http://www.benchmarking.com. Accessed in September 1999.

Berryman, K., Harrington, L., Layton-Rodin, D. and Rerolle, V. (1998). Electronic commerce: Three emerging strategies. *The McKinsey Quarterly*, 1, 152-159.

Bos, G. (1999). *Virtual Supermarkets Index*. Available on the World Wide Web at: http://www.innovell.com/supermarkets.

Burn, J. M. and Barnett, M. L. (2000). Emerging virtual models for global eCommerce: World-wide retailing in the e-grocery business. Special Millennium Issue of *Journal of Global Information Technology Management*, 3(1), 18-32.

El Sawy, O. A., Malhotra, A., Gosain, S. and Young, K. M. (1999). IT-intensive value innovation in the electronic economy: Insights from Marshall Industries. *MIS Quarterly*, 23(3), 305-335.

Eisenhardt, K. E. and Galunic, D. C. (2000). Coevolving. At last, a way to make synergies work. *Harvard Business Review*, Jan-Feb, 91-101.

Elliott, C. (2000). eCommerce and the supply chain. *International Journal of e-Business Strategy Management*, 1(4), 283-288.

Hackney R. A., Ranchhod A. and Griffiths, G. (1999). Internet marketing: New medium, new relevance. *Academy of Marketing*, University of Stirling, July.

Hogarth-Scott, S. and Parkinson, S. (1994). Barriers and stimuli to the use of information technology in retailing. *International Review of Retail, Distribution and Consumer Research*, 4(3), 257-75.

Holmstrom, J., Hoover, Jr., W. E., Louhiluoto, P. and Vasara, A. (2000). The other end of the supply chain. *The McKinsey Quaterly*, 1, 62-71.

Kumar, R. L. and Crook, C. W. A (1999). Multi-disciplinary framework for the management of interorganizational systems. *The Data Base for Advances in Information Systems*, 30(1).

London Economics. (1997). *Competition in Retailing* (Research Paper 13). London: Office of Fair Trading.

Mougayar, W. (1998). *Opening Digital Markets*. McGraw Hill.

Porter, M.E. (1980). *Competing Strategy Techniques for Analysing Industries and Competitors*. New York: Free Press.

Rayport, J. F. and Sviokola, J. (1995). Exploiting the virtual value chain. *Harvard Business Review*, 73(6), 75-86.

Sarkar, M. B., Butler, B. and Steinfield, C. Intermediaries and cybermediaries: A continuing role for mediating players in the electronic marketplace.

Journal of Computer Mediated Communication, 1(3). Available on the World WideWeb at: http://www.ascusc.org/jcmc/vol1/issue3/ sarkar.html.

Strader, T. J., Lin, F. and Shaw, M. J. (1999). Business-to-business electronic commerce and convergent assembly supply chain management. *Journal of Information Technology*, 14, 361-373.

Swaminathan, J. M., Smith, S. F. and Sadeh, N. M. (1998). Modeling supply chain dynamics: A multiagent approach. *Decision Sciences*, 29(3), 607-632.

Ticoll, D., Lowry, A. and Kalakota, R. (1998). Joined at the bit, in blueprint to the digital economy creating wealth in the era of e-business. McGraw-Hill.

Turban, E., Lee, J., King, D. and Chung, M. (1999). *Electronic Commerce: A Managerial Perspective*. Prentice Hall.

Venkatraman, N. and Henderson, J. C. (1998). Real strategies for virtual organizing. *Sloan Management Review*, Fall, 33-48.

Wigand, R. T. and Benjamin, R. I. (1995). Electronic commerce: Effects on electronic markets. *Journal of Computer-Mediated Communication*, 1(3). Available on the World Wide Web at: http://www.ascusc.org/ jcmc/vol1/issue3/wigand.html.

Wileman, A. and Jary, M. (1997). *Retail Power Plays: From Trading to Brand Leadership*. New York: New York University Press.

Younger, R. (1999). *Supply Chain Challenges for Electronic Shopping*. FT Business.

Chapter XIII

Dynamic Digital Process Integration in Business-to-Business Networks

Merrill Warkentin
Mississippi State University, USA

Transparent end-to-end business process integration is the leading edge of today's business-to-business electronic commerce revolution. Firms enter into electronic inter-organizational networks not only to conduct procurement-oriented transactions (supply chain management), but increasingly, they are strategically outsourcing business processes and activities which are not part of the their distinctive competence (strategically core activities) and provided by a new breed of digital process specialists.

The evolution of agent-based inter-organizational systems enables complex direct interaction between heterogeneous information systems, which allow Web-based eServices to act autonomously, communicate independently, discover each other, provide dynamically configured services to one another, and establish composite business systems.

INTRODUCTION: STRATEGIC OUTSOURCING AND INTER-ORGANIZATIONAL SYSTEMS

Early traditional businesses were vertically integrated. Many companies owned or controlled their own sources of materials, manufactured components, performed final assembly, and managed the distribution and sale of their products to consumers. Over time, nearly all firms began to contract with other firms ("outsource") to execute various activities along the chain from raw materials and components supply to manufacturing to distribution and sale in order to concentrate their activities on their core competence. In every industry, new business service providers emerged to fill the need for this outsourcing activity.

The eCommerce system design process includes steps for planning, designing, building, hosting, and operating eBusiness systems. A firm may execute all the activities in this process internally (in-house) or it may choose to utilize the experience and expertise of appropriate specialist firms who can assist in achieving success in eCommerce. For example, an eCommerce firm must design and operate its order fulfillment system and outbound logistics (delivery) functions, or must identify and partner with an external provider of these services. It must provide customer service to the new customers of its Web site. Most eCommerce-related enterprises practice extensive outsourcing of various business processes. While concentrating on core competencies, they develop strategic alliances with partner firms in order to provide activities such as payment processing, order fulfillment, outbound logistics, Web site hosting, customer service, and so forth.

One of the greatest impacts of information technology has been its ability to create linkages between companies. Inter-organizational systems (IOS) are networks of information systems that allow organizations to share information and interact electronically across organizational boundaries (Kaufman, 1966). These systems "enable firms to incorporate buyers, sellers, and partners in the redesign of their key business processes, thereby enhancing productivity, quality, speed, and flexibility" (Applegate et al., 1999). Historically, most IOS were designed to share narrowly defined data and information, such as inventory information, not rich valuable knowledge. The processes had limited ability to adapt, share unusual information, or create new business models. IOS range from simple routine messaging to totally integrated business processes, supported by shared databases and applications. This end-to-end integration is the ultimate form of business-to-business electronic commerce.

Inter-organizational systems exhibit three successive levels of control (Applegate et al., 1999). At the data-control level, IOS participants merely send or receive data or both. EDI systems are primarily data-control IOS. Some systems are unidirectional, while others may allow interactive data sharing. Process-control IOS maintain software that controls the underlying interactivity with partner firms and the related information. However, firms deploying these systems also incur coordination costs. Finally, network control IOS are owned and operated by one or more participants, who incur considerable costs along with the control. Costs arise from activities related to maintenance of integrity, security, and reliability. The Internet has created an entirely new platform for IOS that is nearly ubiquitous, is very inexpensive, and has established protocols for security and reliability.

This chapter is organized as follows. The next few sections will provide examples of specific categories of Web-based eServices, such as system building services, financial processing networks, adserver networks, syndication networks, and infomediaries. Some eService examples from the auction industry are cited. This is followed by a discussion of collaborative commerce, hypermediation, and B2X networks in eCommerce. The importance of partnership management is discussed, and the role of standard protocols is presented. Finally, some managerial guidelines and concluding comments are provided.

SYSTEM-BUILDING SERVICES AND "DIGITAL BUILDING BLOCKS"

After a firm has determined what its electronic commerce strategy will be, it must build the technical and business infrastructure to achieve the goals of that strategy. A business system for electronic commerce includes:

1. *front-end systems* (customer-facing systems)-Web sites, phone trees, wireless access, etc;
2. *back-end systems* (underlying databases and applications to support back-office functions); and
3. *business systems* to ensure its successful operation (policies and procedures and supporting functions to formalize management responsibilities, reporting relationships, recordkeeping requirements, performance evaluation measures, rewards and disincentives, exception reporting, contingency plans, training and helpdesk operations, and all other business functions to ensure that the mission, objectives, and goals are fulfilled).

Various Web-based eServices can be used to establish an online presence. In some cases, these services are utilized by in-house design teams who want to put together a system that incorporates the best-practice electronic components that are available, while in other cases, these services are used by external (third-party) consultants and system integrators who build Web sites for their clients. Some of these system components are very special purpose niche tools, such as tax-calculation software, while others are very broad eCommerce packages to facilitate nearly all aspects of running a successful transactional online system.

Some of these building blocks are licensed and distributed to be incorporated into the system hosted on the client's own servers, while others reside on the service-provider's site, and the real-time service is provided over the Internet.

Some of these externally hosted "digital building blocks" are used according to a subscription pricing model, where the company using the eService pays a standard monthly fee, for example, for the right to use the service. In other cases, the service is actually free. Some of these service providers offer different service levels at different prices, as shown below.

One of the first externally hosted digital building blocks available to Web site designers was the "hit counter," commonly seen on the Web sites of individuals who are proud of the number of visitors they have attracted. From these humble beginnings, an entire industry has been born to provide expert outsourcing for other Web site functionality. One can essentially create a shell site today by plugging in the components that are publicly available. Specialized service providers (outsourcing partners) will provide technical Web site functions and business functions, such as order fulfillments and logistics, discussed in further detail below.

Freefind is a Web site (www.freefind.com) that offers an advanced search and navigation technology that can be integrated into their customers' Web sites in minutes. This hosted search technology requires no download or install–its customers simply sign up and receive the HTML that they insert into their own Web site design. This will display a search button that uses Freefind's servers (in the background, transparently) to perform searches of the Web, the customer's site, or both. It will also track visitor's searches and provide reports. This basic service is free (sponsor-supported), but the company also provides higher service levels for a fee (see www.freefind.com/plans.html). All versions offer automatic daily re-indexing (to ensure more accurate searches), unlimited on-demand re-indexing, and an automatic site map.

Similarly, Picosearch (at www.picosearch.com), Atomz (at www.atomz.com), Bpath (at bpath.whatuseek.com/), and VantageNet, Inc. (at intrasearch.vantagenet.com, see also www.freetools.com) offer free or subscription models for internal search capabilities. The searches are performed on their servers, while the customer only needs to add some HTML code to its Web site in order to add the functionality of an Intra-search feature.

Many of these companies offer other free tools. BeSeen (by LookSmart at www.beseen.com) offers SearchBox, GuestBook, and ChatRoom features for free. Tripod is a free Web-hosting service from Lycos that offers a series of site add-ons to its members, including Javascript libraries, animations, and link management tools. Tripod also supplies "textGEAR" which will randomly insert quotations, tips, factoids, or words of wisdom to the member's site. This feature personalizes sites with dynamic content, makes sites more attractive and interactive, and provides an auto-response option for visitor suggestions.

Table 1 shows the free tools provided by VantageNet, Inc. through the freetools.com Web site (Turban et al., 2002).

A comprehensive list of additional digital building blocks for adding features such as calculators, world clocks, daily jokes, currency exchange calculators, and server performance monitoring is provided by the following meta list: directory.google.com/Top/Computers/Internet/WWW/Authoring/ Online_Tools/.

eCommerce Transaction Processing Building Blocks

An additional building block that can be added to a Web site with ease today is the eCommerce transaction processing function. Companies can purchase code or link their Web sites to other firms that provide automated functions to automate the display of proper forms, query standardized inventory databases, accept and process credit card information, and generate receipts for visitors. One example of this category of digital building blocks is the tools provided by CyberSource at www.cybersource.com/solutions.

There are a number of real-time online financial processing services offered in support of eCommerce companies. For example, there are a number of payment processing systems that are available to Web site owners, and the process of collecting the appropriate legal sales tax and VAR tax is a challenge that is supported by a number of B2B service providers.

Table 1: Digital Building Blocks for Web Site Functions (Source: www.freetools.com)

1. **Polls**. Get instant feedback from site visitors. You pick the Q & A. They vote.
2. **iReviewIt**. Get site visitors to rate and review products, people, places, and more.
3. **Message Boards**. Build a virtual community on your site. Visitors share thoughts and ideas.
4. **Guestbook**. Visitors can post comments about your site (searchable, ban troublemakers, etc.).
5. **LinkSend**. Visitors can quickly and easily tell their friends about your site.
6. **Horoscope**. Visitors can get a daily reading.
7. **Site Search**. Visitors can search your Web site.
8. **Plug-in Email**. Offer your own free email service on your Web site @yoursite.com.
9. **Other services**. The company also offers member services, such as its Browse Tools, SupportBoard, and HelpCenter, where one can view FAQs, retrieve lost passwords, and search help archives.

Tax Calculation and Collection Services

Hosted Sales Tax Calculation Systems. eTailers face a bewildering patchwork of tax rules both nationally and internationally. In the United States alone, they face over 30,000 taxing jurisdictions. In some cases, food and clothing are exempt from sales taxes, in others one or the other or both are taxed, or are taxed only up to some level. In many states, there is a statewide sales tax plus local (city and/or county) sales tax levied that ranges dramatically from one jurisdiction to another. Total sales taxes in the Denver area vary from under 4% to over 8%. Global electronic commerce sales significantly add to the sales tax confusion. There is a temporary sales tax moratorium on Internet sales within the U.S., but it only applies if the seller has no physical presence (a store, a factory or a distribution center) in the state of the buyer. Noncompliance with sales tax collection regulations can lead to fines and penalties. To further complicate matters, the tax rules are dynamic and most companies are not equipped to keep up with the hundreds of changes that can happen monthly.

DPC (at Salestax.com) licenses software that makes is simple to collect and report sales taxes with ease and precision. It promises that its software, which is updated monthly, reduces errors and puts its clients in compliance with the law. The company says that it is in constant contact with all taxing jurisdictions, so it can keep up to date and "sweat the details so you don't have to." DPC's databases, which are keyed to U.S. ZIP Codes (postal codes), have been integrated into numerous eCommerce automation systems on every platform. The company will also provide assistance with the integration of its databases into its client's systems, if necessary. It has also developed relationships with various software vendors and third-party developers who have written modules to facilitate the integration of their databases into other systems. Similarly, **HotSamba** is a B2B service provider that offers its customers (eTailers and mail order catalog sales companies) the CyberSource Payment Services and Tax Services, enabling real-time credit card processing and sales tax calculation online.

Taxware International produces software that operates seamlessly with leading financial and accounting packages on multiple hardware platforms to accurately automate tax compliance. Its SALES/USE Tax System has the only fully populated Product Taxability Matrix in the industry to ensure accurate tax calculation for all products sold on the Internet in all U.S. and Canadian tax jurisdictions. It will also calculate European VAT and other tax rates around the world. Further, this software can be integrated with the VERAZIP system, which acts as a pre-edit for address verification. It matches state, ZIP Code, city and county information to assure that an address is correct and complete so that the SALES/USE Tax System will be able to locate the correct taxing jurisdiction.

In 2001, four U.S. states (Kansas, Michigan, North Carolina and Wisconsin) tested an Internet-based tax calculation and remission system using software and services from several vendors as a cost-effective way to manage the complexities of evolving tax code (Tillet, 2001). The Streamlined Sales Tax Project (SSTP) is designed to create uniformity in the way states administer sales and use taxes. The SSTP test involves tax collection and management software from Taxware.com, Vertex, and esalestax.com that is being integrated by Pitney Bowes Inc. and Hewlett-Packard. Merchants will send live sales transaction data in real time using the Internet to one of four systems in the pilot. The following excerpt explains how the system will work.

After a consumer initiates an online purchase, the eBusiness would use the Internet to access a trusted third-party hosting provider that would determine sales or use taxes on the purchase, based on the locations of the buyer and the seller, as well as applicable state and local tax laws. The third party would provide custom links, typically with XML, between its system and commonly used ERP or eCommerce platforms, making it easier for retailers to connect to the system through the Internet.

For each client, the third party will make a single monthly or quarterly tax payment to a government tax authority. The tax authority would then securely access a database, managed by the third party over the Web, to examine the transaction data for tax compliance. The multi-state approach—in which one or more third parties gets certified to manage tax compliance for businesses that choose to use the service rather than handle tax compliance alone—ultimately makes sense, according to one analyst. "It would be prohibitively expensive to require all retailers to invest in this technology," the analyst said. Online merchants would also save money because the service provider would monitor changes in tax rules and change its compliance database accordingly (Tillet, 2001).

An **end-to-end business solution provider** offers services to build Web sites and eCommerce applications from the conceptual design to deployment. In addition to infrastructure, such companies provide eServices such as payment processing, logistics, and site monitoring. Some vendors that provide such services are bccentral.com (from Microsoft), Webvision.com, Roidirect.com, dellworks.com and Websphere from ibm.com.

ADSERVER NETWORKS

Adserver network operators are firms that create business networks to aggregate the supply and demand for online advertising. If a small Web site seeks to advertise online in order to attract traffic to its site, it cannot easily contact hundreds of high-traffic Web sites to buy ad space. However, an adserver acts as a broker, bringing together the buyer and seller of banner ads, to guarantee that the ad will be displayed or clicked a certain number of times. In the same way, if a high-traffic Web site, such as a portal or search engine, wants to sell banner ad space, it cannot easily contact thousands of potential advertisers. Again, the adserver plays the infomediary role, bringing thousands of buyers to the seller. In fact, the ad space seller does not even interact directly with the seller-the ad is served directly from the adserver's database to the individual client machine. The adserver sells impressions to the buyers of ad space and shares this revenue with the ad space seller.

Because the adserver wishes to maximize the effectiveness of its ad displays to ensure that ads are clicked frequently, it customizes the adserving to target ads to specific individuals. A system employing cookie files, active server pages, and sophisticated data mining software is used to evaluate the clickstream pattern, the content requested, and any information directly provided by the virtual visitor. For example, Michelle visits abcnews.com, which provides general news content with banner ads. DoubleClick.com, the largest adserver, delivers the binary banner ad image to appear at the top of her screen when abcnews.com sends its content to her computer. At the same time, DoubleClick has evaluated information generated from Michelle's previous visits to abcnews.com and many other Web sites in its network (such as espn.com and disney.com), and knows that she enjoys traveling to Mexico, and perhaps that she recently checked airline ticket prices from Philadelphia to Cancun. DoubleClick, which uses sophisticated data mining technology (called "DART"), will serve a banner ad that is specific to Michelle's tastes and interests—perhaps vacation packages to Mexico.

This dynamic transfer of information, shown in Figure 1, is more than a two-way exchange between consumer and a seller. It is more than a three-way exchange between consumer (client PC), the Web site (s)he visits, and the adserver. It is, in fact, an n-way exchange between the consumer, the adserver, and perhaps hundreds or thousands of other Web sites who collaborate in this network to analyze the usage patterns ("clickdata") of each individual user who visits any and all of those sites. The information is maintained within the client's cookie, but is also combined with other profile information sometimes gathered with Webforms. Adserver technology employs both Boolean decision rules and stochastic processes to determine the appropriate custom digital advertising content to deliver to the server (target Web site) in order to deliver to a specific viewer. This must be done in real-time with minimal

Figure 1: Adserver Network (Source: Warkentin et al., 2001)

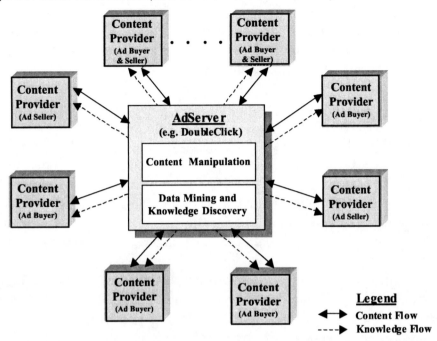

information delivery delays or the user may abandon the visit (Warkentin, Bapna, and Sugumaran, 2000).

Adserver networks demonstrate the dynamic nature of knowledge and information flows between business entities which act to distribute customized digital goods such as banner ads. Network partners must share this knowledge as well as appropriate incentive structures to ensure the success of the entire inter-organizational system. Clearly, the adserver market segment has been enabled by the widespread adoption of the Internet, and DoubleClick's business model would not have even been possible a few years ago. This example of a collaborative inter-organizational system creates tight, long-term alliances between DoubleClick and its partners, which are not easily substituted. The firms have a strong shared interest in the success of the network (Warkentin, Sugumaran and Bapna, 2001).

SYNDICATION NETWORKS

Thousands of consumer-oriented Web sites provide free dynamic content to their virtual visitors. This content may be daily news, sports, weather, or stock quotes, or it may be specialized information, such as the snow reports from various ski reports. The content may be textual, visual, or auditory, such as music. It may also be public domain or proprietary in nature. These Web sites may be general-purpose consumer portals, such as Yahoo or Lycos, or they may be specialized portals designed to appeal to a specific audience, such as ESPN.com or Ski.com. Many such Web sites provide various kinds of content to visitors 1) for free (supported often by the sale of banner ads, affiliate referral fees, or other sources of revenue), 2) for a periodic subscription (such as a monthly charge), or 3) on a pay-per-download basis (typically PDF reports). Dynamic content is what attracts new and returning customers ("eyeballs") and what keeps them longer ("stickiness"), so it contributes to customer loyalty. For banner ad-supported Web sites, the dynamic content may be the primary draw for a site. For transactional sites (selling ski equipment, for example), the dynamic content may be the distinguishing factor bringing certain customers back repeatedly. In other cases, the display of information to an individual occurs within an enterprise portal environment.

Digital content syndication (Werbach, 2000) is the process of aggregating, integrating, packaging and delivering digital content to an intermediary server or directly to a client. The intermediary may be an enterprise portal or a consumer portal, such as a Web site offering news, sports scores, financial information, weather, or other digital content to consumers, along with banner ads, which provide the revenue to support this free content provision. The syndication service provider is itself an intermediary-it collects digital content from numerous originators (newswires, databases, real-time monitors, etc.) and provides it to its customers, the sites that pay for the content. The

Figure 2: Content Syndication Network (Source: Warkentin et al., 2001)

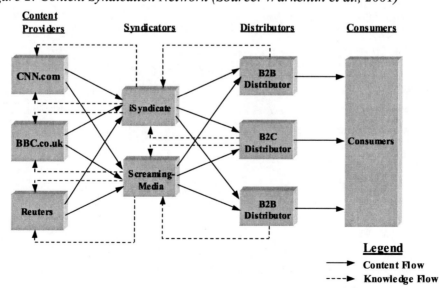

syndicator is not only a broker between disparate sources and users of information; it also provides value-added services by dynamically manipulating and repackaging the content in the format required by the customers. The sources may include all sports information, but the portal may demand content related to a specific basketball team. The syndicator collects various content components from multiple sports sources and integrates and enhances the resulting compilation, reformulating it according to the purchaser's specifications before delivering it dynamically to the portal's server en route to the viewer's client screen. This repackaging may be driven by heuristics concerning actual content component requirements, visual display of content, or protocol requirements. This entire process can happen in real time when an individual clicks on a link to display information about his favorite basketball team. Figure 2 indicates the inter-organizational linkages. For more information about syndication, visit www.moreover.com (See also Warkentin, Sugumaran and Bapna, 2001).

This section has discussed the role of intermediaries and other third-party B2B providers in channeling digital content to the sites who display that content to consumers. In the next section, we will address the next step in the content delivery chain, the task of delivering the digital content to the consumer over the IP environment.

DIGITAL CONTENT
STREAMING SERVICE PROVIDERS

Many eTailers, manufacturers, and portal sites provide digital content, such as news stories, music, video clips, animations, flash media, reference information, financial information, and sports scores, in an effort to reach their target audience with an appealing marketing message. Content providers must be concerned about the download time from the user's perspective, because fickle visitors may click "Stop" before multimedia has time to fully download. It is important that the content providers and marketers find technical solutions to the challenges of ensuring rapid delivery of digital content.

A new category of companies has emerged to provide digital content streaming services through the implementation of complex networks utilizing caching servers which are geographically distributed around the world. Such systems ensure that content is "always near" and will be delivered to client computers quickly and reliably. This service requires an expensive infrastructure of hardware with sophisticated software to control the system. Firms participating in this network must establish dynamic linkages between their servers and the servers of the content streaming service providers to enable real-time automated exchanges of high volume digital content. Some of the companies that are emerging as providers of this Web-based eService include Akamai (Carr, 2000b), Calico, Cabletron, Selectica, and Trilogy.

INFOMEDIARIES AND ONLINE DATA MINING SERVICES

Marketing managers want to understand their customers and potential customers. They want to evaluate their shopping behavior and buying behavior in order to understand how to appeal to them in the future. What do they like? What do they buy? When and where? Traditional retailers evaluate point-of-sale data (grocery scanner data), combined with other available data (like grocery membership club information), in order to generate valuable marketing decision information. (Grocers actually sell this intelligence to food manufacturers.) In today's online environment, there is more potential information than ever before, but the potential can only be realized if the clickstream data can be analyzed, mined to turn it into valuable information, and used to improve services and marketing efforts. A new class of intermediary (called "infomediaries") is emerging to provide these specialized services to Web site owners who do not have the specialized knowledge and systems to perform such data mining.

An infomediary is a business that collects data about consumer behavior, then analyzes and repackages it, and sells the resulting information for marketing and profiling purposes. Some firms use the results of this data mining for their own purposes, while others act strictly for their clients. Other infomediaries are in the business of buying and selling customer information, mostly for the purpose of increasing customer loyalty. Infomediary strategies start with manipulating information until newer information is extracted from it. This new information is sold to customers or exchanged for more information, which is manipulated until newer (even higher value) information is extracted. Combining information yields more information, which can always be sold and yet retained to use again (unlike physical assets).

The infomediary collects consumer information and adds it to thousands or millions of other consumer profiles, then manipulates all this data in ways that are meaningful to consumer product vendors, who use it to do a better job of offering customers products and services that they actually want. Vendors can use the information to identify likely buyers with a much greater degree of precision than ever before—leading to increased sales as well as drastically reduced marketing expenses.

Infomediaries can capture data from the server and act as a B2B provider of real-time data mining services, which can then be used to target banner ads, determine what products to display, or to personalize each individual's display of the company's Web site. One early example of an infomediary is NetPerceptions, which provides its services to retailers and others. By using its Retail Revelations™ technology, a retailer can create demand, improve merchandising programs, and optimize marketing strategies. Its **eCommerce Analyst** tool provides the reporting and analytic tools needed to understand customers more completely. Other companies that provide online data mining services include NetTracker, WebTrends, NetIntellect, HitList, and SurfReport. Infomediaries provide another example of a B2B eService that firms can utilize to extend their ability to execute their eCommerce strategy successfully.

VALUE CHAIN INTEGRATION SERVICES

Early consumer-oriented Web site managers often devoted all their energies into the design of the front-end "customer-facing systems." The "pick and pack and ship" function was viewed as a necessary, but uninteresting business process. However, it is now clear that the back-end systems, from sophisticated customer database functions to the mundane jobs of putting products into boxes and shipping them, are critical to the overall success of the strategy of a firm.

Some firms, such as Amazon.com, handle order fulfillment internally, but outsource the job of outbound logistics (delivery services) to common carriers, such as UPS and FedEx. In other cases, B2C electronic commerce companies (eTailers) will contract with an outsourcing specialist in the third-party logistics area. Firms such as UPS, Line.net (Logistics Information Network Enterprise (Arena)), RightFreight.com, PFS Web, and Efxit.com will provide real-time online eServices such as order management, customer care, distribution services, billing services, inventory management, and information management.

ESERVICES NETWORKS
FOR ONLINE AUCTIONS

An entire group of new eServices providers has emerged to support online auction activity. The eAuction buyers (bidders and winners) and sellers (individuals and businesses) are avid users and strive to maximize their gains from this trading community. Sellers on eAuctions may be individuals who wish to sell "garage sale" type materials, or they may be small businesses using the online auction as their primary marketing channel. An entire industry has emerged to assist these sellers with the management and promotion of their individual auctions. With keen competition for buyers' attention, sellers must differentiate themselves. One method is to enhance their product description with digital imaging. One of these services called iPix.com's PIXcast™ Network now serves over 10 million image views daily and over 500,000 new listings weekly on eBay. Other industries that support the seller include the online appraisal service (eppraisals.com) and firms that will facilitate bid management and tracking, such as auctionhelp.com and andale.com. Other sites help sellers with payment processing (PayPal.com) and creating "virtual storefronts" (auctiva.com). Auctionwatch.com provides sellers with image hosting, counters, shipping, payment, and insurance services, and will manage, launch, and track auctions in one place using Auction Manager (Warkentin, 2001).

On the other hand, eAuction buyers also benefit from new third-party eService providers who facilitate their activities. There are fraud insurance providers and online complaint services to help identify and avoid the "few bad apples" in this space. Auction portals, such as

Figure 3: Linkages to eServices Networks

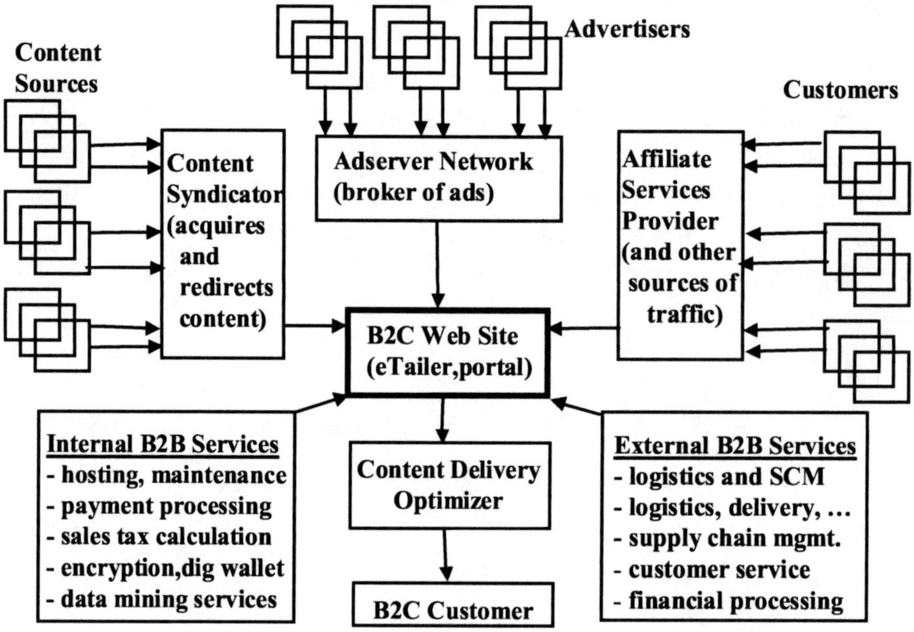

auctionwatch.com, help buyers find items from hundreds of auction and fixed price sites, and can track the buyer's bids and coordinate payment and shipping. Product searchers (BidFind.com) and bidding tools (BidLand.com) help buyers find the best items at the best price. (eBay has tried to stop some of these services from operating.) Finally, there are third-party escrow services (TradeSafe.com) to minimize the risks from auction participation (Warkentin, 2001).

HYPERMEDIATION AND PARTNERSHIP MANAGEMENT IN DIGITAL NETWORKS

In today's rapidly changing eBusiness environment, it is imperative that all organizations pursue and achieve flexible organizational structures that can accommodate partnerships with a variety of external companies in a dynamic agile "virtual organization" (Mowshowitz, 1997). The goal is the development of the truly "agile corporation" in which a firm may engage in continuous reconfiguration as it makes frequent choices about partnerships that best fit the demands of the moment. Many firms form alliances and partnerships in one business area with firms they also compete with in other ways. The Web enables greater collaboration and virtual partnership, and will enable much more in the future as standards are developed (see the next section). With real-time digital interaction between various front-office and back-office functions, two or more firms can quickly form a business-to-business collaborative network with little requirement for exhaustive configuration and design steps as before. With industry standard applications, methods, and data representation schemes, two or more firms can almost "plug into each other" with little or no effort. This process has been termed "collaborative commerce" or C-Commerce. Carr (2000a) suggests that, rather than being primarily a tool for disintermediation, the Web is proving to be a new channel for intermediation and reintermediation. He suggests we are entering an age of hypermediation, in which all firms extensively use the services of other firms provided over the Web in a great pool of outsourcing opportunities. Figure 3 demonstrates the complexity of relationships that can exist even for a simple B2C consumer portal site, and it does not show many of the processes that are required.

Engaging in collaborative commerce activities across dynamic digital networks of partners requires a sophisticated new approach to management. Rather than managing the processes directly, many modern managers must establish and monitor relationships with outsourcing entities that serve the overall mission and objectives of their firms. A firm may engage in "selective outsourcing" to leverage a provider's unique competence for a specific business function or it may practice extensive outsourcing to a single end-to-end service provider or to multiple entities. In either case, it is imperative that the firm establishes a clear understanding with all the outsourcers regarding objectives, outcomes, measures, revenue agreements, information sharing arrangements, and other factors. Rather than initiating an adversarial position, both parties must ensure a true partnership of trust and common interest. However, it would always be wise to "trust, but verify." There are third-party service providers who can become part of the transactional data-exchange network and log activity such as ad impressions served or data points sampled. The "value-based contract" is emerging as one avenue to ensure a successful partnership with outsourcing entities (Garner, 1998). By linking part of a vendor's compensation to the tangible benefits it delivers, the partner is incented to contribute to the firm's goals. There are third-party services that will monitor and log various transactional metrics in an online exchange. For example, they can independently verify the volume of downloads from a site, the number of banner ads displayed, or the clickthroughs from an affiliate's Web site.

Cunningham (2001) offers a framework for determining the partnership arrangements that are appropriate for various circumstances. He identifies inside partnerships, nearside partnerships, and network partnerships that play various roles in B2B eCommerce. Further, he suggests that newer simplified agreements and processes have made it easier to enter into partnerships without time-consuming negotiation.

When evaluating selective process outsourcing versus total end-to-end service providers, carefully consider the trade-offs. Rather than managing multiple relationships, a single provider may provide a streamlined approach to partnership management. However, if some of those services are not the "best of class," a firm may prefer to use separate vendors for each outsourced process. This latter approach may ensure higher levels of service, creating a more successful overall eCommerce solution, but at the cost of greater partnership coordination. The firm may have to operate multiple protocols and systems, which is organizationally confusing and expensive.

Keenan Vision has identified a vision of Business-to-Exchange (B2X) networks within which a firm's computer's could "plug in" to online services and utilize them on a pay-for-use basis without complicated negotiation and system configuration management (Keenan Vision, 2000). Figure 4 shows a B2X hub which could connect an enterprise to many exchanges, all using standard communications and applications protocols. The ability to "snap together" various applications and

Figure 4: Business-to-Exchange Networks (Source: B2X Hub Architecture, keenanvision.com, April 24, 2000)

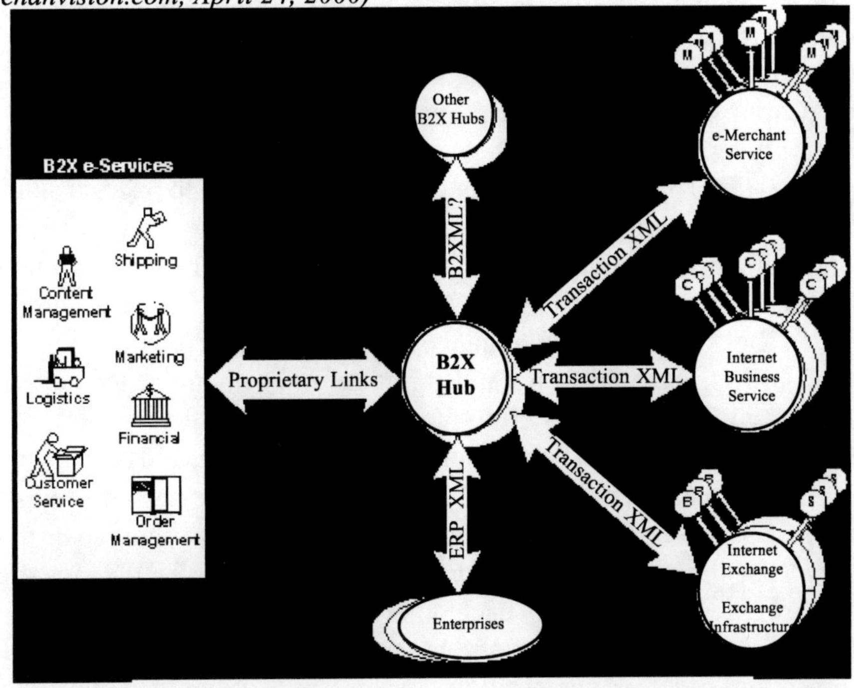

e-Merchant, Internet Business Services and Internet Exchanges may be serviced by one B2X hub

functionalities would provide a venture with the ability to take an idea and form a complete transactional Web-based virtual corporation in a short time. Membership in the exchange would provide access to an entire range of value-added services, and the site designers could plug in the services via API and URL insertion "instead of a custom system integration job."

We are witnessing the evolution of agent-based inter-organizational systems that enable complex direct interaction between heterogeneous information systems, which allow Web-based eServices to act autonomously, communicate independently, discover each other, provide dynamically configured services to one another, and establish composite business systems.

THE ROLE OF STANDARDS

In order to establish effective collaborative commerce networks, organizations must be able to connect their servers, their applications, and their databases easily. Autonomous intelligent agents must be able to dynamically search and utilize new processes and services. For this level of tight integration, there must be standard protocols and data representation schemes. There must be a dependable infrastructure that crosses organizational boundaries and can provide the features typically found behind the firewall. A seamless environment for process integration requires a cooperative effort between industry groups and Web service providers.

The universally recognized standard notation of Hypertext Markup Language (HTML) is only useful for displaying visual Web pages to human eyes, but does not address the need to interconnect back-end database systems and applications. For that purpose, the industry is pursuing several alternatives for standardized data representation. Most of these standards are built upon the eXtensible Markup Language (XML) Protocol (previously known as SOAP). XML is the "alphabet and grammar" of eCommerce interactivity.

Universal Data Discovery Interface (UDDI) is used for registering and publishing Web services. The creation of Microsoft, IBM, and Ariba, UDDI is intended to be an Internet standard for creating an online business registry, and defines a standard for how business is conducted between two or more partners. (For more information, consult www.uddi.org.) UDDI specifications allow companies to query each other's capabilities automatically. The alliance has also announced the Web Services Description Language (WSDL)- the cornerstone of UDDI-which allows businesses to describe their offerings in a standard way (Sturdevant, 2000). The WSDL is used for describing the application programming interface (API) of a Web service, therefore enabling systems to discover each other independently. RosettaNet is another promising standard for establishing seamless effective inter-organizational information systems. This model provides a common business interface for exchanging information between trading partners without implementing entity-specific business practices. Based on XML, it offers the hope of drastic efficiency gains for supply chain participants.

SUMMARY

The new era of business-to-business electronic commerce is one which will witness the evolution of new markets, new industries, and new business forms. The most significant inter-organizational information systems will probably not be the trading exchanges, though they are already an important new economic reality. The most significant aspect of B2B eCommerce will be the networks of services and applications created by specialized providers and delivered dynamically over the Internet Protocol environment.

The environment would create a virtual "data tone/applications tone," like today's standard "dial tone," so that a new venture could "plug in" and "snap-together" new features into existing systems, which are found in the global registry created with UDDI. Web services will be defined as "chunks of business logic and function that are published, described, discovered, and invoked on the Internet" (Dube and Sink, 2000). Extreme efforts formerly needed to link systems and applications will be eliminated, and the Web will become as much a place for exchanging services and applications as it is now for exchanging information, goods, and ideas.

Real-time business-to-business integration results in competitive advantage when business partners can easily and transparently exchange information and integrate applications in real time over the Internet. In fact, thousands of companies have now implemented automated application-to-application integration that crosses traditional organizational boundaries using open standards of data representation over the Internet, rather than proprietary standards and networks.

Ultimately, firms will be able to create collaborative business networks that automate end-to-end process integration and seamless workflow within and between organizations. The network effect from this hypermediated environment will result in an explosion in real-time business intelligence as infomediaries and other data mining entities evaluate the data stream from this highly integrated business environment. This will dramatically improve overall market efficiencies by ushering in collaborative demand planning. The effects on the participants will be exceeded by the aggregate advantages for the entire economy.

Managing the outsourcing process provides unique managerial challenges. Selecting appropriate service providers can be difficult–large, well-known providers may be safer choices, but may be expensive and less flexible. The expanding number of B2B services with multiple service levels and options creates another complex set of decisions. Useful metrics are often not available in a particular industry, and a firm may have to assess competitors or establish new contractual arrangements to ensure success. Effective partner relationship management becomes imperative. Creating a culture of shared purpose, backed by contractual verification can provide some assurance of success. A firm should investigate joint venture arrangements with service providers, especially for infrastructure and automated processes. There may be an opportunity to provide value to other members of the community and generate additional revenues from the provision of services over the network.

This brave new world of business-to-business interoperability will surely provide new challenges and opportunities not yet seen. To be effective in this environment, an eCommerce manager must be vigilant in the pursuit of knowledge about industry trends, standards, technologies, and competitor activities. The dynamic nature of these evolving process networks will speed the pace with which the business environment evolves. The choices of outsourcing arrangements may have to be constantly evaluated for improvements. But if managed effectively, these new "plug and play" eServices will provide companies with real potential to concentrate on their core competencies and continue to provide expanded value to their customers.

REFERENCES

Applegate, L. M., McFarlan, J. W. and McKenney, J. L. (1999). *Corporate Information Systems Management* (5e), New York: Irwin-McGraw-Hill.

Bichler, M., Segev, A. and Bean, C. (1998). An electronic broker for business-to-business electronic commerce in the Internet. *International Journal of Cooperative Information Systems*, 7(4).

Carr, N. G. (2000a). The future of commerce-hypermediation: Commerce as clickstream. *Harvard Business Review*, January-February.

Carr, N. G. (2000b). On the edge: An interview with Akamai's George Conrades. *Harvard Business Review*, May-June.

Cross, K. (2000). The ultimate enablers: Business partners. *Business 2.0*, February.

Cunningham, M. J. (2001). Maximizing the power of partners. *eBusiness Advisor*, 19(1), 32-41.

Dube, J. and Sink, D. (2000). Do you need Web services? *eBusiness Advisor*, 18(2), 16-21.

Garner, R. (1998). Strategic outsourcing: It's your move. *Datamation*, 44,(2), 32-41.

Greening, D. R. (1999). Self-service syndication with ICE: Building informative Web pages and catalogs automatically. *Web Techniques*, 11.

Kaufman, F. (1966). Data systems that cross company boundaries. *Harvard Business Review*, January-February.

KeenanVision.com. (2000). *The Keenan Report Number 6: B2X Emerges as New Industry to Service Exchange Transactions*. Available on the World Wide Web at: http://www.keenanvision.com/html/content/ex2000/exchange2000. htm. Accessed on April 24, 2000.

Mowshowitz, A. (1997). A virtual organization. *Communications of the ACM*, 40(9), 30-37.

Pickering, C. (2000). Outsourcing the store. *Business2.0*, October.

Raisch, W. D. (2001). *The eMarketplace: Strategies for Success in B2B eCommerce*. New York: McGraw Hill.

Sturdevant, C. (2000). UDDI standard: A ticket to global B2B?. *eWEEK*, November. Available on the World Wide Web at: http://www.zdnet.com/products/stories/reviews/0,4161,2649000,00.html.

Tillett, L. C. (2001). States test systems for eCommerce taxation. *Internetweek*, January 16.

Turban, E., King, D., Lee, Jae, Warkentin, M. and Chung, H. Michael (2002). Electronic Commerce 2002: A Managerial Perspective. Upper Saddle River, NJ: Prentice Hall.

Voss, C. (2000). Developing an eService strategy. *Business Strategy Review*, Spring.

Warkentin, M. (2001). The next big thing in eCommerce. *Decision Line*, 32(1), 7-10.

Warkentin, M., Bapna, R. and Sugumaran, V. (2000). The role of mass customization in enhancing supply chain relationships in B2C eCommerce markets. *Journal of Electronic Commerce Research*, 1(2), 1-17.

Warkentin, M., Sugumaran, V. and Bapna, R. (2001). eKnowledge networks for inter-organizational collaborative eBusiness. *Logistics Information Management*, 14(1-2), 149-162.

Werbarch, K. (2000). Syndication: The emerging model for business in the Internet era. *Harvard Business Review*.

Yang, J. and Papazoglou, M. (2000). Interoperation support for electronic business. *Communications of the ACM*, 43(6), 39-47.

About the Authors

Merrill Warkentin is Associate Professor of MIS in the College of Business and Industry at Mississippi State University. He has authored over 100 articles, chapters, and books. His research, primarily in eCommerce, virtual teams, expert systems, and system security, has appeared in such journals as *MIS Quarterly, Decision Sciences, Information Systems Journal, Journal of Knowledge Engineering & Technology, Journal of Electronic Commerce Research, Logistics Information Management, ACM Applied Computing Review, Expert Systems*, and *Journal of Computer Information Systems*. Professor Warkentin is a co-author of *Electronic Commerce: A Managerial Perspective (2e)* (Prentice Hall, 2002) and Editor of *Business-to-Business Electronic Commerce: Challenges and Solutions* (Idea Group Publishing, 2002). He is currently on the editorial board of *Information Resources Management Journal*. Dr. Warkentin has served as a consultant to numerous companies and organizations, and has been a featured speaker at over one hundred industry association meetings, executive development seminars, and academic conferences. He has been a Lecturer at the Army Logistics Management College and since 1996, he has served as National Distinguished Lecturer for the Association for Computing Machinery (ACM). Professor Warkentin holds BA, MA, and Ph.D. degrees from the University of Nebraska-Lincoln. He can be reached at mwarkentin@acm.org.

***

Norm Archer holds the Wayne C. Fox Chair in Business Innovation and is Professor of Management Science and Information Systems in the Michael G. DeGroote School of Business at McMaster University, Canada. He is also director of the McMaster E-commerce Research Centre (MERC) (http://merc.mcmaster.ca). His research interests are in topics that relate to electronic commerce, including business-to-business implementations, intelligent agents and the human-computer interface. He has published in a number of journals, including *Internet Research*; *International Journal of Management Theory and Practice*; *IEEE Transactions on Systems, Man and Cybernetics*;

International Journal of Human-Computer Studies, International Journal of Technology Management and many others. Professor Archer can be contacted at archer@mcmaster.ca.

Janice M. Burn is Foundation Professor and Head of the School of Management Information Systems at Edith Cowan University in Perth, Western Australia, and Director of the We-B research centre–Working for e-Business. In 2000 she assumed the role of World President of the Information Resources Management Association (IRMA). She has previously held senior academic posts in Hong Kong and the UK. Her research interests relate to information systems strategy and benefits evaluation in virtual organizations with a particular emphasis on cross cultural challenges in an e-business environment. She is recognised as an international researcher with more than 150 refereed publications in journals and international conferences. She is on the editorial board of six prestigious IS journals and participates in a number of joint research projects with international collaboration and funding.

Robert M. Colomb is currently a reader in information systems with the Department of Computer Science and Electrical Engineering, The University of Queensland; lecturing in advanced databases, information science, and human-computer interface. His research interests are in the general area of how an information space presents itself to a user population and conversely how a user can interact with the space in order to satisfy information requirements. He has more than 75 publications, including two books, and has supervised eight completed PhD and MSc programs. From 1985 to 1990, he was manager of the Knowledge Based Systems Engineering program of the CSIRO Division of Information Technology. The group had a mission to develop tools to help people exploit knowledge, and worked in software engineering of artificial intelligence systems, knowledge processing technology, and hypermedia systems. In 1987 he was awarded a PhD in computer science from the University of New South Wales for the application of content addressable memory to the programming language Prolog. Prior to resuming his studies, he had an extensive and varied career in the computer industry, including commercial, operating systems, programming tools, technical, planning and communications applications; as well as consulting in a variety of areas, both in the United States and Australia. When he came to Australia in 1971, he spent a few years outside the computer industry doing, among other things, running a fruit shop in a small country town. He has a BS in mathematics from the Massachusetts Institute of Technology, awarded in

1964.

Omar A. El Sawy is Professor of Information Systems at the Marshall School of Business at the University of Southern California. He holds a PhD from Stanford Business School, an MBA from the American University in Cairo and a BSEE from Cairo University. His current interests include redesigning value chain processes for e-business in fast response environments. Professor El Sawy is the author of more than 60 papers, serves on five journal editorial boards and is a four-time winner of the Society for Information Management's International Paper Awards Competition. He is the author of the recent book Redesigning Enterprise Processes for e-Business (McGraw-Hill, 2001).

John M. Gallaugher is an Assistant Professor of Information Systems in the Boston College School of Management. Professor Gallaugher's research interests include electronic commerce, information systems strategy and information systems economics. His research has appeared in *Communications of the ACM, Information & Management, International Journal of Electronic Commerce* and *Electronic Markets*, among others. Professor Gallaugher has worked and consulted in the Fortune 50 and is a frequent invited speaker to large corporations on topics of eCommerce and IS strategy.

Jorge Gasós is scientific officer for electronic commerce in the European Commission's Information Society Directorate-General. He is in charge of the research area on "Intelligent Applications for Electronic Commerce" in the Electronic Commerce Unit, that includes research and developments in agent technologies. He has published a large number of papers and book chapters in leading international journals and publications, mainly in the area of artificial intelligence. Jorge Gasós previously held research positions in Spain, Japan and Belgium, where he focused his work on artificial intelligence applications. He holds a PhD in Computer Science from the Polytechnic University of Madrid (Spain).

Judith Gebauer is a Research Fellow and Lecturer at the Fisher Center for IT and Marketplace Transformation (CITM) at the Haas School of Business, University of California, Berkeley. Her research focuses on emerging technologies to support inter-business relationships and the impacts on organizations and industry structures. Dr. Gebauer coordinates a major CITM research project on Internet-based procurement, and also teaches eBusiness classes at the Haas School. She received both her PhD

(1996) and a Master's in Economics (1991) from the University of Freiburg in Germany. More information is available from haas.berkeley.edu/~gebauer. She can be reached at gebauer@haas.berkeley.edu.

Seng Kwong Gwee received his B Sc (Computer Science) from the University of Oregon and his MBA from Brunel University. He is currently the Director of SME.com at the Productivity & Standards Board (PSB) in Singapore, overseeing eCommerce adoption in the small and medium-size enterprises (SMEs). He is actively promoting E-business technology, supply chain management and electronic commerce to local enterprises in Singapore. Prior to his secondment to PSB, he was the Director of the Manufacturing and Distribution Cluster at Infocomm Development Authority of Singapore (IDA). His main task was to deploy IT projects that supported the strategic intent of the Manufacturing 2000 Project in line with the Singapore Government's overall IT2000 program.

Ray Hackney is Director of Business Information Technology Research within the Manchester Metropolitan University, UK. He holds a Cert. Ed, BSc (Hons), MA and PhD from leading universities and has contributed extensively to research in the field of information systems with publications in numerous national and international conferences and journals. He has taught on a number of MBA programs including MMU, Manchester Business School and the Open University. He leads the organising committee for the annual BIT and BITWorld Conference series, and is a member of the Strategic Management Society and Association of Information Systems. Dr. Hackney has served on the Board of the UK Academy for Information Systems since 1997 and is also the Vice President of Research for IRMA (USA), Associate Editor of the *JGIM, JEUC, JLIM* and *ACITM*. He is also a reviewer for a number of publishers, journals and conferences. His research interests are the strategic management of information systems within a variety of e-business and organisational context.

Ahmad Kayed is currently a PhD student in information systems with the Department of Computer Science and Electrical Engineering at the University of Queensland. His research interests are in electronic commerce, tendering process, ontology, knowledge acquisition, e-broker, software agents, and EDI/XML. From 1989 to 1993, he joined Arab Community College (Jordan) as a computer instructor. From 1993 to 1996, he was a project manager for financial systems at IdealSoft within IdealGroup. This project achieved the Best Software Award (METS 1994 & 1996). From 1996 to 1998, he joined the Centre for British Teachers (CfBT) Oman branch as computer lecturer. In 1989 he was awarded a BSc in computer science and MSc (1992) in math/statistics from Jordan University, Amman-Jordan. When he came to Australia in 1998, he joined the University of Queensland Brisbane to complete his PhD.

Ann Majchrzak is Professor of Information Systems at the Marshall School of Business at the University of Southern California. She holds a PhD in Social Psychology from the University of California, Los Angeles. She was previously with the Institute of Safety and Systems Management at the University of Southern California. Her research interests focus on the development of change plans that optimize the synergy between computer-based technologies, human capabilities, organizational structure and business strategy. She has applied her research in such industry sectors as manufacturing, assembly and engineering design. She has used her research to generate tools to help technology and organizational designers, including HITOP, ACTION and TOP Modeler (www.topintegration.com). Her tools have been used in Europe, Australia, North and South America, and with such companies as Ford, Hewlett-Packard, General Motors, Texas Instruments and Hughes. Dr. Majchrzak has served on three National Academy of Sciences committees, written seven books, including *The Human Side of Factory Automation*, has a 1996 *Harvard Business Review* article on "Building a Collaborative Culture in Process-Centered Organizations" and is the 2000 winner of SIM-International Paper Award Competition. Her current research interests include development of knowledge management tools and processes, and the design of stakeholder participation processes in IS development.

Darren Meister is an Assistant Professor at Queen's School of Business, Queen's University. He teaches in the areas of information systems and change management. A Rotary Foundation Scholar, Dr. Meister received a Master of Applied Science and a PhD in Management Sciences from the University of Waterloo. His research interests focus on the management of technology-based change, primarily identifying organizational actions that facilitate volitional adoption. His work has been published in journals such as the *International Journal of Technology Management* and *Group Decision and Negotiation*. He is a past Director with Electronic Commerce Canada.

Michael P. Papazoglou is a Full Professor and Director of the Infolab at Tilburg University in the Netherlands. His scientific interests include cooperative information systems, heterogeneous database systems, object-oriented systems and modeling, distributed computing, digital and electronic commerce where he has authored approximately 100 journal articles and refereed conference papers and edited 10 books. He has chaired several prestigious conferences and serves on several scientific committees and advisory boards for international journals. His research has been funded by the European Commission, the Australian Research Council, the Japanese Society for the Promotion of Science and Departments of Science and Technology in Europe and Australia. Professor Papazoglou is a golden core member of the IEEE and a recipient of the prestigious IEEE Certificate of Appreciation for his contributions to computer science as distinguished visitor of the IEEE.

Paul A. Pavlou is a PhD Candidate of Information Systems at the Marshall School of Business in the University of Southern California (USC). He holds a Master's degree in Electrical Engineering from USC, and a Bachelor's degree in Managerial Studies and Electrical Engineering from Rice University (magna cum laude). His current research interests are mostly in the area of electronic commerce, dealing with interorganizational and consumer relationships, the role of trust and marketing communications. Mr. Pavlou is the author of several papers that appeared as journal articles, book chapters and conference proceedings.

Suresh C. Ramanathan is the President & CEO of Koryak, an eBusiness consulting firm that specializes in addressing the needs of B2B and manufacturing companies. He left Deloitte Consulting as a Senior Manager in January 2000 to co-found Koryak. While at Deloitte Consulting, he assisted numerous clients with his procurement and information technology knowledge and project management expertise. Prior to Deloitte Consulting, he was with Alcoa, where he reengineered the procurement process and contributed to numerous successful information technology initiatives.

ManMohan S. Sodhi is Senior Director at Gandiva Inc. and has previously worked at Scient and Andersen Consulting (Accenture) on client projects concerning eBusiness and supply-chain management. He is interested in B2B eCommerce and supply-chain planning, and writes a column, *Cyberspace*, pertaining to these issues for *ORMS Today*. He is the current President of the Logistics Section of INFORMS and founded the news group sci.ops-research.

He has a doctorate in Management Science from the Anderson School of Management at UCLA and has taught operations management at the University of Michigan Business School.

Albert Wee Kwan Tan was an Assistant Director in Infocomm Development Authority of Singapore (IDA), responsible for upgrading the IT capability of the manufacturing and logistics industries. The projects that he was involved include electronic procurement for MRO parts, electronic fulfillment for companies in the chemical industry and a logistics portal for health care industry. He has also provided numerous ERP consulting for both discrete and process companies in Asia to streamline their supply chain while working for Oracle Corporation. He is currently teaching e-Business and IT management courses at the Institute of Systems Science of the National University of Singapore. Mr. Tan received his Master of Business Studies from National University of Ireland and is a certified member of APICS (CPIM).

Paul Timmers is head of sector for electronic commerce in the European Commission's Information Society Directorate-General. He is closely involved in electronic commerce policy and programme development at the European Commission and has been working with several national governments on electronic commerce policies. He regularly publishes about electronic commerce, including the recent book *Electronic Commerce: Strategies and Models for Business-to-Business Trading*, (Wiley & Sons Ltd). He is a frequent speaker at international conferences and a visiting professor at several business schools and universities. Paul Timmers previously held management positions in the IT industry and has co-founded a software company. He holds a PhD in theoretical physics (University of Nijmegen, NL) and an MBA (Warwick Business School, UK).

Aphrodite Tsalgatidou is a Professor at the Department of Informatics of the University of the Athens, Greece. She holds an MSc and a PhD in Computer Science from the University of Manchester (UMIST), UK. Her scientific interests include requirements engineering, business process modeling and reengineering, workflow systems, virtual enterprises and (mobile) electronic commerce, and she has published several articles on these topics. She has chaired two conferences on eCommerce and business process reengineering, she is the managing editor of two electronic journals, she serves on more than 30 scientific committees and on the advisory boards for two international journals.

Jian Yang is an Assistant Professor at Infolab, Tilburg University. Her current research interest includes e-service development and representation, data warehousing, querying and searching Web-based information, and interoperability issues in digital libraries and eCommerce. She has published more than 30 papers in international journals and conferences on the above topics as well as others. Before she joined Infolab, Dr. Yang worked as a senior research scientist at CSIRO Australia where she led the Internet Marketplace research group, and as a lecturer at Australian Defence Force Academy. She received her PhD in Computer Science from Australian National University in 1995.

Index